Building a Future-Proof Cloud Infrastructure

A Unified Architecture for Network, Security, and Storage Services

Silvano Gai

With Contributions by
Roger Andersson,
Diego Crupnicoff, and Vipin Jain

✦ Addison-Wesley

Many of the designations used by manufacturers and sellers to distinguish their products are claimed as trademarks. Where those designations appear in this book, and the publisher was aware of a trademark claim, the designations have been printed with initial capital letters or in all capitals.

The author and publisher have taken care in the preparation of this book, but make no expressed or implied warranty of any kind and assume no responsibility for errors or omissions. No liability is assumed for incidental or consequential damages in connection with or arising out of the use of the information or programs contained herein.

Microsoft and/or its respective suppliers make no representations about the suitability of the information contained in the documents and related graphics published as part of the services for any purpose. All such documents and related graphics are provided "as is" without warranty of any kind. Microsoft and/or its respective suppliers hereby disclaim all warranties and conditions with regard to this information, including all warranties and conditions of merchantability, whether express, implied or statutory, fitness for a particular purpose, title and non-infringement. In no event shall Microsoft and/or its respective suppliers be liable for any special, indirect or consequential damages or any damages whatsoever resulting from loss of use, data or profits, whether in an action of contract, negligence or other tortious action, arising out of or in connection with the use or performance of information available from the services. The documents and related graphics contained herein could include technical inaccuracies or typographical errors. Changes are periodically added to the information herein. Microsoft and/or its respective suppliers may make improvements and/or changes in the product(s) and/or the program(s) described herein at any time. Partial screenshots may be viewed in full within the software version specified.

Microsoft® and Windows® are registered trademarks of the Microsoft Corporation in the U.S.A. and other countries. Screenshots and icons reprinted with permission from the Microsoft Corporation. This book is not sponsored or endorsed by or affiliated with the Microsoft Corporation.

For information about buying this title in bulk quantities, or for special sales opportunities (which may include electronic versions; custom cover designs; and content particular to your business, training goals, marketing focus, or branding interests), please contact our corporate sales department at corpsales@pearsoned.com or (800) 382-3419.

For government sales inquiries, please contact governmentsales@pearsoned.com.

For questions about sales outside the U.S., please contact intlcs@pearson.com.

Visit us on the Web: informit.com/aw

Library of Congress Control Number: 2019956931

ISBN-13: 978-0-13-662409-7

ISBN-10: 0-13-662409-X

2 2020

Editor-in-Chief
Mark Taub

Product Manager
James Manly

Managing Editor
Sandra Schroeder

Senior Project Editor
Lori Lyons

Copy Editor
Paula Lowell

Production Manager
Vaishnavi/codeMantra

Indexer
Erika Millen

Proofreader
Abigail Manheim

Editorial Assistant
Cindy Teeters

Cover Designer
Chuti Prasertsith

Compositor
codeMantra

To the women in my family: Antonella, Eleonora,
Evelina, and Carola;
and to Jacopo

Contents at a Glance

Contents

Chapter 4: Network Virtualization Services

List of Figures

Figure Credits

Figure 2-8: Cisco Nexus 9000 Series Switches © Cisco system, Inc

Figure 3-5: Hyper V Architecture © Microsoft corporation

Figure 3-7: Virtio: An I/O virtualization framework for Linux by M. Jones © IBM Corporation

Figure 3-10: Xen arc diagram © The Linux Foundation

Figure 3-12: Kata Containers: Secure, Lightweight Virtual Machines for Container Environments by Scott M. Fulton, III © The New Stack

Figure 4-1: OpenFlow Switch Specification © The Open Networking Foundation

Figure 4-2: gRIBI © 2020 GitHub, Inc, https://github.com/opencon/gribi

Figure 4-3: DPDK © DPDK Project

Figure 4-4: Linux Foundation Collaborative Projects, "OVS: Open vSwitch," © 2016 A Linux Foundation Collaborative Project. http:// www.openvswitch.org/

Figure 4-5: Open v Switch © 2016 A Linux Foundation Collaborative Project

Figure 4-9: The Linux Foundation Projects, 'Vector Packet Processing (VPP)' © Cisco Systems, Inc.

Figure 6-11: Supplement to InfiniBandTM Architecture Specification, Volume 1, Release 1.2.1, Annex A17, RoCEv2, © 2010 by InfiniBandTM Trade Association. https://cw.infinibandta.org/document/dl/7781

Figure 6-12: © Copyright 2017. Mellanox Technologies

Figure 6-13: Top 500, Development over time, © 1993-2019 TOP500.org. https://www.top500.org/statistics/overtime/

Figure 7-1: Original data up to the year 2010 collected and plotted by M. Horowitz, F. Labonte, O. Shacham, K. Olukotun, L. Hammond, and C. Batten New plot and data collected for 2010–2017 by K. Rupp – Creative Commons Attribution 4.0 International Public License

Figure 7-2: Moore's law © Our World In Data

Figure 8-1: PCI Express® Basics & Background by Richard Solomon © PCI-SIG

Table 8-1: Specifications of PCI-SIG © PCI-SIG

Figure 8-4: Used with permission from Hewlett Packard Enterprise

Figure 8-5: Used with permission from Open Compute Project Foundation

Figure 8-6: Used with permission from Open Compute Project Foundation

Figure 8-9: Virtio: An I/O virtualization framework for Linux by M. Jones © IBM Corporation

Figure 10-3: Used with permission from Pensando

Figure 11-1: P4 Language Tutorial © P4.org

Figure 11-2: P4 Language Tutorial © P4.org

Figure 11-3: P416 Portable Switch Architecture (PSA) © P4.org

Figure 11-4: P4 Language Tutorial © P4.org

Figure 11-5: P4Runtime Specification © P4.org

Preface

The Motivation for Writing this Book

I decided to write this book after the success of the *Cisco Unified Computing System (UCS) Data Center* book, which I wrote with Roger Andersson and Tommi Salli.

I attribute the excellent response to that book to the significant amount of material that we included on protocols, technologies, and system evolution. We discussed several significant changes that were happening in data centers, from the blade server architecture to the dominance of Ethernet, to the trend toward I/O consolidation. We also made some predictions on the long-term evolution, some of which turned out to be right, while others didn't.

In the eight years that followed, the pace of changes has dramatically increased, and I thought it was time to provide an updated view of the technology trends as independently as possible from actual products.

This book focuses on core services like segment routing, NAT, firewall, microsegmentation, load balancing, SSL/TLS termination, VPNs, RDMA, storage, and storage services such as compression and encryption. These services are vital components whenever multiple users share any cloud architecture, be it private, public, or hybrid. In particular, this book is about distributed services platforms that can be implemented with multiple service modules located in different hardware components, such as NICs, appliances, or switches. Distributing these service modules as closely as possible to the final applications enables very high performance, low latency, low jitter, deep observability, and rapid troubleshooting.

Who Should Read This Book

This book targets all IT professionals who want to learn about the evolution of service architectures. In particular, this book is helpful to:

- Network engineers, for the L2, L3 forwarding, Clos networks, VLAN, VXLAN, VPN, and network services

- Cloud engineers, for multi-tenancy, overlay networks, virtual switching, and GFT

- Security experts, for firewalls, encryption, key management, and zero trust

- Application engineers, for load balancing, virtualization, and microservice architecture

- High-performance computing engineers, for RDMA applications

- Storage engineers, for NVMe and NVMe-oF, compression, deduplication, and encryption in motion and at rest

After reading this book, the reader will comprehend the problems with the current reality of discrete centralized appliances and will understand the need to migrate services as closely as possible to the applications. They will then have the right knowledge to evaluate different commercial solutions, compare them by asking pertinent questions, and make the right selection for her/his business.

Chapter Organization

Chapter 1, "Introduction to Distributed Platform," introduces the need for a Distributed Services Platform that offers superior security, cloudlike scale, hardware performance, and low latency and yet be software programmable. A platform that is easy to manage, operate, troubleshoot, and works for bare metal, virtual machine, and container workloads. The chapter explores the need for domain-specific hardware, programmable through a domain-specific language for network, security, and storage services, to satisfy the insatiable demand for processing, as Moore's law hits the limits of physics.

Chapter 2, "Network Design," presents standard network designs for clouds and enterprise data centers, reviewing L2/L3 forwarding algorithms used both in classical switch routers and in hypervisors, the requirements posed by Clos networks with their leaf and spine architecture, the role of overlays and how to secure them, segment routing, and the need for "tromboning" in the presence of discrete appliances.

Chapter 3, "Virtualization," is about the trend in public, private, and hybrid clouds and virtualization; it covers the differences between bare metal, virtual machines, and containers. It describes virtualization solutions like VMware and KVM, with particular emphasis on their network and service implications. It introduces the microservice architecture and container technologies as a possible implementation, with examples on Docker and Kubernetes. It concludes with examples of OpenStack and NFV.

Chapter 4, "Network Virtualization Services," introduces networking virtualization services, starting with SDN and OpenFlow trends and more recent efforts like gRIBI. It discusses DPDK, virtual switches and OVS, offloading techniques like tc-flower, DPDK RTE flow, eBPF, and VPP and tries to provide a taxonomy of these many efforts. Popular services like load balancing and NAT are also presented. The chapter ends with a discussion about telemetry.

Chapter 5, "Security Services," introduces security services. Starting with popular services like firewall, the discussion evolves into microsegmentation, followed by a deep dive on security with symmetric and asymmetric encryption, key storage, unique key generation, digital certificates, hashing, TLS/TCP implementations, and VPNs.

Chapter 6, "Distributed Storage and RDMA Services," presents RDMA and storage services. RDMA was born in the world of high-performance computing, but it is now used also in enterprise and cloud networks. NVMe is the new storage standard that replaces SCSI for high-performance storage drives. NVMe is also overlaid on RDMA to provide networkwide access to storage resources in an arrangement called NVMe over Fabrics (NVMe-oF). NVMe-oF can also use TCP as an alternative to RDMA. This chapter describes this landscape with the addition of essential storage services such as encryption of data at rest, compression, and data deduplication.

Chapter 7, "CPUs and Domain-Specific Hardware," discusses servers used in clouds and data centers, looking in particular to the dramatic reduction in performance growth in recent years that calls for domain-specific hardware to take over service functions. Moore's law, Dennard scaling, Amdahl's law, and 42 years of microprocessor data are analyzed to understand the economics of the server better and to help the reader decide how to partition the server functions.

Chapter 8, "NIC Evolution," describes the evolution of network interface cards (NICs) from simple devices in charge of sending and receiving one packet at a time, to more complex and sophisticated entities capable of effectively supporting multicore CPUs, multiple types of traffic, stateless offloads, SR-IOV, and advanced parsing/classification capabilities. The term SmartNICs has recently appeared to indicate NICs that incorporate even more processing power to enable offload of networking processing from the host CPU. Understanding this evolution is essential because the NIC represents one of the possible footprints for a distributed services platform.

Chapter 9, "Implementing a DS Platform," introduces distributed services platforms, outlining their goals, constraints, and implementation. Obtaining a standard set of functionalities with a granular distribution is key to scaling the architecture to a vast number of users while creating scalability and maintaining low latency, low jitter, and minimum CPU load. The chapter compares possible implementations and trade-offs in greenfield and brownfield deployment scenarios.

Chapter 10, "DSN Hardware Architectures," describes possible hardware implementations of these Distributed Services Platforms, considering three main approaches: sea of processors, field programmable gate arrays (FPGAs), and application-specific integrated circuits (ASICs). It compares the advantages and disadvantages of each approach and draws some conclusions.

Chapter 11, "The P4 Domain-Specific Language," presents the P4 architecture that makes it possible to implement ASICs that are data plane–programmable at runtime, an important feature that marries the programmability of devices like FPGAs with the performance and power-saving capability of ASICs. The chapter ends with an analysis of future directions to make P4 more usable and flexible.

Chapter 12, "Management Architectures for DS Platforms," discusses the architectural components and design choices to build a modern management infrastructure, leveraging the concepts of distributed systems, stateless microservices, and API-driven software. It presents design trade-offs for building secure, highly available, high performance, and scalable software. It further discusses the practical aspects of a management system, like ease of deployment, troubleshooting, diagnosing, and integration with existing software ecosystems. Finally, the chapter touches upon federating the declarative intent across multiple clusters.

Help Improve This Book

If you uncover any remaining resilient bugs, please contact the authors by email at dsplatforms@ip6. com. We welcome general comments to the text and invite you to send them by email also.

I hope this book provides useful information that you can apply to your daily activity.

—Silvano Gai

With Contributions by

- Diego Crupnicoff contributed all of Chapter 6, "Distributed Storage and RDMA Services" and helped review the book.

- Vipin Jain and Roger Andersson contributed Chapter 12, "Management Architectures for DS Platforms" and helped review the book.

- Francis Matus provided part of Chapter 7, "CPUs and Domain-Specific Hardware" on the historical evolution of processors as well as data for Chapter 10, "DSN Hardware Architectures."

About the Authors

Silvano Gai, who grew up in a small village near Asti, Italy, has more than 35 years of experience in computer engineering and computer networks. He is the author of several books and technical publications on computer networking as well as multiple Internet Drafts and RFCs. He is responsible for 50 issued patents. His background includes seven years as a full professor of Computer Engineering, tenure track, at Politecnico di Torino, Italy, and seven years as a researcher at the CNR (Italian National Council for Scientific Research). For the past 20 years, he has been in Silicon Valley where, in the position of Cisco Fellow, he was an architect of the Cisco Catalyst family of network switches, of the Cisco MDS family of storage networking switches, of the Nexus family of data center switches, and the Cisco Unified Computing System (UCS). Silvano is currently a Fellow with Pensando Systems.

Roger Andersson has spent more than 28 years in the computer and storage industry with work experience that spans across EMC/Data General, Pure Storage, Veritas/Symantec and Nuova Systems/Cisco UCS, focusing on software automation, OS provisioning, and policy-driven management at scale. Roger's roles started in hardware engineering, moved to software engineering, and for the past 16 years has been in technical product management roles. Roger is currently working at Pensando as a Technical Product Manager focusing on Distributed Service Management at scale. Roger was born in Stockholm, Sweden.

Diego Crupnicoff has been a Fellow at Pensando Systems since May 2017. Prior to that, Diego served as VP Architecture at Mellanox Technologies where he worked since its inception in 1999, driving chip and system architectures for multiple generations of Ethernet and RDMA products. Diego has been a member of the InfiniBand Trade Association since its early days and took part in the definition of the InfiniBand RDMA Standard. Among other roles, Diego chaired the IBTA Technical Working Group for many years. He was also among the founding directors of the OpenFabrics Alliance and chaired its Technical Advisory Council for several years. Over the past two decades, Diego has participated in multiple other SDOs and Tech Committees, including the IEEE802, IETF, T11, NVME, and the ONF. Diego is an inventor in multiple patents on the areas of computer networks and system architecture. He holds a B.Sc. in Computer Engineering (Summa Cum Laude) and an M.Sc. in EE. (Summa Cum Laude), both from the Technion - Israel Institute of Technology.

Vipin Jain is a passionate engineer with 20 years of industry experience. Over the years, he has contributed in the areas of switching, routing, network protocols, embedded systems, ASIC architecture, data path design, distributed systems, software-defined networking, container networking, orchestration systems, application security, open source, cloud infrastructure, and DevOps.

He holds numerous patents and has been a speaker at many conferences, author of IETF RFCs, and been a developer evangelist for his open source work. He enjoys coding for work and for fun. He also enjoys snowboarding, hiking, kayaking, and reading philosophy. He holds a bachelor's degree in Computer Science from NIT Warangal, India. He has worked in multiple successful startups in technical and management leadership roles. He is founder and CTO at Pensando Systems.

Acknowledgments

I would like to thank the following people for their contributions to this book:

- I am in debt to the MPLS team (Mario Mazzola, Prem Jain, Luca Cafiero, and Soni Jiandani) and to Randy Pond for having let me participate in the design of some of the most fantastic networking products of the last 20 years.

- John Evans and Boris Shpolyansky have spent many hours reviewing the chapters and providing countless insights.

- Rami Siadous, Bob Doud, Stuart Stammers, Ravindra Venkataramaiah, Prem Jain, Kangwarn Chinthammit, Satya Akella, Jeff Silberman, David Clear, and Shane Corban have provided many valuable comments.

- Chris Ratcliffe helped me organize my ideas and my terminology. He is a master in messaging.

- Mike Galles, Francis Matus, and Georges Akis kept me honest on all the hardware discussions.

- Krishna Doddapaneni made countless measurements on the performance of different technologies and summarized the results for this book.

- The members of the Pensando Advisory Board for many technically challenging discussions.

- Dinesh Dutt is a great friend who has helped me define the structure of this book.

- Alfredo Cardigliano provided material and insights on DPDK.

- Nital Patwa helped me to better understand the implications of integrating ARM cores in an SoC.

- Elese Orrell and Darci Quack are the graphic designers. They were effortless to work with, and I like the result.

- Brenda Nguyen and Rhonda Biddle for their support.

- Wikipedia made writing this book so much easier that I will donate the first $1,000 of royalties to this fantastic source of information.

- All the other people who gave me advice, suggestions, ideas, and reviews: my deeply felt thank you.

Chapter 1

Introduction to Distributed Platforms

In the last ten years, we have observed an increasingly rapid transition from monolithic servers to virtualization. Initially, this happened inside enterprise networks, creating the need for virtual networking, but it has quickly evolved into modern cloud architectures that add the dimension of multitenancy and, with multitenancy, increased demand for security. Each user requires network services, including firewalls, load balancers, virtual private networks (VPNs), microsegmentation, encryption, and storage, and needs to be protected from other users.

This trend is very evident in cloud providers, but even larger enterprises are structuring their networks as private clouds and need to secure network users from each other.

Software-based services are often the solution. The server CPU implements a Distributed Services Architecture in software. A virtual machine or a container comprises the software that implements the service architecture. All network traffic goes through this software and, after the appropriate processing, packets are delivered to their final destinations (other virtual machines or containers). Similar processing happens on the reverse path.

A pure software solution is limited in performance, and it has high latency and jitter. Moreover, it is very problematic in bare-metal environments where the entire server is dedicated to a user or an application, and there is no place to run the services architecture.

> A distributed services platform is a set of components unified by a management control plane that implements standard network services, such as stateful firewall, load balancing, encryption, and overlay networks, in a distributed, highly scalable way with high performance, low latency, and low jitter. It has no inherent bottleneck and offers high availability. Each component should be able to implement and chain together as many services as possible, avoiding unnecessary forwarding of packets between different boxes that perform different functions. The management control plane provides role-based access to various functions and is itself implemented as a distributed software application.

We offer a new term, *distributed services node (DSN)*, to describe the entity running various network and security services. A DSN can be integrated into existing network components such as NICs (network interface cards), switches, routers, and appliances. The architecture also allows for a software implementation of the DSN, even though only hardware is capable of providing the security and performance needed by today's networks.

Keeping DSNs closer to applications provides better security; however, DSNs should be ideally implemented at a layer that is immune to application, operating system, or hypervisor compromise.

Having multiple DSNs, as distributed as possible, increases scalability dramatically and effectively removes bottlenecks.

This architecture is practical only in the presence of a management system capable of distributing and monitoring service policies to all DSNs.

Figure 1-1 provides a graphical representation of a distributed services platform.

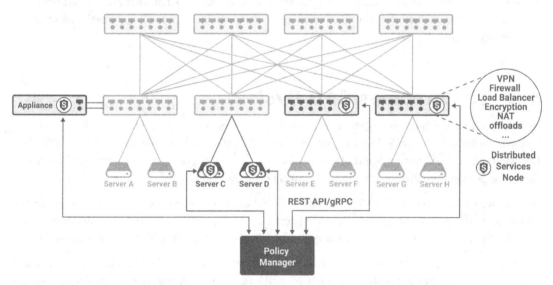

FIGURE 1-1 A Distributed Services Platform

1.1 The Need for a Distributed Services Platform

A real distributed services platform should solve not only performance issues but should also provide:

- A consistent services layer common to bare-metal servers, virtual machines, and containers

- Pervasive security without any entitlements within the perimeter; that is, decouple security from network access

- A security solution that is immune to compromised OSes or hypervisors

- Services orchestration and chaining to simplify management while enabling the delivery of different combinations of services

- Better utilization of resources, higher performance, lower latency, and latency isolation

- Tools capable of troubleshooting the network flows going through multiple services

- Built-in telemetry for edge-to-edge network troubleshooting, rather than debugging individual systems, applications and segments, to give the infrastructure the ability to proactively report potential issues and offending actors

- A comprehensive set of infrastructure services that are easy to manage and that can be used together, including features such as microsegmentation, load balancing, a firewall, encryption service, storage virtualization, and infrastructure services such as RDMA and TCP/TLS proxy

- Programmability in the management, control, and data planes so that software-defined features can be rolled out without requiring hardware swapout or extended hardware development and release cycles

1.2   The Precious CPU Cycles

In recent years, single-thread performance has only grown a few percentage points a year due to the slowdown in Moore's law as well as Dennard scaling issues (see Chapter 7, "CPUs and Domain-Specific Hardware"). Similarly, increasing the number of cores per CPU only partially helps, due to the problems pointed out in Amdahl's law on parallelization.

Another important aspect is that CPU architectures and their associated operating systems are not the best matches for implementing services at the packet level: an example is interrupt-moderation, which reduces the number of interrupts to increase throughput, but has the side effect of jitter explosion.

As processors become more complex, processor cycles are becoming more precious every day and should be used for user applications and not for network services. A purely software-based solution might use a third of the available cores on an enterprise-class CPU to implement services; this is unacceptable in cases of high load on servers. It creates a big pushback for software-based services architectures.

1.3   The Case for Domain-Specific Hardware

Domain-specific hardware can be designed to be the best implementation for specific functions. An example of successful domain-specific hardware is the graphic processor unit (GPU).

GPUs were born to support advanced graphics interfaces by covering a well-defined domain of computing—matrix algebra—which is applicable to other workloads such as artificial intelligence (AI) and machine learning (ML). The combination of a domain-specific architecture with a domain-specific language (for example, CUDA and its libraries) led to rapid innovation.

Another important measure that is often overlooked is power per packet. Today's cloud services are targeted at 100 Gbps, which for a reasonable packet size is equivalent to 25 Mpps. An acceptable power budget is 25 watts, which equates to 1 microwatt per packet per second. To achieve this minuscule amount of power usage, selecting the most appropriate hardware architecture is essential. For example, Field-Programmable Gate Arrays (FPGAs) have good programmability but cannot meet this stringent power requirement. You might wonder what the big deal is between 25 watts and 100 watts per server. On an average installation of 24 to 40 servers per rack, it means saving 1.8 to 3.0 kilowatts of power per rack. To give you an example, 3 kilowatts is the peak consumption of a single-family home in Europe.

When dealing with features such as encryption (both symmetric and asymmetric) and compression, dedicated hardware structures explicitly designed to solve these issues have much higher throughput and consume far less power than general-purpose processors.

This book should prove to the reader that a properly architected domain-specific hardware platform, programmable through a domain-specific language (DSL), combined with hardware offload for compression and encryption, is the best implementation for a DSN.

Although hardware is an essential aspect of a distributed services platform, a distributed services platform also uses a considerable amount of software.

The management and control planes are entirely software, and even the data plane must be software defined. The hardware is what provides the performance and lowers latency and jitter when used in conjunction with software. When we compare performance and delays, the differences can be enormous. Leading solutions exist in which the first packet of a flow incurs a 20-millisecond delay and other solutions in which the same packet is processed in 2 microseconds: a difference of four orders of magnitude.

1.4   Using Appliances

Today the most common implementation of services is through appliances, typically deployed centrally. These network devices implement services such as firewall, load balancing, and VPN termination. These are discrete boxes, and the traffic is sent to them explicitly in a technique called *tromboning* (see section 2.7). These devices become natural bottlenecks for traffic and impose a weird routing/ forwarding topology. They are very high-cost, high-performance devices, and even the most capable ones have limitations in performance when compared to the amount of traffic that even a small private cloud can generate. These limitations, plus the fact that a packet must traverse the network multiple times to go through service chaining, result in reduced throughput and high latency and high jitter.

A distributed services platform avoids these large centralized appliances and relies on small high-performance distributed services nodes (DSNs) located as closely as possible to the final applications they serve. They are also multifunctional; that is, they implement multiple services and can chain them internally, in any order, without needing to traverse the network numerous times.

1.5 Attempts at Defining a Distributed Services Platform

The first question we should ask ourselves is, "Which services should this architecture support?" A precise classification is difficult, if not impossible, but Figure 1-2 is an example of some of the services typically associated with a domain-specific platform.

From 10,000 feet, we can see two groups of services: infrastructure services and value-added services.

Infrastructure services are things such as Ethernet and bridging, IP and routing, storage access through a modern protocol like NVMe, RDMA transport, TCP termination, and overlay network processing.

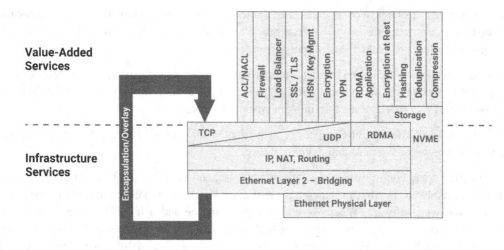

FIGURE 1-2   Services

Value-added services include a firewall, load balancer, encryption (both symmetric and asymmetric, both in flight and at rest), key management and secure storage, classical VPNs like IPsec, and more modern ones such as SSL/TLS, storage compression, and deduplication.

In this book, we will present infrastructure and value-added services together because they are deployed together in the majority of the cases.

The first attempt at a truly "distributed" network architecture can be traced back to software-defined networking (SDN). SDN is a paradigm that was introduced initially on switches and routers but was expanded to servers. It offers the capability to control and program the NIC virtual forwarding functions.

The main focus of SDNs is on infrastructure services. They do not currently address value-added services, but they create a framework where DSNs are under the central coordination of a common manager and work together toward a common goal.

There is also an open-source effort within the container community, called *service mesh*, that defines the services, such as load balancing, telemetry and security, distributed across the clusters of nodes and combined with a management control plane. The approach uses a software proxy sitting next to an application to provide layer 4 or layer 7 load balancing features and TLS security between applications and provide telemetry for all the traffic that passes through the proxy. The management control plane provides integration with orchestration systems, such as Kubernetes, and also provides a security framework to do key management for applications and define authorization primitives that can police interapplication communication. Although the effort started for containers, the concepts and code can be leveraged for virtual machines. There are many implementations of service mesh, such as Istio, Nginx, Linkerd, and some commercial closed-source implementations.

It is definitely possible to provide a much superior service mesh with DSNs by offering better security via keeping private keys within the hardware root of trust, by improving performance by an order of magnitude, and by reducing interapplication latency, without losing the software programmability.

The distributed services platform also attempts to address a few additional elements:

- Provide immunity from host/application/hypervisor compromises; that is, the enforcer shouldn't be compromised if the enforcee is compromised

- Provide services beyond the network, for example, storage, RDMA, and so on

- Offer low latency, high throughput, and latency isolation without impacting application performance

- Exhibit cloudlike scale to handle millions of sessions

A distributed services platform may be used alongside service mesh, which is an application layer concept, as opposed to an infrastructure layer concept. For example, the distributed services platform may provide isolation, security, and telemetry at the virtualization infrastructure layer, whereas service mesh can provide application layer TLS, API routing, and so on.

1.6 Requirements for a Distributed Services Platform

A truly distributed services platform requires the availability of DSNs that are placed as closely as possible to the applications. These DSNs are the enforcement or action points and can have various embodiments; for example, they can be integrated into NICs, appliances, or switches. Having as many services nodes as possible is the key to scaling, high performance, and low delay and jitter. The closer a DSN is to applications, the lesser the amount of traffic it needs to process, and the better the power profile becomes.

Services may appear to be well defined and not changing over time, but this is not the case. For example, new encapsulations or variations of old ones or different combinations of protocols and encapsulations are introduced over time. For this reason, DSNs need to be programmable in the management, control, and data planes. The control and management planes may be complicated, but they are not data intensive and are coded as software programs on standard CPUs. Data plane programmability is a crucial requirement because it determines the performance and the scaling of the architecture. Network devices that are data plane programmable are still pretty rare, even if there have been some attempts in the adapter space with devices that are typically called SmartNIC and in the switching/routing space using a domain-specific programming language called P4.

An excellent services platform is only as good as the monitoring and troubleshooting features that it implements. Monitoring has significantly evolved over the years, and its modern version is called *telemetry*. It is not just a name change; it is an architectural revamp on how performance is measured, collected, stored, and postprocessed. The more dynamic telemetry is and the less likely it is to introduce latency, the more useful it is. An ideal distributed services platform has "always-on telemetry" with no performance cost. Also, compliance considerations are becoming extremely important, and being able to observe, track, and correlate events is crucial.

Where do services apply? To answer this question, we need to introduce a minimum of terminology. A common way to draw a network diagram is with the network equipment on top, and the compute nodes at the bottom. If you superimpose a compass rose with the North on top, then the term North-South traffic means traffic between the public network (typically the Internet) and servers; the term East-West implies traffic between servers (see Figure 1-3).

Historically the North-South direction has been the focus of services such as firewall, SSL/TLS termination, VPN termination, and load balancing. Protecting the North-South direction is synonymous with protecting the periphery of the cloud or data center. For many years, it has been security managers' primary goal because all the attacks originated on the outside, and the inside was composed of homogeneous, trusted users.

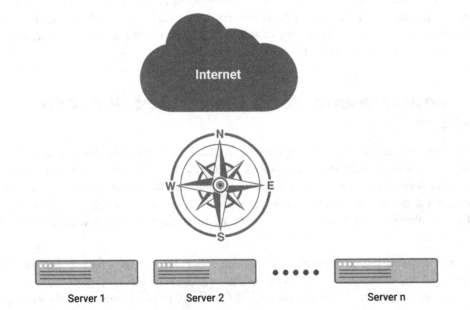

FIGURE 1-3   North-South vs. East-West

With the advent of public clouds, the change in the type of attacks, the need to compartmentalize large corporations for compliance reasons, the introduction of highly distributed microservice architectures, and remote storage, East-West traffic is now demanding the same level of services as the North-South connections.

East-West traffic requires better services performance than North-South for the following reasons:

- Usually, the North-South traffic has a geographical dimension; for example, going through the Internet creates a lower bound to the delay of milliseconds, due to propagation delays. This is not the case for East-West traffic.

- East-West traffic is easily one order of magnitude higher in bytes than North-South traffic, a phenomenon called "traffic amplification," where the size of the response and internal traffic can be much larger, that is, "amplified," compared to the inbound request. For this reason, it requires services with higher throughput.

- With the advent of solid-state disks (SSDs), the storage access time has dramatically decreased, and delays associated with processing storage packets must be minimal.

- In microservice architectures, what on the North-South direction may be a simple transaction is in reality composed of multiple interactions between microservices on the East-West direction. Any delay is critical because it is cumulative and can quickly result in performance degradation.

Institutions with sensitive data, such as banks or healthcare providers, are considering encrypting all the East-West traffic. It implies, for instance, that each communication between two microservices must be encrypted and decrypted: If the encryption service is not line-rate and low-latency, this will show up as degraded performance.

1.7 Summary

This introductory chapter delineated what a distributed services platform could be, the continuously evolving requirements of the cloud world, the rising importance of the East-West traffic, and the need for domain-specific hardware and common management.

Starting with the next chapter, we will cover all these aspects in detail.

Chapter | 2

Network Design

Why a chapter on network design in a book about distributed network services? The reality is that network design has evolved a lot in the recent years to accommodate the new scale and bandwidth requirements introduced initially in cloud networks but that are now also present in enterprise data center networks.

For many years the classical way to structure a network was with an Access-Aggregation-Core model, using a mixture of bridging, routing, and VLANs. It was primarily a layer 2–based design, with the layer 2/3 boundary at the core of the network. These layer 2, spanning tree–based, loop-free designs inherently limited the ability of the network to horizontally scale to address the increasing East-West bandwidth demand. Applications have evolved with each new generation requiring more bandwidth and lower latency than the previous one. New applications are more "media-rich" (think of the evolution from pure text to images, to videos, to high-definition, image rendering, and so on) but there is also a new way of structuring applications as microservices (see Chapter 3, "Virtualization"), increasing the data exchanged between the different parts of an application.

In enterprise data center networks, servers have evolved from 1 Gbps connectivity to 10 Gbps and are now in the process of upgrading to 25 Gbps. In a cloud infrastructure, the number of supported customers far exceeds that of data centers, with servers connected at 40/50 Gbps and moving to 100 Gbps soon, posing significant requirements on data center and cloud networks. As a result, 200 and 400 Gbps interswitch links are now becoming common.

Speed is not the only thing that has changed. Applications have evolved from monoliths to multi-tiered (web server, application, database) scale-out applications, using distributed databases, stateless distributed microservices, creating a lot more demand for East-West network capacity and, more importantly, network services. Typically, the East-West traffic is 70 percent of overall traffic and is forecast to reach 85 percent by 2021 [1].

With this increase in scale and bandwidth and the change in application architecture, the access-aggregation networks have been discontinued in favor of Clos networks that have many advantages, as explained later in this chapter, but they are layer 3 routed networks and therefore they strictly limit the role of layer 2 bridging. To continue to support legacy applications that have layer 2 adjacency requirements, various tunneling technologies have been introduced, with VXLAN becoming the most prevalent and widely deployed industry standard (see section 2.3.4 for details).

This chapter drills down on these topics, and in particular it describes:

- The difference between bridging and routing

- Routing implementation techniques, such as LPM and caches

- Clos networks that enable most public cloud architectures and large enterprise data centers

- The importance of tunneling techniques and how to secure them

- Segment routing and traffic engineering techniques

- The role of discrete appliances and the traffic trombone

After you read this chapter, it should be evident that proper network design and implementation of routing and tunneling in hardware can significantly reduce the load on server CPU cores. The availability of flexible hardware will allow the encapsulations to evolve further as new abstractions are created, ensuring less hardcoding and yet providing the performance, low latency, and low jitter for various networking and distributed services.

Understanding network design is also crucial to understanding the limitations of the appliance model and where to best place the distributed service nodes.

2.1 Bridging and Routing

The debate between bridging and routing supporters has been very active for the last 25 years. With Ethernet being the only surviving technology at layer 2, the term *bridging* is today a synonym of Ethernet bridging, with its behavior defined by the Institute of Electrical and Electronics Engineers (IEEE) in IEEE 802.1 [2] and implemented by *bridges*. On the other hand, IP is the only surviving technology at layer 3, and *routing* is the synonym of IP routing with its behavior defined by IETF [3] (Internet Engineering Task Force) RFC (Request For Comment) standards and implemented by *routers*.

Switch and *switching* are terms that do not exist in standards; they were generally introduced to indicate a multiport layer 2 bridge. Over the years, their use has expanded to layer 3 switching (which we should correctly call *routing*) and also to stateful layer 4 forwarding as used by firewalls, load balancers, and other layer 4 functions.

Independent of naming, understanding the difference between layer 2 (L2) forwarding and layer 3 (L3) forwarding is essential.

2.1.1   L2 Forwarding

Ethernet packets (properly called *frames*) have a straightforward structure that contains six fields: destination MAC address, source MAC address, 802.1Q tag, Ethertype (protocol inside the data field), data, and frame check sequence (FCS). The 802.1Q tag contains the VLAN identifier (VID) and the priority.

Of these fields, the only ones used in L2 forwarding are the VID and the destination MAC address that are concatenated and used as a key to search a MAC address table with an exact match technique. If the key is found, the table entry indicates where to forward the frame. If the key is missing, the frame is flooded to all the ports (except the one where it came in) in an attempt to make the maximum effort to deliver the frame to its final destination.

Usually, this exact match is implemented by using a hashing technique that has the capability of dealing with collisions; for example, through rehashing. Efficient hardware implementations exist for these hashing schemes.

This L2 forwarding requires a forwarding topology structured as a tree to avoid loops and packet storms. L2 forwarding uses the spanning tree protocol to prune the network topology and obtain a tree. One of the disadvantages of spanning tree is that it dramatically reduces the number of links usable in the network, blocking any connection that can cause a loop, thus substantially reducing the network bandwidth. For this reason, in modern network design, the role of bridging is strictly confined to the periphery of the network, whereas the network core uses L3 routing. We continue this discussion later in this chapter when speaking of Clos networks and VXLAN.

2.1.2   L3 Forwarding

Layer 3 forwarding is different from L2 forwarding: if the packet needs to be sent across subnets, the destination IP address is searched in an IP routing table using a longest prefix match (LPM) technique. The routing table does not include all the possible IP addresses, but it contains prefixes. For example, in IPv4, the routing table may contain:

```
10.1.0.0/16 - port 1
10.2.0.0/16 - port 2
10.1.1.0/24 - port 3
```

The /*n* indicates that only the first *n* bits from the left are significant in any matching. Now let's suppose that a packet has a destination IP of 10.1.1.2. The first entry has a 16-bit match, and the third entry has a 24-bit match, but it is mandatory to select the longest one (the one that is more specific)—that is, the third one—and therefore forward the packet on port 3.

If the LPM does not find a match in the forwarding table for the IP destination address, the packet is dropped. Not forwarding packets for which there is not a routing table entry is a significant difference compared to L2 forwarding, and it removes the requirement for a tree topology. In L3 forwarding the active network topology can be arbitrarily meshed. Temporary loops are acceptable and packets are discarded when they exceed their time to live (TTL).

LPM can be done in software using a variety of data structures and algorithms [4]. Linux uses a level-compressed trie (or LPC-trie) for IPv4, providing good performance with low memory usage. For IPv6, Linux uses a more traditional Patricia trie [5].

2.1.3 LPM Forwarding in Hardware

LPM forwarding in HW is the most common implementation of layer 3 forwarding. It is used by almost all modern routers (including layer 3 switches) [6], [7].

Figure 2-1 shows the simplicity of this approach. Each packet is processed independently of all the other packets; a full forwarding decision occurs in constant time. The packet per second (PPS) is very predictable, consistent, and independent of the type of traffic.

FIGURE 2-1 LPM Forwarding

There are a few different ways to accomplish LPM in hardware. All of them require performing a "ternary match"; that is, a match where some of the bits are "don't care" (represented by the letter "X").

For example, the route 10.1.1.0/24 is encoded as

```
00001010 00000001 00000001 XXXXXXXX
```

which means that the last 8 bits are "don't care" (ignored) in the matching process.

Ternary matches are more challenging to implement in hardware compared to the binary matches used in L2 forwarding. For example, some commercial routers use a microcode implementation of Patricia trie. Others use a hardware structure called ternary content-addressable memory (TCAM) [7] that supports ternary matches. The TCAM also contains a priority encoder not just to return any matching entry, but to return the longest one to comply with LPM. Unfortunately, TCAMs take up significant silicon space and have high power consumption.

Pure IPv4 destination routing requires a 32-bits-wide forwarding table called a forwarding information base (FIB) to host all the routes, mostly the internal ones because the routes associated with the outside world are summarized in a few entries pointing to a few default gateways.

The FIB width can grow due to several factors:

- The presence of multiple routing tables (see section 2.1.4 for a discussion of virtual routing and forwarding [VRF])

- Using IPv6 in addition to IPv4; that is, 128-bit addresses instead of 32-bit addresses

- Supporting multicast routing

One additional advantage of this approach is that it is straightforward to upgrade the FIB as a result of a route change. If a routing protocol (for example, Border Gateway Protocol, or BGP [8]) changes a few routes, the associated entries in the FIB are updated without creating any traffic disruption.

2.1.4 VRF

Virtual routing and forwarding (VRF) is a layer 3 network virtualization technology that permits multiple instances of a routing table to exist in a router and work simultaneously. This allows different kinds of traffic to be forwarded according to different routing tables. Each routing instance is independent of the others, thus supporting overlapping IP addresses without creating conflicts.

In VRF, each router participates in the virtual routing environment in a peer-based fashion; that is, each router selects the routing table according to some local criteria, the most common being the incoming interface (either physical or logical).

In the full implementation, VRF selects the routing table according to a "tag" inside the packet. Common tags are the VLAN ID or an MPLS label.

VRF requires the use of a routing protocol that is "VRF aware," such as BGP.

2.2 Clos Topology

A Clos network is a multistage network that was first formalized by Charles Clos in 1952 [9]. In its simplest embodiment, it is a two-stage network like the one shown in Figure 2-2. It can be scaled to an arbitrary number of stages, as explained later.

In their current usage and parlance, two-stage Clos networks have leaves and spines. The spines interconnect the leaves, and the leaves connect the network users. The network users are mostly, but not only, the servers. In fact, any network user needs to be attached to the leaves and not to the spines, including network appliances, wide-area routers, gateways, and so on. The network users are typically stored in racks. Each rack in its top unit usually contains a leaf, and therefore a leaf is often called a top of rack (ToR) switch.

The Clos topology is widely accepted in data center and cloud networks because it scales horizontally and it supports East-West traffic well. There are multiple equal-cost paths between any two servers, and routing protocols can load balance the traffic among them with a technique called equal cost multipath (ECMP). Adding additional spines increases the available bandwidth.

Clos networks are not suited for layer 2 forwarding, because the spanning tree protocol will prune them heavily, thus defeating their design principle. For this reason, the spanning tree protocol is not used between the spines and the leaves, but it is confined at the leaf periphery (southbound, toward the network users).

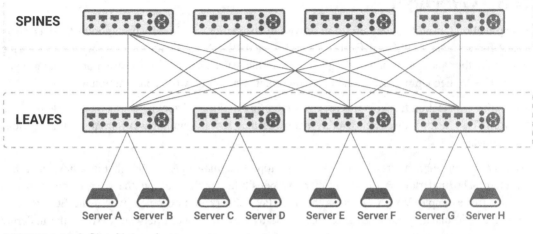

SPINES

LEAVES

Server A   Server B   Server C   Server D   Server E   Server F   Server G   Server H

FIGURE 2-2   A Clos Network

Each leaf owns one or more IP subnets, and it acts as the default gateway for these subnets. The subnets can be in the same or different VRFs.

Layer 3 routing protocols that support ECMP are used between the leaves and the spines, mainly BGP, with some deployment of Open Shortest Path First (OSPF) [10] and Intermediate-System to Intermediate-System (IS-IS) [11].

VXLAN encapsulation (see section 2.3.4) provides layer 2 connectivity across a Clos network if required.

When using ECMP to distribute the load, it is essential not to create out-of-order packet delivery that can severely impact, for example, the performance of TCP-based applications. The flow hashing technique eliminates packet reordering. The five-tuple containing source and destination IP addresses, protocol type and source, and destination ports is hashed to select a path. Different implementations may use all or a subset of the five fields.

To further scale a Clos network both in terms of users and bandwidth, it is possible to add another tier of spines, thus creating a three-tier Clos network. Functionally, these new spines are equivalent to the other spines, but they are usually called super-spines. Three-tier Clos networks can be virtual chassis-based or pod-based, but they are outside the scope of this book. A book [12] from my dear friend Dinesh Dutt contains a detailed discussion of all topics related to Clos networks.

From a hardware perspective, super-spines, spines, and leaves can be the same type of box, resulting in a considerable simplification, because this reduces the number of spare parts that are needed and it simplifies the management and provisioning.

Clos networks are very redundant, and servers can be connected to two leaves if desired. Losing one switch in a Clos network is often a non-event, and, for this reason, each box does not need to have high availability or support inline software upgrade capability. Each switch can be upgraded independently from the others and replaced if required, without significantly disrupting network traffic.

2.3 Overlays

Encapsulation has proven very useful in providing abstractions in the networking industry over many years; for example, MPLS, GRE, IP in IP, L2TP, and VXLAN. The abstraction offered by layering allows for the creation of another logical networking layer on top of a substrate networking layer. It provides for decoupling, scale, and most importantly, newer network consumption models.

Network virtualization technologies require supporting multiple virtual networks on a single physical network. This section discusses overlay networks that are a common way to satisfy the previous requirements.

An *overlay network* is a virtual network built on top of an *underlay network*; that is, a physical infra-structure. The underlay network's primary responsibility is forwarding the overlay encapsulated packets (for example, VXLAN) across the underlay network in an efficient way using ECMP when available. The underlay provides a service to the overlay. In modern network designs, the underlay network is always an IP network (either IPv4 or IPv6), because we are interested in running over a Clos fabric that requires IP routing.

In overlays, it is possible to decouple the IP addresses used by the applications (overlay) from the IP addresses used by the infrastructure (underlay). The VMs that run a user application may use a few addresses from a customer IP subnet (overlay), whereas the servers that host the VMs use IP addresses that belong to the cloud provider infrastructure (underlay).

An arrangement like the one described is shown in Figure 2-3 where the VMs use addresses belonging to the 192.168.7.0/24 subnet and the servers use addresses belonging to the 10.0.0.0/8 subnet.

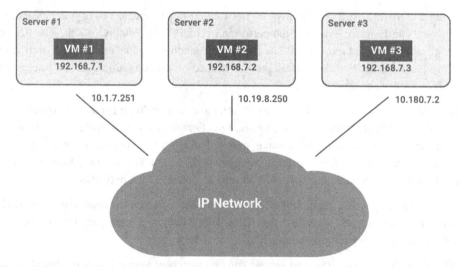

FIGURE 2-3 Customers and Infrastructure IP Addresses

Overlay networks are an attempt to address the scalability problem and to provide ease of orchestration fitting an agile model for network consumption, both critical for large cloud computing deployments. In the previous example, the packets exchanged between the virtual machines with source and destination addresses belonging to the subnet 192.168.7.0/24 are encapsulated into packets exchanged between the servers with source and destination addresses belonging to the subnet 10.0.0.0/8. The packets are said to be *tunneled*. The encapsulation is also referred to as *tunneling*, and the term *tunnel endpoints* (the points where the encapsulation is added or removed) is used.

In any overlay scheme there are two primary considerations:

- The first one is a data plane consideration: the structure of the encapsulated frame and the operations required to put a packet in the tunnel (encapsulate) and to remove a packet from the tunnel (decapsulate). Data plane considerations are of primary importance from a performance perspective. Forwarding decisions control tunneling operations, and this implies that they need to be integrated with LPM and flow tables; thus encapsulation and decapsulation should be incorporated into the forwarding hardware to achieve high performance.

- The second consideration is a control and management plane: tunnel creation and maintenance, address mapping, troubleshooting tools, and so on.

In this section, we focus on the data plane, and you will see that all the encapsulation schemes considered have the general structure shown in Figure 2-4, where the concepts of underlay and overlay are apparent.

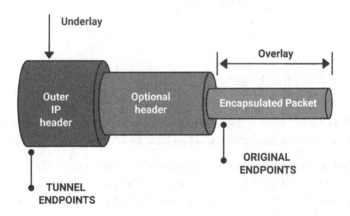

FIGURE 2-4 Generic Encapsulation

Let's consider the example of Figure 2-3, and let's assume that VM #2 wants to send a packet to VM #3. The original IP header contains Source Address (SA) = 192.168.7.2 and Destination Address (DA) = 192.168.7.3; the outer IP header contains SA = 10.19.8.250 and DA = 10.180.7.2. The content of the "other optional headers" depends on the encapsulation scheme.

In the continuation of this chapter, we will consider three encapsulation schemes: IP in IP, GRE, and VXLAN.

2.3.1 IP in IP

One of the first standards that deals with encapsulation of IPv4 in IPv4 is RFC 1853 [13], which is dated October 1995, pretty ancient history in Internet years—an essential fact to consider when examining the choices made in that standard.

In 1995 the speed of the lines was still pretty slow, the topology was sparsely connected and typically lacking parallel links, and optimizing the usage of each byte in the packet was a primary concern. Software or microcode was used to implement routers, so when designing a protocol, being "hardware friendly" was not a consideration.

IPv4 in IPv4 was the first encapsulation defined, and it did not have any optional header. In the outer IP header, the field Protocol was set to 4 to indicate that another IPv4 header was next. Normally the field Protocol is set either to 6 to indicate a TCP payload or to 17 to indicate a UDP payload. The value 4 also gave the name "Protocol 4 encapsulation" to this scheme (see Figure 2-5).

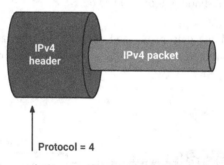

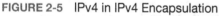

Protocol = 4

FIGURE 2-5   IPv4 in IPv4 Encapsulation

The same protocol 4 encapsulation is also usable for IPv4 inside IPv6. Merely set the field Next Header of the IPv6 header to 4 to indicate that the next header is an IPv4 header.

Another encapsulation is called *Protocol 41 encapsulation*. It is very similar to the previous one; the only difference is that the inner IP header this time is an IPv6 header. To encapsulate IPv6 in IPv4, set the Protocol of the outer IPv4 header to 41; to encapsulate IPv6 in IPv6, set the next header of the outer IPv6 header to 41 (see RFC 2473 [14]).

There are much more popular IPv6 in IPv4 encapsulations that are not covered in this book.

2.3.2 GRE

In 1994 Cisco Systems introduced Generic Routing Encapsulation (GRE) and published it as informational RFC 1701 [15], [16]. The goal was to be able to encapsulate a wide variety of network layer protocols inside virtual point-to-point links over an IP network. When GRE was designed, this was an important feature due to the relevant number of layer 3 protocols that were present on LANs (for example, AppleTalk, Banyan Vines, IP, IPX, DECnet, and so on). Although nowadays this feature is less relevant because the only surviving protocols are IPv4 and IPv6, it is still important, because with virtualization there is a need to carry layer 2 traffic inside a tunnel. Efforts such as Network Virtualization using Generic Routing Encapsulation (NVGRE) [17] and L2 GRE try to satisfy this virtualization requirement.

In a nutshell, GRE adds an extra header between the outer IP header and the original IP header, as shown in Figure 2-6.

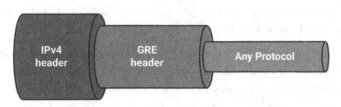

FIGURE 2-6   GRE Encapsulation

2.3.3 Modern Encapsulations

Encapsulation requirements have evolved. Minimizing overhead is no longer critical. Although it remains essential to be hardware friendly and to support richly connected networks in which multipathing is used to achieve high throughput, the network should not reorder packet arrivals, as was discussed in section 2.2.

Routers achieve ECMP and avoid packet reordering by using a hash over the five-tuple, but the five-tuple is well defined only for TCP, UDP, and SCTP. SCTP is not very common; therefore, modern encapsulation must be based either on TCP or UDP.

TCP is not a choice because it is complicated to terminate and carrying a TCP session inside a TCP tunnel has been shown to perform very poorly due to the interaction between the inner and outer TCP congestion control algorithms [18], [19]. Research has shown that using a TCP tunnel degrades the end-to-end TCP throughput, creating, under some circumstances, what is called a TCP meltdown [20].

UDP has become the de facto standard for modern encapsulation schemes. For example, VXLAN (described in the next section) and RoCEv2 (described in Chapter 6, "Distributed Storage and RDMA Services") use UDP. In these applications, the UDP checksum is not used.

2.3.4 VXLAN

Before entering into the details, let's have a 10,000-feet view of why VXLAN is essential. As we mentioned in the introduction, access-aggregation networks allowed layer 2 domains (that is, layer 2 broadcast domains) to span multiple switches. The VID (VLAN identifier) was the standard way to segregate the traffic from different users and applications. Each VLAN carried one or more IP subnets that were spanning multiple switches.

Clos network changed this by mandating routing between the leaves and the spines and limiting the layer 2 domains to the southern part of the leaves toward the hosts. The same is true for the IP subnets where the hosts are connected. To solve the problem of using a Clos network, while at the same time propagating a layer 2 domain over it, VXLAN was introduced. In a nutshell, VXLAN carries a VLAN across a routed network.

In essence, VXLAN enables seamless connectivity of servers by allowing them to continue to share the same layer 2 broadcast domain. Although VLANs have historically been associated with the spanning tree protocol, which provides a single path across a network, VXLAN can use the equal cost multi-path (ECMP) of the underlying network to offer more bandwidth.

It was designed primarily to satisfy the scalability requirements associated with large cloud computing deployments. The VXLAN standard is defined in RFC 7348 [21] and the authors' list, showing that it is a concerted effort among router, NIC, and virtualization companies, indicating the strategic importance of this overlay. Figure 2-7 shows VXLAN encapsulation.

VXLAN uses UDP encapsulation, and the destination UDP port is set to the well-known value of 4789.

The source UDP port should be randomly set, creating entropy that can be used by routers to load balance the traffic among multiple parallel links.

In a first example, the encapsulation endpoint can set the source UDP port to be equal to a hash of the original source IP address (the one in the inner IP header, typically belonging to a VM). In this way, all the packets belonging to a VM will follow one link, but other VMs may use different links. This choice implements load balancing at the VM level.

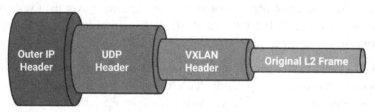

FIGURE 2-7   VXLAN Encapsulation

In a second example, the encapsulating endpoint may set the UDP source port to a hash of the five-tuple of the inner IP header. In this way, all the packets belonging to a single flow will follow the same path, preventing out-of-order packets, but different flows may follow different paths.

VXLAN is also used as a technology for encapsulating layer 3 unicast communication between application layers; this is evident in the newer revision of the VXLAN specification that allows for IP encapsulation within VXLAN natively.

Finally, VXLAN encapsulation adds a Virtual Network ID (VNID) to the original L2 frame, a concept similar to a VLAN-ID, but with a much broader range of values, because the VNID field is 24 bits, compared to the VLAN-ID field that is only 12 bits (see Figure 2-8).

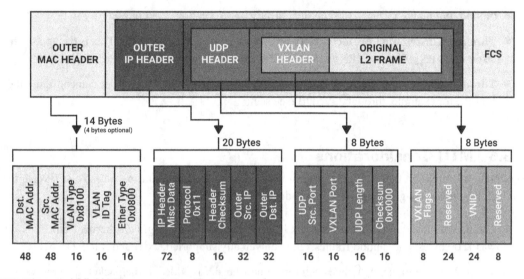

FIGURE 2-8 VXLAN Encapsulation Details

The VXLAN encapsulation adds 50 bytes to the original layer 2 Ethernet frame, which needs to be considered in the context of the network underlay; see section 2.3.5 on MTU.

VNID can be used to put the packets from multiple tenants into the same VXLAN tunnel and to separate them easily at the tunnel egress point. Figure 2-9 shows a VXLAN tunnel endpoint, or VTEP, in the leaf switches and the VXLAN tunnel overlaid on the underlying Clos network.

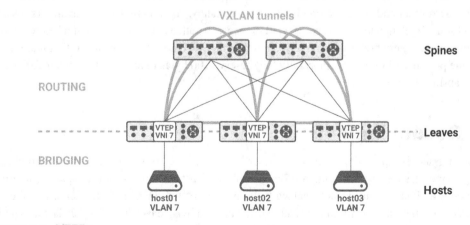

FIGURE 2-9 VTEPs

VTEPs are configured by creating a mapping between the VLAN VID and the VXLAN VNID (Figure 2-9 shows using the same number for VID and VNID, but this is not necessary). For traffic to flow, the VTEPs need to create forwarding table entries. They can do this in three ways:

- **"Flood and learn":** This is the classical layer 2 approach discussed in section 2.1.1

- **Through a distributed protocol that announces address reachability:** This is the approach taken in EVPN (Ethernet VPN) where BGP is used to advertise address reachability

- **Through an SDN (Software Defined Networking) approach:** A controller can configure the VTEPs; for example, through OVSDB (see section 4.3.1)

2.3.5   MTU Considerations

Maximum transmission unit (MTU) is a term that indicates the maximum packet size at layer 3 that can be transmitted on a given link. The MTU depends on two factors:

- The size of the data field at the data link layer. In the case of an original Ethernet frame, this size was 1500 bytes, but "jumbo frames," now universally supported, extended it to 9216 bytes.

- The presence of tunneling, since each time a new header is added to the packet, the payload is reduced by the size of the additional header.

Historically, the IPv4 protocol had the capability of fragmenting the packet under this circumstance, but modern IPv4 routers typically don't fragment IP packets—they drop them if they exceed the link MTU, increasing the difficulty to troubleshoot malfunctioning. In IPv6 fragmentation is not supported.

Path MTU discovery (PMTUD) is a standardized technique for determining the MTU on the path between IP hosts. It is standardized in RFC 1191 [22], in RFC 1981 [23], and in RFC 4821 [24]. It can help in avoiding MTU issues in overlay networks. It requires ICMP to discover the actual usable MTU on a network from an end host to an end host. Unfortunately, some network administrators disabled ICMP, and some implementations were affected by bugs, so path MTU discovery got a bad reputation. Many network managers prefer to manually configure the MTU to a lower value so that there are no issues in the presence of tunneling. Normally they reserve 100 bytes to account for packet size growth due to encapsulation.

2.4   Secure Tunnels

The tunneling and encapsulation techniques described up to this point solve a variety of problems, including address issues, layer 2 domain propagation, multicast and broadcast propagation, multiprotocol support, and so on, but do not deal with the privacy of the data. In fact, even when the data undergoes encapsulation, it is still in the clear and can be read by an eavesdropper. This lack of security may be acceptable inside the data center, but it is not tolerable when the transmission happens on a public network, in particular on the Internet.

The conventional way to secure tunnels is with the addition of encryption. Section 5.11 describes the encryption algorithms used by secure tunnels.

2.5   Where to Terminate the Encapsulation

Hosts, switches, and appliances terminate different kinds of tunnels.

Software running on the host may terminate encapsulations, and this is common in virtualized environments that do not require high performance. The network interface card in the server may provide some degree of hardware support to terminate tunnels. Appliances are commonly used to terminate all sorts of encapsulations. Initially, appliances were stand-alone boxes with physical interfaces, but recently they are also sold as "virtual appliances"; for example, as virtual machines to run in a virtualized environment. Top of Rack (ToR) switches can also terminate all kinds of encapsulation; for example, they support VLAN to VXLAN mapping to allow layer 2 traffic to propagate over a layer 3 Clos network, as explained in section 2.3.4.

Terminating simple encapsulations is relatively easy, even if not all the hardware solutions recognize all the encapsulation schemes. Complexity arises because, after terminating the encapsulation, other actions need to happen, like bridging or routing and potentially adding another encapsulation. When authentication and encryption are present, the requirement for dedicated hardware to achieve high performance is real. The need for specialized hardware becomes even more evident if the tunneling scheme requires terminating TCP, as in the case of TLS.

2.6   Segment Routing

Source routing is a technology known for decades in which the sender of the packet decides the path the packet should take to its destination. Segment routing (SR) [25] is a form of source routing where the source node defines the forwarding path as an ordered list of "segments." There are two kinds of Segment Routing:

- SR-MPLS, which is based on Multiprotocol Label Switching (MPLS)
- SRv6, which is based on IPv6

The underlying technology used by SR-MPLS is Multiprotocol Label Switching (MPLS), a routing technique that directs data from one node to the next based on "labels" rather than network addresses. Alternatively, SR can use an IPv6 data plane, as is the case in SRv6.

Segment routing divides the network into "segments" where each node and link could be assigned a segment identifier, or a SID, which is advertised by each node using extensions to standard routing protocols like IS-IS, OSPF and BGP, eliminating the need to run additional label distribution protocols such as MPLS LDP.

SR imposes no changes to the MPLS data plane. In SR the ordered list of segments is encoded as a stack of labels. The first segment to process is on the top of the stack. Upon completion of a segment processing, the segment is removed from the stack.

For example, in the absence of SR the routing between the Source and the Destination in Figure 2-10 is composed of two ECMPs: A - D - F - G and A - D - E - G (assuming all links have the same cost). In the presence of SR it is possible to forward the packet across other links. For example, if the source specifies a stack E/C/A, where A is the top of the stack, the packet is forwarded to A that pops its label, resulting in a stack containing E/C. Then A sends the packet to C, C will pop its label and forward the packet to E, which delivers it to its destination.

Using SR, it is possible to implement traffic engineering to allow the optimal usage of network resources by including links that are not part of the ECMP paths provided by IP routing.

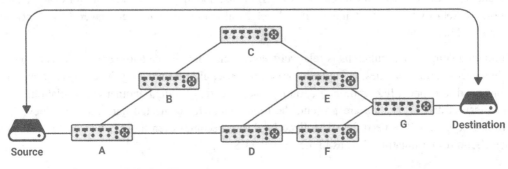

FIGURE 2-10   Segment Routing Example

Segment routing offers the following benefits:

- Network slicing, a type of virtual networking architecture with the ability to express a forwarding policy to meet a specific application SLA (for example, latency, bandwidth)
- Traffic engineering
- Capability to define separate paths for disjoint services
- Better utilization of the installed infrastructure
- Stateless service chaining
- End-to-end policies
- Compatibility with IP and SDN

2.7 Using Discrete Appliance for Services

This section contains an example of a communication between two servers that goes through a firewall and a load balancer, an operation customarily called *service chaining*.

Figure 2-11 shows a Server C that needs to communicate with Server E through a load balancer (Virtual Server Z). For security, the communication between Server C and Virtual Server Z also needs to go through a firewall. This can be achieved with a layer 2 or with a layer 3 approach.

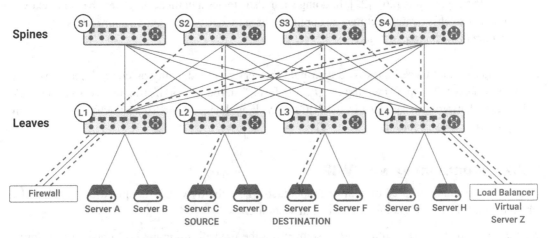

FIGURE 2-11 Example of Trombone at Layer 2

2.7.1 Tromboning with VXLAN

The first example is based on a layer 2 approach where the firewall is deployed in transparent mode, acting as the default router for the server C subnet. Please note that a host and its default router need to be in the same subnet. This is impossible without some encapsulation, because in a Clos network each leaf has native IP addresses in its own subnet. The network manager maps each subnet to a VLAN and enables VLAN trunking toward the firewall, so that the firewall may act as the default gateway for hosts in different subnets. In our case, the network manager uses a VLAN with VLAN-ID = 7 from server C to the leaf switch L2. The leaf switch L2 maps VLAN 7 to a VXLAN segment with VNID = 7 (to keep the example simple). The encapsulated frame goes through S2 to L1, L1 removes the VXLAN encapsulation and passes the packet on VLAN 7 to the firewall that receives it and applies the appropriate policies. If the packet complies with the policies, the firewall forwards it to the virtual server Z; that is, the load balancer using the same process. Again, L1 encapsulates the packet in VXLAN, L1 forwards to S4, S4 forwards to L4, L4 decapsulates and gives the packet to the load balancer that decides to send it to server E, where the same encapsulation/decapsulation process happens again.

This process has two major deficiencies:

- For server C to communicate with server E, the packet has to cross the network three times instead of one. We have spent 30 years in trying to optimize packet routing at layer 3, and now we throw it out of the window because we need to support discrete appliances.

- The firewall acts as an inter-VLAN router between L2 domains, and a significant amount of traffic is funneled through the firewall in a technique colorfully described as traffic trombone or traffic tromboning [26], [27]. In doing so, it also creates a bottleneck. Given the complexity of today's network architectures, an appliance-based security tromboning approach is an unrealistic option.

The solution to both these issues is to distribute the service functionality as close to the servers as possible. Chapter 9, "Implementing a DS Platform," introduces a distributed service network architecture that provides services in the NICs or rack appliance or the ToR switches to solve both these problems in a scalable way.

2.7.2   Tromboning with VRF

This second example is based on a layer 3 approach where the firewall is deployed in routed mode, which uses the VRF configuration described in section 2.1.4.

We start with the more straightforward case of using the firewall in Figure 2-12 only for the North-South security policy enforcement case.

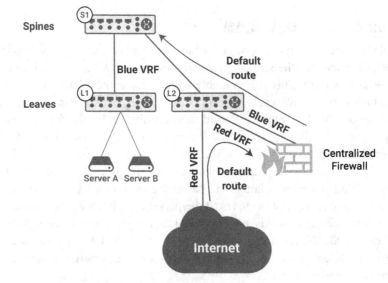

FIGURE 2-12   Example of Trombone at Layer 3

We define two VRFs: the Red VRF associated with the Internet (external) traffic and the Blue VRF associated with the data center internal traffic. All the switches in our network participate in the Blue VRF, while the leaf L2 is also a part of the Red VRF. L2 distinguishes between the Blue and the Red VRFs based on the physical ports. More sophisticated association schemes are possible, but not required for this example. The firewall has interfaces on both the Blue VRF (internal network) and the Red VRF (external network), so it is the only point of contact between the two VRFs, and thus all the traffic to/from the Internet must transit through the firewall.

The Internet-facing edge router injects the default route. The firewall receives it on the Red link and then pushes into the Blue link. The firewall has no notion of VRFs; it just maintains two BGP sessions: one on the Red link and the other on the Blue link.

Only Leaf 2 runs BGP in the Internet-facing Red VRF, with two sessions: one peering with the Internet-facing router and the other peering with the firewall on the Red link. All other routers run BGP in the Blue VRF. For example, Leaf 2 runs BGP in the Blue VRF with peering sessions to the firewall on the Blue link and Spine 1.

This default route causes all the external traffic from the Blue VRF to go through the firewall. The firewall applies its security policy and forwards the traffic through the Red VRF to the Internet. Similarly, in the opposite direction, the traffic coming from the Internet reaches the firewall on the Red VRF, and the firewall applies its security policy and forwards the traffic through the Blue VRF to its internal destination.

It is possible to use the same principle also for the East-West security policy enforcement case. In this case we need to define more VRFs. Let's suppose that we have four groups of servers that we want to keep separate on the East-West direction—we define four VRFs on all the switches of the Clos network, plus one external VRF on the leaf L2. The firewall will have five layer 3 interfaces defined, one per VRF. These interfaces don't need to be physical ports; they can be different VLANs in different subinterfaces on the same physical port.

Compared to the previous case, we have not used any VXLAN encapsulation, and the firewall is not the default gateway of the server. The firewall injects the default route, whereas the default gateway for the server remains its leaf switch (in Figure 2-12 Server A has leaf L1 as the default gateway).

2.7.3   Hybrid Tromboning

The two previous approaches can be combined into a hybrid approach. VXLAN can be used as described in section 2.7.1, but the firewall does not need to be the default gateway. The firewall injects the default routes as described in section 2.7.2.

2.8   Cache-Based Forwarding

The technique discussed in this section is not used in routers, but it has some implementation on the hosts, often in conjunction with a NIC.

Cloud providers have a large number of tenants and, even if routing and access control lists (ACLs) requirements for each tenant are moderate, when multiplied by the number of tenants there is an explosion in the number of routes and ACLs, which can be difficult to accommodate on the host with traditional table lookups.

Some cloud providers decided to implement a cache-based forwarding scheme in the server NIC hardware instead of maintaining an entire forwarding database.

A flow cache is a binary data structure capable of exactly matching packets belonging to a particular flow. The word "exactly" implies a binary match easier to implement both in hardware or software, unlike a ternary match such as LPM.

A flow cache contains an entry for each known packet flow. The flow can be defined with an arbitrary number of fields, thus supporting IPv6 addresses, different encapsulations, policy routing, and firewalling. New cache entries may be created by a separate process if a packet does not match any flow in the flow cache (this is called "a miss").

Figure 2-13 shows the organization of this solution. Any packet that causes a miss in the flow cache is redirected to a software process that applies a full decision process and forwards or drops the packet accordingly. This software process also adds an entry in the flow cache (dashed line) so that subsequent packets can be forwarded or dropped as the previous packets of the same flow.

Let's suppose that an average flow is composed of 500 packets: one will hit the software process, and the remaining 499 will be processed directly in hardware with a speed-up factor of 500 compared to a pure software solution. Of course, this solution should guarantee that packets that are processed in software and in hardware don't get reordered.

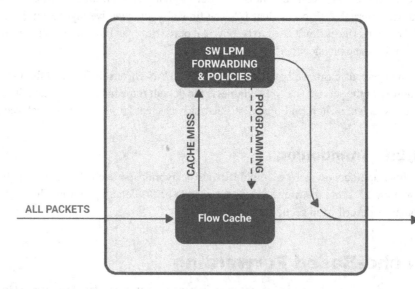

FIGURE 2-13   Cache-based Forwarding in HW

In this case, the packet per second (PPS) is not predictable and constant, because it depends on the type of traffic. Recent advances such as persistent connections in the HTTP/HTTPS protocols (that account for the majority of the traffic) tend to make the flows longer and, therefore, can play in favor of this solution.

Another consideration is that multiple protocols exchange only a couple of packets per flow. These are auxiliary protocols like Domain Name Server (DNS), Time Server, and so on. For these protocols, it is not meaningful to create a cache entry, because it only consumes cache resources without generating a significant increase in performance.

The width of the cache may be significant, due to these factors:

- Doing source routing in addition to destination routing: two addresses instead of one
- Using IPv6 in addition to IPv4: 128-bit addresses instead of 32-bit addresses
- Using overlay techniques (see section 2.3) like IP in IP or VXLAN: more headers to parse
- Doing policy routing on layer 4 headers: the need to parse protocol types and source and destination ports
- Implementing firewalls and load balancers

In an extreme case, the cache width was 1700 bits, making the hardware extremely complicated; that is, more square millimeters of silicon, higher cost, and more power.

An attractive property of this solution is ease of merging multiple services into a single cache entry; for example, it is possible to remove an encapsulation, route the packet, apply firewall rules, and collect statistics with a single cache entry.

Of course, as with all cache solutions, there is the issue of cache maintenance; for example, aging old entries. A bigger problem happens when a route changes. In fact, there is no easy way to know which cache entries are affected and therefore the conventional approach is to invalidate the whole cache. Immediately after clearing the cache, there is a drop-in performance that, even if transient, is significant. For this reason, cache-based forwarding is not used in backbone routers that are subject to frequent route changes. In the case of a peripheral network service point, one can argue route changes are a rare event, and therefore cache invalidation is acceptable. Chapter 3, "Virtualization," describes a few implementations of software switches that use this technique. In some cases, the first packet is processed on the server CPU core; in other instances it is processed in cores embedded in a NIC, providing different grades of offload.

2.9 Generic Forwarding Table

Generic forwarding table (GFT) is an approach used in Microsoft Azure [28], [29] that follows the model described in the previous section. Azure has a virtual machine offering based on Hyper-V, the Microsoft Hypervisor (see section 3.2.2). Hyper-V includes a software switch to forward packets between the virtual machines and the network. To implement GFT, Microsoft built VFP (Virtual Filtering Platform) to operate on top of Hyper-V software switch. VFP has the concept of unified flows, matching a unique source and destination L2/L3/L4 tuple, potentially across multiple layers of encapsulation, along with the capability of adding, removing, or modifying headers.

A custom Azure SmartNIC includes a field programmable gate array (FPGA) to accelerate the forwarding operations by implementing the flow cache in hardware [30].

The cache redirects any packet that has a miss to VFP, which in turn forwards the packet in software and programs the cache.

Currently, VFP runs on the primary server CPU, but there is no technical reason why the SmartNIC itself cannot have a CPU to host VFP, thus freeing server CPU cycles.

2.10 Summary

In this chapter, we discussed the network design concepts that are at the basis of designing a distributed network service architecture. We discussed L2 versus L3 forwarding, two different implementations of L3 forwarding, the impact of Clos networks, and the requirements for routing in the network core. This requires the introduction of overlay networks and a way of securing them. We have also analyzed how the presence of appliances creates the tromboning issue and how a distributed services architecture solves that. Finally, we have discussed segment routing as a way to increase network utilization and predictability.

In the next chapter, we discuss in a similar and parallel way the impact of virtualization on a distributed network service architecture.

2.11 Bibliography

[1] Cisco Global Cloud Index: Forecast and Methodology, 2016–2021, https:// www.cisco.com/c/en/us/solutions/collateral/service-provider/global-cloud-index-gci/white-paper-c11-738085.pdf

[2] https://1.ieee802.org

[3] RFC Editor, "Internet Official Protocol Standards," RFC5000, May 2008.

[4] W. Eatherton, Z. Dittia, and G. Varghese. Tree Bitmap: Hardware/Software IP Lookups with Incremental Updates. ACM SIGCOMM Computer Communications Review, 34(2):97–122, 2004. Online at http://cseweb.ucsd.edu/~varghese/PAPERS/ccr2004.pdf

[5] Park, Hyuntae, et al. "An efficient IP address lookup algorithm based on a small balanced tree using entry reduction." Computer Networks 56 (2012): 231–243.

[6] Waldvogel, M., Varghese, G., Turner, J.S., & Plattner, B. (1997). Scalable High Speed IP Routing Lookups. SIGCOMM.

[7] Pagiamtis, K.; Sheikholeslami, A. (2006). "Content-Addressable Memory (CAM) Circuits and Architectures: A Tutorial and Survey." IEEE Journal of Solid-State Circuits. 41 (3): 712–727. Online at https://www.pagiamtzis.com/pubs/pagiamtzis-jssc2006.pdf

[8] Lougheed, K. and Y. Rekhter, "Border Gateway Protocol 3 (BGP-3)", RFC 1267, DOI 10.17487/RFC1267.

[9] Clos, Charles. "A study of non-blocking switching networks". Bell System Technical Journal. 32 (2): 406–424. doi:10.1002/j.1538-7305.1953. tb01433.x. ISSN 0005-8580. Mar 1953, Retrieved 22 March 2011.

[10] Moy, J., "OSPF Version 2", STD 54, RFC 2328, DOI 10.17487/RFC2328, April 1998.

[11] Zinin, A., "Cooperative Agreement Between the ISOC/IETF and ISO/IEC Joint Technical Committee 1/Sub Committee 6 (JTC1/SC6) on IS-IS Routing Protocol Development", RFC 3563, DOI 10.17487/RFC3563.

[12] Dutt, Dinesh. "Cloud-Native Data Center Networking Architecture: Protocols, and Tools." O'Reilly, 2019.

[13] Simpson, W., "IP in IP Tunneling," RFC 1853, DOI 10.17487/RFC1853, October 1995.

[14] Conta, A. and S. Deering, "Generic Packet Tunneling in IPv6 Specification," RFC 2473, DOI 10.17487/RFC2473, December 1998.

[15] Hanks, S., Li, T., Farinacci, D., and P. Traina, "Generic Routing Encapsulation (GRE)," RFC 1701, DOI 10.17487/RFC1701, October 1994.

[16] Farinacci, D., Li, T., Hanks, S., Meyer, D., and P. Traina, "Generic Routing Encapsulation (GRE)," RFC 2784, DOI 10.17487/RFC2784, March 2000.

[17] Garg, P., Ed., and Y. Wang, Ed., "NVGRE: Network Virtualization Using Generic Routing Encapsulation," RFC 7637, DOI 10.17487/RFC7637, September 2015.

[18] O. Titz, "Why TCP over TCP is a bad idea." http://sites.inka.de/sites/bi-gred/devel/tcp-tcp.html

[19] Honda, Osamu & Ohsaki, Hiroyuki & Imase, Makoto & Ishizuka, Mika & Murayama, Junichi. (2005). Understanding TCP over TCP: effects of TCP tunneling on end-to-end throughput and latency. Proc SPIE. 104.10.1117/12.630496.

[20] OpenVPN, "What is TCP Meltdown?," https://openvpn.net/faq/what-is-tcp-meltdown

[21] Mahalingam, M., Dutt, D., Duda, K., Agarwal, P., Kreeger, L., Sridhar, T., Bursell, M., and C. Wright, "Virtual eXtensible Local Area Network (VXLAN): A Framework for Overlaying Virtualized Layer 2 Networks over Layer 3 Networks," RFC 7348, DOI 10.17487/RFC7348, August 2014.

[22] Mogul, J. and S. Deering, "Path MTU discovery," RFC 1191, DOI 10.17487/RFC1191, November 1990.

[23] Lottor, M., "Internet Growth (1981–1991)," RFC 1296, DOI 10.17487/RFC1296, January 1992.

[24] Mathis, M. and J. Heffner, "Packetization Layer Path MTU Discovery," RFC 4821, DOI 10.17487/RFC4821, March 2007.

[25] Filsfils, C., Ed., Previdi, S., Ed., Ginsberg, L., Decraene, B., Litkowski, S., and R. Shakir, "Segment Routing Architecture," RFC 8402, DOI 10.17487/RFC8402, July 2018.

[26] Ivan Pepelnjak, "Traffic Trombone (what it is and how you get them)," ip-space.net, February 2011. https://blog.ipspace.net/2011/02/traffic-trombone-what-it-is-and-how-you.html

[27] Greg Ferro, "VMware 'vFabric' and the Potential Impact on Data Centre Network Design—The Network Trombone" etherealmind.com, August 2010, https://etherealmind.com/vm- ware-vfabric-data-centre-network-design

[28] Greenberg, Albert. SDN for the Cloud, acm sigcomm, 2015.

[29] Firestone, Daniel et al. "Azure Accelerated Networking: SmartNICs in the Public Cloud." NSDI (2018), pages 51–66.

[30] Daniel Firestone. "VFP: A virtual switch platform for host SDN in the public cloud." In 14th USENIX Symposium on Networked Systems Design and Implementation (NSDI 17), pages 315–328, Boston, MA, 2017. USENIX Association.

Chapter | 3

Virtualization

The previous chapter discussed how network design has an impact on a distributed network service architecture, but it is nothing compared to the effect of virtualization techniques like virtual machines (VMs) and containers, which are crucial components of cloud infrastructures and modern data centers. VMs and containers are not synonymous, and they don't have the same scope:

- VMs provide machine virtualization and packaging that helps instantiate a machine on demand, with specified CPU, memory, disk, and network.

- Containers provide application packaging and application runtime within a server.

In general, virtualization techniques allow for higher workload density, and when using microservices, to partition monolith functions into smaller units, to replicate them effectively, and to move them around as needed. These workloads are also dynamic; that is, they are created and terminated often, and this creates a need for automating the network services. This causes an explosion in the number of IP addressable entities and the need to offer granular network services to these entities; for example, firewalling and load balancing. At this point, the reader may deduce that a solution that addresses virtualized loads solves all problems. Unfortunately, this is far from the truth. In enterprise data centers, a large number of the servers are "bare metal"; that is, without any virtualization software. Even public clouds, where initially the load was 100 percent virtualized, are now moving to offer bare-metal servers that remain important for specific applications, like databases, or allow bring-your-own-hypervisor; for example, VMware. Almost all cloud providers offer bare-metal servers in addition to VMs. Therefore, any distributed network service architecture must support equally well all bare-metal server, virtual machine, and container environments.

The remainder of this chapter describes these environments. The discussion is organized into sections on virtualization and clouds, virtual machines and hypervisors, containers, and the microservice architecture.

At the end of this chapter, it should be apparent that most networks use a combination of techniques with some applications running on bare metal and others on virtual machines, and some rewritten following the microservice architecture and thus are suitable for containers. This chapter also outlines an example of a management and provisioning system (OpenStack) and an instance on a virtualized application in the Telco space (NFV).

3.1 Virtualization and Clouds

In the old days, some computers were running multiple concurrent applications to increase computer utilization. Unfortunately, this proved impractical because different applications require different libraries, OSes, kernels, and so on and running various applications on the same computer provided almost no separation from a security, management, and performance perspective. Many computers became dedicated to a single application, which resulted in very low CPU and memory utilization. Server virtualization was invented to solve these and other issues.

Server virtualization addresses several needs:

- Multiple OS environments can exist simultaneously on the same machine, isolated from each other.

- A physical server can run various logical servers (usually called virtual machines or VMs). Running a VM per CPU core is a standard practice.

- It reduces the number of physical servers by increasing server utilization, thus reducing the cost associated both to server CAPEX and OPEX; for example, space and electrical power.

- Applications can take advantage of multiple cores without the need to rewrite them in a multi-threaded and parallel way. Server virtualization allows users to run multiple copies of the same application on different VMs.

- Virtualization enables testing and staging environments to be run in parallel with production, and this is a considerable simplification.

- Machine provisioning, snapshots, backup, restore, and mobility become much more straightforward.

- Virtualization software offers centralized management and provisioning.

- Because each virtual machine is a complete server, including the OS and the kernel, there is better application isolation and security than in shared environments.

- Hardware independence is obtained by presenting a "standardized hardware" to all the virtual machines.

Of course, there are also drawbacks, mainly in the area of high RAM usage and application performance predictability, but these must be minor because server virtualization has become a de facto reality on which many corporations rely for their day-to-day operations.

Virtualization allows for greater sharing of resources; for example, all the VMs may share a single 100G NIC. However, whenever there is sharing, there is the potential for abuse. In a multitenant cloud, a so-called "noisy neighbor" may consume most of the available resources (PCI bandwidth, for example) and impact other tenants on the server. This is a problem even if the "noise" is transient.

VMware was the first commercially successful company to virtualize the x86 architecture [1], and nowadays its presence in the data center is relevant. KVM (Kernel-based Virtual Machine) is one of the few public domain hypervisors, and it is used as a starting point for many offerings in the cloud space.

Public clouds are now a very mature offering, with players such as Amazon Web Services (AWS)—a subsidiary of Amazon.com, Azure—a cloud computing service created by Microsoft, Oracle Cloud Infrastructure, IBM Cloud, Google Cloud Platform, Alibaba Cloud, OVH, and others.

Private clouds are the new way of organizing an enterprise data center so that virtual servers, in the form of virtual machines, can be easily and quickly provisioned. Clouds provide more agility and cost savings. The sentence "cloud-native data center infrastructure" is used to describe these realities.

Hybrid clouds, shown in Figure 3-1, are the current frontier.

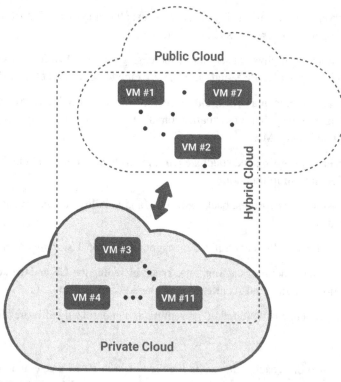

FIGURE 3-1   A Hybrid Cloud

Hybrid clouds are a combination of private and public clouds to achieve load balancing, fault tolerance, computing peak absorption, data partitioning, and so on. In a perfect hybrid cloud architecture, a virtual machine can be located in the private part or the public part and can be moved from one place to another without having to rewrite code, change addresses or policies, or being concerned about security issues. In advanced cases, this move can happen while the virtual machine is running.

Hybrid clouds pose incredible challenges that are only partially addressed by current solutions.

Clouds have also made multitenancy a de facto reality. Cloud providers must protect users from each other because applications of different users can run on the same physical server and use shared storage resources and shared network services. Different users may use the same private IP addresses that, if not appropriately dealt with, may create conflicts on the network. Finally, in a cloud environment, the provider must take care of securing access to the user applications, both in terms of firewalling and encryption and to offer other value-added services such as load balancing.

Multi-tenancy is a reality not only in the public cloud but also inside large enterprises to separate and protect different activities from each other; for example, for legal compliance.

Multi-tenancy requires an on-demand virtual infrastructure instantiation per tenant, including network, storage, compute, security, and other services.

These new requirements have created a need to layer this new virtual infrastructure as closely as possible to the workload. A distributed services platform is the best solution for these needs.

3.2 Virtual Machines and Hypervisors

Today two major virtualization solutions are available:

- Virtual machines and hypervisors (described in this section)
- Containers (described in section 3.3)

At first glance, these may look like two simple variations of the same solution, but when you dig deeper, they are substantially different.

The idea behind virtual machines is to take a physical server, including OS, kernel, userspace, libraries, and applications and transform it into a virtual server that runs inside a virtual machine. No assumption is made on what the physical server does or on how the application or applications are structured inside the server. With the advent of packaging, portability, and tooling around it, virtualizing applications has become easier. Multiple tools are available to migrate a physical server into a virtual machine without changing anything.

The idea behind containers is different. Containers can be used to repackage an application or to convert it into a microservice architecture. When it is being repackaged, the application and its runtime environment are encapsulated in a container without requiring any rewriting; for example, a Python application that requires Python 2.6 can be packaged in a container, run alongside another application requiring Python 4.5 wrapped in a different container. Containers also offer the possibility to convert an application to microservices, but this means reorganizing the application often with substantial rewriting, to follow the new microservice architecture described in section 3.4. In a nutshell, the application is divided into multiple independent modules that communicate with each other using standardized APIs. A container instantiates each module.

If an application is built as a microservice, it can be horizontally scaled out by instantiating multiple copies, each being a stateless service.

If a module is a performance bottleneck, the same module may be instantiated in multiple containers.

Although it is partially possible to use virtual machines as containers and vice versa, the full potential of the solution is achieved when each technique is used for its proper purpose.

In the remainder of this section, we drill down on these two concepts:

- The hypervisor, which creates an environment where the virtual machine runs

- The virtual machine, which encapsulates a physical server including the operating system (kernel and userspace), the libraries, and the applications

Figure 3-2 shows two types of hypervisors: bare metal and hosted.

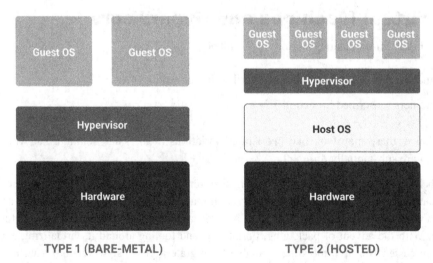

TYPE 1 (BARE-METAL)   TYPE 2 (HOSTED)

FIGURE 3-2   Different Types of Hypervisors

A bare-metal hypervisor [2] is a native operating system that runs directly on the hardware, with direct access to the hardware resources, thus providing scalability, robustness, and performance.

The disadvantage of this approach is that the hypervisor must have all the drivers required to support the hardware over which it is running.

In contrast, a hosted hypervisor is an extension to an existing operating system, with the advantage of supporting the broadest range of hardware configurations.

Another way to classify hypervisors is by looking at the kind of virtualization they offer: full virtualization or paravirtualization.

Full virtualization provides a total abstraction of the underlying physical server and requires no modification in the guest OS or application; that is, in the virtual machine. Full virtualization is advantageous when migrating a physical server to a virtual machine because it provides complete decoupling of the software from the hardware but, in some cases, it can incur a performance penalty.

Paravirtualization requires modifications to the guest operating systems that are running in the virtual machines, making them "aware" that they are running on virtualized hardware. Performance may improve, but it is not as generic as full virtualization.

Hypervisors contain one or more virtual switches, also known as vSwitches, that are software entities in charge of switching packets among virtual machines and through the network interface cards (NICs) to the outside world (see Figure 3-3).

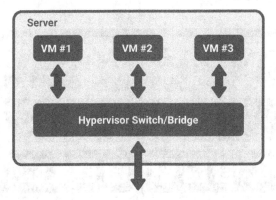

FIGURE 3-3 A Virtual Switch

A vSwitch usually acts as a layer 2 bridge, offers virtual Ethernet interfaces to the VMs, and connects to one or more NIC. The external connectivity, in the presence of multiple NICs, can be configured in two primary modes of NIC teaming: active-standby and active-active. Active-standby is self-explanatory. Active-active on hypervisors has the following flavors:

- **vEth-based forwarding:** Traffic arriving on a virtual Ethernet (vEth) port is always sent to a given uplink unless a failure is observed.

- **Hash-based forwarding:** This can be MAC address, IP address, or flow based.

The active-active mode can implement static bonding or dynamic (LACP)-based bonding.

vSwitches are essential in the context of a distributed services platform because they represent a place where it is possible to implement a distributed network service architecture. Their functionality can also be moved into hardware to increase performance. We describe various virtual switch approaches and standards in section 4.3 in Chapter 4, "Network Virtualization Services."

Although the hypervisor is the real enabler of VMs, commercial companies monetize their investments on the management and service offerings. Often services are offered as virtual appliances; that is, as VMs that implement a particular function, such as firewall, VPN termination, and load balancer. These virtual appliances are very flexible, but they often lack the deterministic performance and latency of physical appliances that use dedicated hardware.

In the next sections, we consider two commercial and two open source virtualization systems.

3.2.1 VMware ESXi

Founded in 1998, VMware was one of the first commercially successful companies to virtualize the x86 architecture [3]. VMware ESXi is the hypervisor of VMware. It is a bare-metal hypervisor that supports full virtualization. Figure 3-4 shows an ESXi server with two VMs. The ESXi presents a hardware abstraction to each VM.

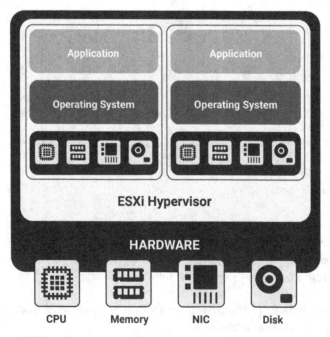

FIGURE 3-4   VMware ESXi

Each VM has its OS, including the kernel, and it has the perception of running on the real hardware.

Not having a host OS, ESXi needs drivers for all the server hardware components, and this may limit its deployability in the presence of uncommon HW. VMware offers certified compatibility guides that list system, I/O, storage/SAN, and backup compatibility.

The basic version of ESXi has a free license, and VMware offers many additional features under a paid license. These include

- **VMware vCenter:** A centralized management application to manage virtual machines and ESXi hosts centrally as well as features typically needed to enable business continuity, such as vMotion; that is, the capability to do live migration of VM from one ESXi host to another.

- **VMware vSAN:** A storage aggregation layer to create a single storage pool shared across all hosts in the vSAN cluster.

- **VMware NSX:** A distributed network virtualization that includes switching, routing, firewalling, and other network and security services.

VMware is a software company. At the time of writing it implements all its solutions in software, and this has worked well so far because the speed of the Intel processors has continually increased. Unfortunately, this trend is slowing down, as shown in Chapter 7, "CPUs and Domain-Specific Hardware," and time will tell whether VMware will have to move some of its functionality to domain-specific hardware.

Finally, a significant evolution is the native support of VMware in the cloud. For example, VMware Cloud on AWS is an integrated cloud offering, jointly developed by AWS and VMware, in which the customer can provision, on the AWS cloud, servers that run the VMware software. This offering has the capability of supporting a hybrid cloud and moving VMs from the private part to the public portion and vice versa. Tools also exist to migrate applications to and from the cloud. Similar announcements are expected with other cloud providers.

3.2.2 Hyper-V

Microsoft Hyper-V [4] is a bare-metal hypervisor that can create virtual machines on x86 64-bit systems. It was first released alongside Windows Server 2008 and has been available without additional charge since Windows Server 2012 and Windows 8. Microsoft also released a standalone version, called Hyper-V Server 2008, that is available as a free download, but with the command line interface only. Figure 3-5 shows the Hyper-V architecture.

Hyper-V implements isolation of virtual machines in terms of a partition. Each VM runs in a separate child partition. A root or parent partition contains the Windows OS, which is responsible for the management of the server, including the creation of the child partitions; that is, of the VMs.

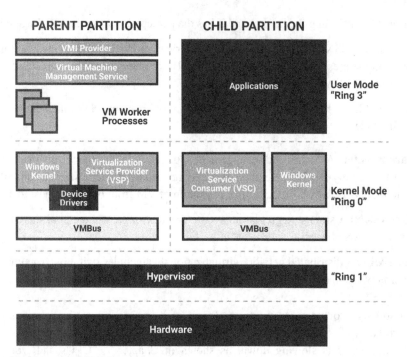

FIGURE 3-5   The Hyper-V Architecture

The virtualization software runs in the parent partition and has direct access to the hardware devices. The parent partition has several roles:

- Controls the physical processors, including memory management and interrupts
- Manages the memory for the child partitions
- Handles the devices connected to the hypervisor such as the keyboard, mouse, and printers
- Presents the device to the child partitions as virtual devices

When a child partition accesses a virtual device, the virtual device forwards the request via the VMBus to the devices in the parent partition, which will manage it. The VMBus is a logical channel that enables interpartition communication. The response also travels back via the VMBus. Hyper-V also offers "Enlightened I/O," a mechanism that allows the VMBus to interact with the hardware directly for high speed I/O operations.

Even though not shown in the picture, Hyper-V has the capability of creating virtual switches that provide virtual network adapters to its virtual machines and teamed physical network adapters to serve as uplinks toward the network switches.

By default, Hyper-V also provides virtualization support for Linux guests and Microsoft has submitted Hyper-V drivers to the Linux kernel. Hyper-V Linux support can be extended by installing the Linux Integration Components.

Hyper-V is also the hypervisor at the base of Microsoft's Azure offering. In section 2.9 we discussed the relationship between the Hyper-V virtual switch and the Azure SmartNIC.

3.2.3   QEMU

QEMU (Quick EMUlator) [5] [6] is a complete, standalone open-source software capable of operating as a machine emulator, or virtualizer.

When operating as a machine emulator, QEMU transforms binary code written for a given processor into another one (for example, it can run x86 code on an ARM processor). QEMU emulates a processor through dynamic binary translation and provides a set of different hardware and device models to run a variety of guest operating systems. QEMU includes a long list of peripheral emulators: network, display adapters, disks, USB/serial/parallel ports, and so on.

When used as a virtualizer, QEMU runs code on the native architecture; for example, x86 code over an x86 platform. In this configuration, it is typically paired with KVM (see the next section) to implement a hypervisor.

QEMU used as an emulator is slower than QEMU used as a virtualizer because it involves translating binary code. QEMU virtualizer runs virtual machines at near-native speed by taking advantage of CPU virtualization features such as Intel VT or AMD-V.

3.2.4   KVM

KVM (for Kernel-based Virtual Machine) [7], [8] is an open-source hosted hypervisor, full virtualization solution that can host multiple virtual machines running unmodified Linux or Windows images. Figure 3-6 shows the KVM architecture.

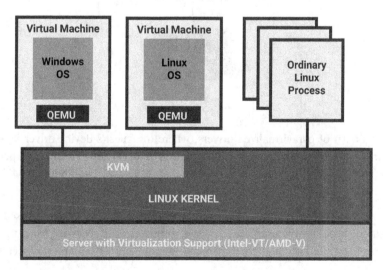

FIGURE 3-6   The KVM Architecture

A Linux host OS is booted on the bare-metal hardware. The kernel component of KVM is included in mainline Linux as of 2.6.20. KVM uses either Intel VT or AMD-V virtualization extensions. KVM consists of a loadable kernel module, kvm.ko, that provides the core virtualization infrastructure and a processor-specific module, kvm-intel.ko or kvm-amd.ko. This code is responsible for converting the Linux kernel into a hypervisor. KVM also supports PPC, S/390, ARM, and MIPS processors.

In conventional Linux-style, KVM does one thing, and it does it right. It leaves process scheduling, memory management, and so on to the Linux kernel. Any improvements done by the Linux community to these features immediately benefit the hypervisor as well.

KVM does not provide virtualized hardware; it leverages QEMU. The userspace component of KVM is included in QEMU (see the previous section). Each virtual machine created on a host has its own QEMU instance. The guest runs as part of the QEMU process.

KVM exposes its API to userspace via ioctls, and QEMU is one of the users of this API.

QEMU is also integrated with Virtio, as shown in Figure 3-7.

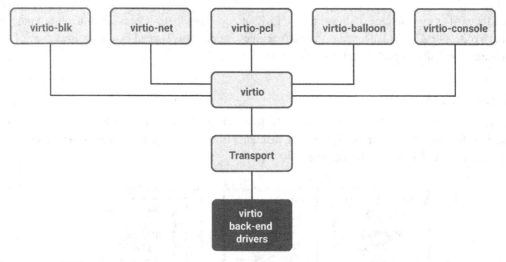

FIGURE 3-7   Virtio

Virtio [9], [10] is a set of paravirtualized drivers, where the guest's device driver is aware that it is running in a virtual environment and cooperates with the hypervisor to obtain high-performance; for example, in network and disk operations. Virtio is tightly integrated with both QEMU and KVM, as shown in Figure 3-8.

In particular, the vhost driver in the Linux kernel implements a fast, kernel-based Virtio device emulation. Usually, the QEMU userspace process emulates I/O accesses from the guest. Vhost puts Virtio emulation code into the kernel, reducing the number of buffer-copy operations and thus improving performance. Section 8.5 further discusses Virtio-net because it has applicability also outside KVM/QEMU.

QEMU and KVM support both the classical virtual switch model and SR-IOV, a standard described in section 8.4, to move the virtual switch into the NIC for high networking performance. Figure 3-9 shows the two cases. The TAP device shown in Figures 3.8 and 3.9 is a virtual ethernet interface that works at layer 2 and is associated with a specific guest/VM.

Finally, from a management perspective, libvirt [11] provides a hypervisor-neutral API to manage virtual machines, including storage and network configurations.

Public cloud companies such as AWS and Google use KVM in production.

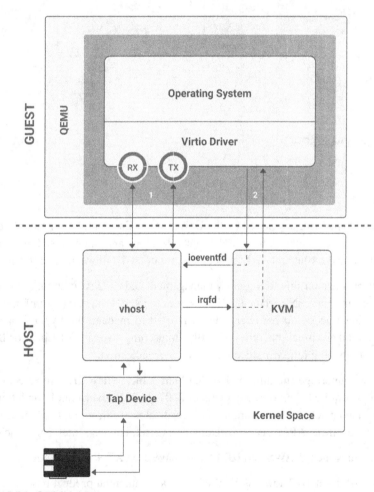

FIGURE 3-8   KVM, QEMU, Virtio

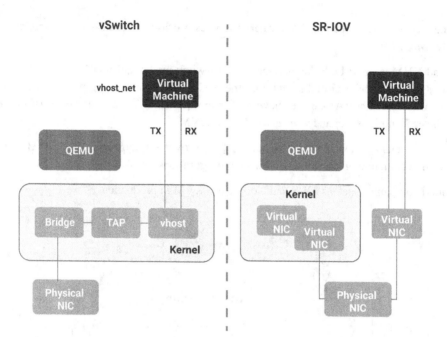

FIGURE 3-9   vSwitch with SR-IOV

3.2.5 XEN

XEN is a bare-metal hypervisor developed by the University of Cambridge Computer Laboratory [12], [13]. In the open-source community, the XEN Project develops and maintains Xen. Xen is currently available for Intel 32- and 64-bit and ARM processors. Figure 3-10 shows its architecture.

The XEN hypervisor is responsible for memory management and CPU scheduling of virtual machines, also known as "domains" in XEN parlance. XEN reserves to itself domain 0 ("dom0"), the only virtual machine that has direct access to hardware. dom0 is used to manage the hypervisor and the other domains; that is, the other virtual machines. Usually, dom0 runs a version of Linux or BSD. For user domains, XEN supports both full virtualization and paravirtualization.

Around 2005, a few Cambridge alumni founded XenSource, Inc. to turn XEN into a competitive enterprise product. Citrix acquired XenSource in October 2007. In 2013 the Linux Foundation took charge of the Xen project and launched a new community website at xenproject.org. Current project members include AlibabaCloud, AMD, ARM, AWS, BitDefender, Citrix, Huawei, Intel, and Oracle.

Public cloud companies such as AWS and IBM Cloud have used XEN in production.

Citrix hypervisor [14], formerly known as XenServer, is a commercial product based on XEN.

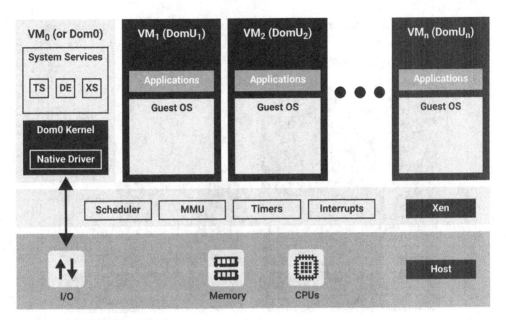

FIGURE 3-10 The XEN Architecture

3.3 Containers

Container-based virtualization, or *containers* for short [15], is a virtualization technique that matches well the microservice architecture described in the next section. It is a virtualization method that avoids launching an entire VM just to run an application.

In traditional virtualization, a VM not only contains the application, but it also includes the OS and the kernel. In container virtualization, all the applications running on the same host share the same kernel, but they may have a customized view of the OS and its distribution packaging; for example, libraries, files, and environment variables. Linux OS offers LXC (LinuX Containers), a set of capabilities of the Linux kernel that allow sandboxing processes from one another by using resource isolation, kernel namespaces, and kernel groups.

The most relevant kernel techniques used by containers are:

- **Namespaces:** pid namespace, network namespace, mount, ipc, user, and so on
- **Chroot:** Allows for a different root file system for an application instead of that of the base OS
- **Control groups:** Allows isolation of resources among various processes; for example, CPU, memory, disk, and network I/O

Containers also rely on a union-capable file system such as OverlayFS. Containers expand or replace LXC to achieve additional advantages.

Figure 3-11 shows the difference between a hosted hypervisor and container virtualization.

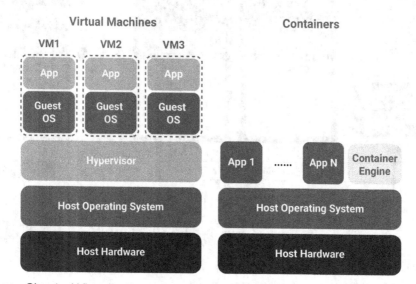

FIGURE 3-11   Classical Virtualization versus Container Virtualization

Container efforts can be classified as runtime mechanisms to execute multiple containers on the same physical server and as management and provisioning efforts to simplify the deployment and monitoring of a large number of containers, also known as *orchestration*. Docker is a well-known solution for the first aspect, whereas Kubernetes addresses the second aspect.

3.3.1 Docker and Friends

This section describes container runtimes; that is, software systems that allow multiple containers to run on the same server. Among them, Docker is probably the most well-known.

Docker [16] started in France as an internal project within dotCloud, a platform-as-a-service company. The software debuted to the public in 2013 and, at that time, it was released as open source.

Docker replaces LXC with runC (formerly known as libcontainer), uses a layered filesystem (AuFS), and manages networking. Compared to hypervisor virtualization, it offers less isolation, but it is much lighter to run, requiring fewer resources. The conventional wisdom is that you can run on a physical server up to ten times more containers compared to virtual machines. The comparison is partly unfair because a container typically runs just a microservice, not the entire application. Docker is not the only container runtime solution available. Other similar solutions are containerd (now part of the Cloud Native Computing Foundation) [17]; OCI (Open Container Initiative) [18]; Rocket, part of CoreOS [19] (a lightweight OS that can run containers efficiently, recently acquired by Red Hat); and Mesos [20] a container scheduler similar to Kubernetes.

3.3.2 Kata Containers

In the previous sections, we have discussed how containers share the OS kernel and achieve isolation through kernel namespaces and groups. In some applications, having a common kernel shared by two or more containers is considered a security risk—a classic example being a financial application. The Kata Container project [21] tries to solve this issue and promises " ... *the speed of containers, and the security of VMs ...*"

Figure 3-12 compares the classical container approach with Kata Containers.

In Kata Containers, each container has its kernel, thus providing the same level of isolation as virtual machines. Of course, this also comes at the cost of a more substantial infrastructure.

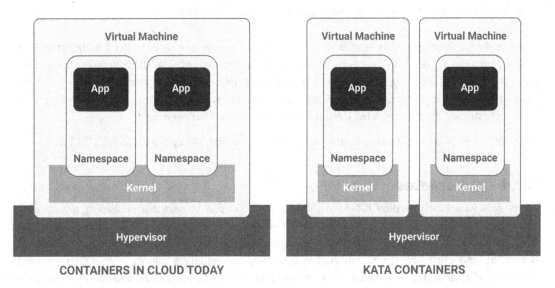

FIGURE 3-12 Kata Containers

Companies offering virtual machine solutions have done a significant amount of work to mitigate their disadvantages in comparison to containers. Today's offerings range from virtual machines to Kata Containers, to standard containers with trade-offs present in each choice.

3.3.3 Container Network Interface

Containers are more dynamic than virtual machines and much more dynamic than bare-metal servers. Containers are deployed in great numbers, and they are created and destroyed continuously. The lightweight nature of containers enables "elasticity," where services are scaled on demand. Service scaling should be automatic, so, naturally, container connectivity should be automated through an API. The Container Network Interface (CNI) answers this need [22]. It is a simple interface between the container runtime and network implementation. It is a way for an orchestrator to connect a workload to the network. It was developed as part of Rocket at CoreOS. It is a generic plugin-based networking solution for application containers on Linux. The plugability allows for normalizing the user-visible semantics for various network providers; for example, users of the orchestrator can use the same interface regardless of whether it is running in a public cloud as a service or in an on-premise network.

Currently, it is composed of a simple set of four APIs:

- ADD network for a container
- DEL network for a container
- CHECK status of the network for a container
- VERSION, which provides the supported CNI versions by the driver

These APIs are blocking APIs; for example, container orchestrator would wait for the underlying network provider to finish the network plumbing, including assigning an IP address, to ensure that network is ready before an application can be started to use the network. This semantic makes it a perfect place to instantiate any security and other policies before the workload is brought up. Kubernetes and other orchestration systems selected CNI; it has become the industry standard.

A similar effort exists in the storage space; it is called Container Storage Interface (CSI) [23].

3.3.4 Kubernetes

Kubernetes (commonly written K8s) [24], [25] is an important project that is shaping the future of containers. Kubernetes is container orchestration software for automating deployment, scaling, and management of containerized applications. Google designed it based on the experience of creating Borg [26], and currently, the Cloud Native Computing Foundation maintains it. Other container orchestration systems exist, such as Mesos, but Kubernetes is the most popular and the most promising one. It manages containerized applications across multiple hosts in a cluster. Figure 3-13 shows the Kubernetes cluster components.

Figure 3-14 illustrates how microservices are deployed using Kubernetes.

A Kubernetes cluster is composed of at least three nodes. Each node may be a VM or a bare-metal server. Each node contains the services necessary to run pods (see later) and is managed by the master node(s). Services on a node include the container runtime (typically Docker), kubelet (the primary node agent), and kube-proxy (the network proxy).

The master node(s) contains the cluster control plane. Multinode high-available masters are common in production. The API server is the front-end of the Kubernetes control plane. The master node(s) includes the API server, the front-end of the Kubernetes control plane; the "etcd" database, a highly available key-value store used for all cluster data; the scheduler; and various controllers.

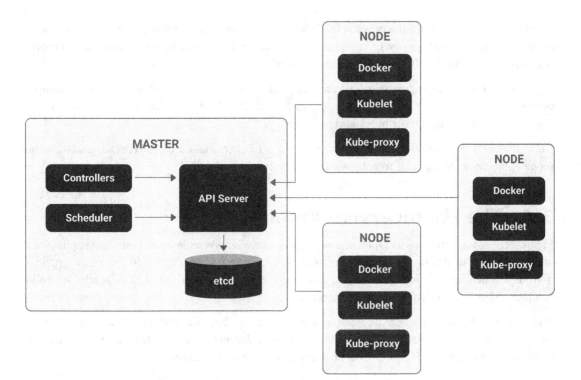

FIGURE 3-13 Kubernetes Cluster Components

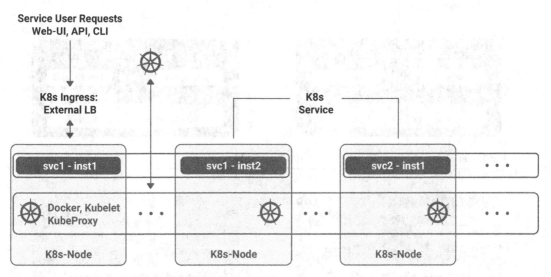

FIGURE 3-14 Microservices Deployed using Kubernetes

Another critical concept in Kubernetes is the "pod." A pod is an atomic unit of deployment that cannot be split. A pod encapsulates one or more containers that share the same resources and local network. A pod is highly available. If it dies, it gets rescheduled.

A pod is the unit of replication in Kubernetes. In production, it is common practice to have multiple copies of a pod running for load balancing and fault tolerance. When an application is overloaded, it is possible to increase the number of instances of a pod.

Kubernetes is a vast system with many components; a full explanation of Kubernetes is outside the scope of this book. Kubernetes maintains a nice documentation site [27].

3.4 The Microservice Architecture

In this section, we shift gears and look at how to apply virtualization techniques best when applications are written from scratch or substantially rewritten. The most recent paradigm is to write these applications as a collection of microservices [28] and to use microservices as the "LEGO blocks" to build complex and scalable software or newer services.

There is no official definition of what a microservice is but, for this book, we assume this: "*A microservice implements a small unit of a conceptual business function that can be accessed via a well-defined interface.*" Figure 3-15 depicts a microservice architecture.

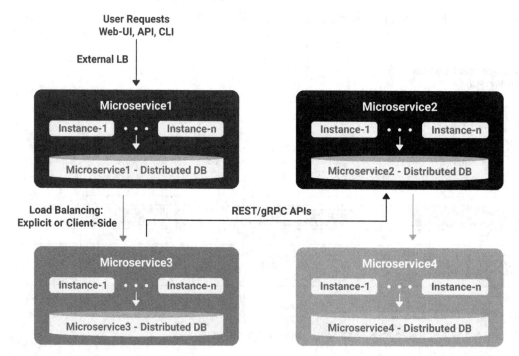

FIGURE 3-15   A Microservice Architecture

Commonly accepted attributes of a microservice architecture are:

- Services are fine-grained.

- Protocols are lightweight.

- Application decomposition in microservices improves modularity.

- Applications are easier to understand, develop, and test.

- Continuous application delivery and deployment is easily enabled.

- Because microservices communicate through a clean API, they can be coded using different programming languages, databases, and so on.

- They can be independently scaled as the load increases by creating multiple instances and load balancing among them.

- They are usually built as stateless, restartable services, each backed by a shared database.

- They create a small failure domain with a scale-out model.

- Microservices are fast and easy to spin up and tear down.

The API used by microservices is either a REST API (see section 3.4.1) or gRPC (see section 3.4.2). Sometimes microservices support both APIs. REST API and gRPC usually run on top of HTTP/HTTPS protocols. HTTPS enables the applications to provide authenticated access to a given microservice. These APIs are generally backward compatible, so components can be swapped out with newer revisions without impacting other parts.

Microservices are implemented as stateless instances; that is, they can be quickly terminated/started to scale up/down with the application load. This allows a load balancer to sit in front and route any incoming URLs/APIs to various back-end instances.

Microservices are popular with developers because they are faster to develop, test, rebuild, and replace, thanks to their independence from each other and clear APIs. Teams can be smaller and more focused and adopt new development technologies more efficiently.

Microservices are natively designed for the cloud; they can be run on-premise or in the cloud. They take advantage of the container architecture and modern tooling; see section 3.3.

Microservices use mature schedulers such as Kubernetes (see section 3.3.4) and built-in telemetry, security, and observability. Microservices also have disadvantages. The main one is that they don't work well for existing or "brownfield" applications; that is, they require applications to be rewritten.

Troubleshooting can also be challenging due to the need to track interservice dependencies. There are tools for helping this aspect but, of course, they consume resources and add overhead.

There is also additional latency because function calls inside a process are replaced with RPCs over the IP network, with all the associated overhead.

Highly optimized standardized tooling like protobuf/gRPC (see section 3.4.2) can help to compensate for this overhead. Also, RPC load balancers add an extra hop before a service can be reached. Client-side load balancing (for example, finagle, gRPC-lb) can help alleviate this.

Another critical design consideration is that partitioning an application in microservices with improper abstractions can be worse than keeping it monolithic. Inappropriate partitioning results in increased RPC calls, which exposes internal functioning, and troubleshooting interservice dependencies becomes a nightmare, especially in the presence of circular dependencies. Any microservice architecture should account for time spent creating the correct business abstractions.

Microservices are also complicated to deploy and operationalize without proper tooling like Kubernetes (see section 3.3.4).

3.4.1   REST API

Roy Fielding first introduced REST (Representational State Transfer) in 2000 in his dissertation [29]. It is a software architecture that defines a set of constraints that must be satisfied to create RESTful web services. REST is a client-server architecture that separates the user interface from the application logic and storage. Each REST request is stateless; that is, it contains all the information necessary to process it, and it cannot refer to any state stored on the server. Session state is, therefore, kept entirely on the client. Each response must also indicate if the data is cacheable; that is, if the client can reuse it. Requests are sent from the client to the server, commonly using HTTP. The most common methods are GET, PUT, POST, and DELETE. Typically, the responses are formatted in HTML, XML, or JSON.

REST aims to achieve performance, reliability, and reusability by using a stateless protocol and standard operations. REST is not a synonym of HTTP: REST principles are stricter and can be applied independently of HTTP.

A common approach is to start from an object model and generate the REST APIs automatically. Swagger [30] has been both a tool to create the API and a modeling language that has now evolved into OpenAPI Specification (OAS) [31]. YANG [32] (Yet Another Next Generation) is another data modeling language that can be used for this purpose.

3.4.2   gRPC

gRPC [33] is an open source remote procedure call (RPC) system developed initially at Google. gRPC is coupled with *protocol buffers* [34].

Protocol buffers are Google's "language-neutral, platform-neutral, extensible mechanism for serializing structured data." An interface description language (IDL) describes the structure of the data, and a program creates the source code for generating and parsing the byte stream. gRPC can use protocol buffers as both its IDL and as its underlying message interchange format.

gRPC uses HTTP/2 for transport and provides features such as authentication, bidirectional streaming, flow control, blocking or nonblocking bindings, cancellation, and timeouts.

REST API and gRPC are similar in functionality, and they can be generated simultaneously from the same IDL or modeling language, but they have differences, too:

- REST API encodes textual representation, making it easy to be human readable; for example, the "curl" utility can be used to execute a REST API and interact with a system.

- gRPC uses a binary representation, making it more compact and high performance, and it has built-in load balancing.

In general, gRPC is suitable for internal service-service communication, whereas REST is useful for external communication.

3.5 OpenStack

When a company wants to build a cloud, some of the significant problems to solve are the provisioning, management, and monitoring of the cloud infrastructure. Several commercial companies offer software for this purpose. OpenStack is an open-source project that attempts to address the problem in its globality.

OpenStack [35] is an open-source software platform for provisioning, deployment, and management of VMs, containers, and bare-metal servers. It is a modular architecture dedicated to builders and operators of cloud infrastructures.

The OpenStack Foundation manages the project under the principles of open source, design, development, and community.

It is one of the most significant open source projects, but it is difficult to grasp its actual penetration in production environments.

Figure 3-16 shows the OpenStack architecture.

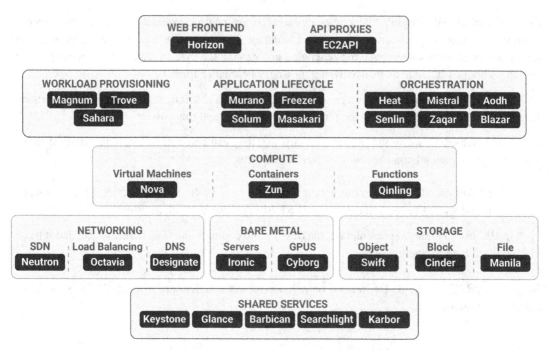

FIGURE 3-16   The OpenStack Architecture

Among the many modules that constitute OpenStack, the most relevant are:

- **Keystone (Identity Service):** A service for authenticating and managing users and roles in the OpenStack environment. It authenticates users and services by sending and validating authorization tokens.

- **Neutron (Networking):** A service for physical and virtual networking in an OpenStack cloud. It includes many standard networking concepts such as VLANs, VXLANs, IP addresses, IP subnets, ports, routers, load balancers, and so on.

- **Nova (Compute):** A service for physical and virtual computing resources, mainly instances (for example, virtual machines) and hosts (for example, hardware resources, mostly servers). Nova can also be used to snapshot an instance or to migrate it.

- **Glance (Image Service):** A service to register, discover, and retrieve virtual machine images.

- **Cinder (Block Storage):** A service to connect storage volumes to compute instances. Cinder supports different storage protocols, like iSCSI, to access the storage volumes.

- **Swift (Object Storage):** A service that implements object storage on commodity hardware. Swift is highly scalable and redundant.

- **Ironic (bare-metal):** A service for server bare-metal provision.

The book *OpenStack Cloud Computing* [36] provides a good overview of OpenStack and shows the role of Ansible [37] in OpenStack configuration and automation. Figure 3-16 shows that many more modules are available in addition to the ones listed previously.

3.6 NFV

This section contains an example of application of virtualization, called Network Function Virtualization (NFV), mainly used in the telecommunications community.

The architecture of telephone networks has dramatically evolved with the introduction of cellular technology. Each new generation (2G, 3G, 4G, LTE, 5G) has added more features, deemphasizing classical phone calls in favor of Internet traffic, apps, and services. Initially, telecommunications companies have tried to implement these services using discrete appliances, like firewalls, NATs, load balancers, session border controllers, message routers, CDNs, WAN optimizers, and so on, but with the explosion of traffic and services, this approach has become impractical.

According to the ETSI (European Telecommunications Standards Institute) [38], new service creation often demands network reconfiguration and on-site installation of new dedicated equipment, which in turn requires additional floor space, power, and trained maintenance staff. The goal of NFV is to replace hardware appliances with virtualized network functions to allow networks to be agile and capable of responding to the needs of new services and traffic. In the extreme case, most of these functions can be moved to the cloud.

NFV is a network architecture that virtualizes entire classes of network node functions into building blocks that connect and are chained together to create communication services. It uses traditional server virtualization and virtual switches, as previously discussed, but it also adds virtualization of load balancers, firewalls, devices offering network address translation (NAT), intrusion detection and prevention, WAN acceleration, caching, Gateway GPRS Support Nodes (GGSN), Session Border Controllers, Domain Name Services (DNS), and other layer 4 services.

Figure 3-17 shows an example of NFV. A different gray tone indicates distributed services for a diverse group of users.

New standards like 5G, the latest generation of cellular mobile communications, exacerbate these needs by supporting many more applications and, therefore, many more user groups with different needs; for example, IoT (Internet of Things) and autonomous vehicles.

ETSI has been very active in trying to standardize NFV in one of its working groups, the ETSI ISG NFV [39]. Open Source Mano is also an ETSI-hosted initiative to develop an Open Source NFV Management and Orchestration (MANO) software stack aligned with ETSI NFV [40].

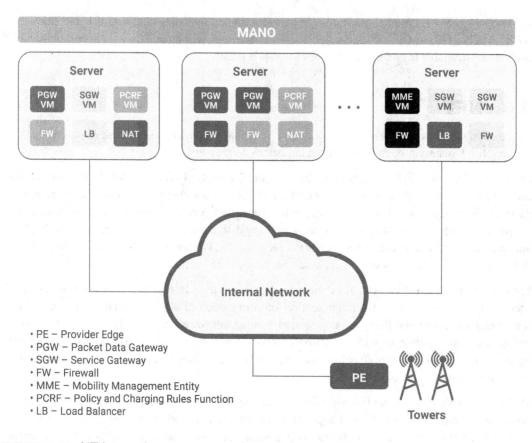

FIGURE 3-17   NFV example

3.7 Summary

This chapter shows that any distributed network service architecture should support a mixture of bare-metal servers, virtual machines, and containers and be integrated with management and orchestration frameworks. Where to place the distributed services nodes depends on multiple factors, including virtualized versus bare-metal workload, the amount of bandwidth required, and the kind of services needed. The remainder of the book describes these topics in detail.

The next chapter focuses on network virtualization services.

3.8 Bibliography

[1] Bugnion, E., Devine, S., Rosenblum, M., Sugerman, J., and Wang, E. Y. 2012. Bringing virtualization to the x86 architecture with the original VMware Workstation. ACM Trans. Comput. Syst. 30, 4, Article 12 (November 2012), 51 pages.

[2] Alam N., Survey on hypervisors. Indiana University, Bloomington, School of Informatics and Computing, 2009.

[3] VMware ESXi: The Purpose-Built Bare Metal Hypervisor, https://www.vmware.com/products/esxi-and-esx.html

[4] Anthony Velte and Toby Velte. 2009. *Microsoft Virtualization with Hyper-V* (1 ed.). McGraw-Hill, Inc., New York, NY, USA.

[5] Fabrice Bellard. 2005. QEMU, a fast and portable dynamic translator. In Proceedings of the annual conference on USENIX Annual Technical Conference (ATEC '05). USENIX Association, Berkeley, CA, USA, 41–41.

[6] QEMU, https://www.qemu.org

[7] Habib I., "Virtualization with KVM," Linux Journal, 2008:8.

[8] Linux KVM. https://www.linux-kvm.org

[9] Virtio, https://wiki.libvirt.org/page/Virtio

[10] Using VirtIO NIC - KVM, https://www.linux-kvm.org/page/Using_VirtIO_ NIC

[11] ibvirt. https://libvirt.org

[12] Paul Barham, Boris Dragovic, Keir Fraser, Steven Hand, Tim Harris, Alex Ho, Rolf Neugebauer, Ian Pratt, and Andrew Warfield. 2003. Xen and the art of virtualization. In Proceedings of the nineteenth ACM symposium on Operating systems principles (SOSP '03). ACM, New York, NY, USA, 164–177. DOI: https://doi.org/10.1145/945445.945462

[13] XEN, https://xenproject.org

[14] Citrix hypervisor, https://www.citrix.com/products/citrix-hypervisor

[15] What is a Linux Container, RedHat, https://www.redhat.com/en/topics/containers/whats-a-linux-container

[16] Docker, https://www.docker.com

[17] Cloud Native Computing Foundation, containerd, https://containerd.io

[18] The Linux Foundation Project, OCI: Open Container Initiative, https://www.opencontainers.org

[19] CoreOS, https://coreos.com

[20] Mesos, http://mesos.apache.org

[21] Kata Containers, https://katacontainers.io

[22] GitHub, "Container Network Interface Specification," https://github.com/containernet working/cni/blob/master/SPEC.md

[23] GitHub, Container Storage Interface (CSI) Specification, https://github. com/container-storage-interface/spec

[24] kubernetes or K8s, https://kubernetes.io

[25] Kelsey Hightower, Brendan Burns, and Joe Beda. 2017. *Kubernetes: Up and Running Dive into the Future of Infrastructure* (1st ed.). O'Reilly Media, Inc.

[26] Verma, A., Pedrosa, L., Korupolu, M., Oppenheimer, D., Tune, E., & Wilkes, J. (2015). Large-scale cluster management at Google with Borg. EuroSys. https://pdos.csail.mit.edu/6.824/papers/borg.pdf

[27] Kubernetes documentation, kubernetes.io/docs/home

[28] Sam Newman. 2015. *Building Microservices* (1st ed.). O'Reilly Media, Inc.

[29] Fielding, Roy Thomas, "Chapter 5: Representational State Transfer (REST)." Architectural Styles and the Design of Network-based Software Architectures (Ph.D.). University of California, Irvine, 2000.

[30] Swagger, https://swagger.io

[31] Open API. https://www.openapis.org

[32] Bjorklund, M., Ed., "YANG—A Data Modeling Language for the Network Configuration Protocol (NETCONF)," RFC 6020, DOI 10.17487/RFC6020, October 2010.

[33] gRPC, https://grpc.io

[34] Protocol Buffers, https://developers.google.com/protocol-buffers

[35] OpenStack Foundation. https://www.openstack.org

[36] Kevin Jackson. 2012. *OpenStack Cloud Computing Cookbook*. Packt Publishing.

[37] Ansible, https://www.ansible.com

[38] ETSI, http://www.etsi.org

[39] NFV, http://www.etsi.org/technologies-clusters/technologies/nfv

[40] Mano, http://www.etsi.org/technologies-clusters/technologies/nfv/open-source-mano

Chapter | **4**

Network Virtualization Services

Three main types of services are required to successfully implement a cloud infrastructure: networking, security, and storage services. These services are essential services to implement any multitenant architecture, be it private or public.

This chapter explains the networking services with particular emphasis on network virtualization. Chapter 5, "Security Services," describes the security services.

In a distributed services platform, these two services can be located in different places, because they are not strictly related to the I/O and memory architecture of the server. Chapter 6, "Distributed Storage and RDMA Services," describes two other services, RDMA and storage, which are best hosted in the server because they are more tightly coupled with the I/O and memory of the server.

4.1 Introduction to Networking Services

Adding networking services to a cloud or data center network is associated with several challenges. Among them:

- **Where to locate the services:** They can be implemented in the server software, in the server hardware, or in a network device external to the server.

- **Complexity:** Traditional mechanisms of inserting service appliances are met with operational complexity, needing complicated automation, and imposing limitations associated with a single or dual point of failure.

- **Lack of management:** Integration with existing management tools and orchestration systems like VMware and Kubernetes can provide ease of deployment and simplification to the end user.

- **Lack of visibility:** Deploying telemetry in the infrastructure is also a big part of securing it. Knowing the application-level insights can be beneficial to the architects, as well as application developers to plan capacity, and to understand security postures.

- **Lack of troubleshooting tools:** Today's tools are still very cumbersome to use, involving multiple touch points and having to be turned on when required, making it a tedious process; hence the need for always-on telemetry and troubleshooting.

- **Limited performance:** Implementing network, security, telemetry and other services in software running on the server CPU steals precious cycles from user applications. A perfect server should use 100 percent of its CPU cycles to run user applications! The availability of domain-specific hardware that implements a correct standard networking model will remove these loads from the server CPU.

Because some of the recent technology trends in networking have been particularly chaotic, especially concerning server networking, we will try to clarify the historical reasoning behind them and their future directions.

The final part of the chapter describes some new trends in telemetry and troubleshooting. Even the best service implementation will fall short if not accompanied by state-of-the-art troubleshooting and telemetry features.

4.2 Software-Defined Networking

At the end of the previous century, all the crucial problems in networking were solved. On my book-shelf I still have a copy of *Interconnections: Bridges and Routers* by Radia Perlman [1] dated 1993. In her book, Perlman presents the spanning tree protocol for bridged networks, distance vector routing, and link state routing: all the essential tools that we use today to build a network. During the following two decades there have been improvements, but they were minor, incremental. The most significant change has been the dramatic increase in link speed. Even Clos networks, the basis of the modern data center leaf-spine architecture, have been known for decades (since 1952).

In 2008, Professor Nick McKeown and others published their milestone paper on OpenFlow [2]. Everybody got excited and thought that with software-defined networking (SDN), networks were going to change forever. They did, but it was a transient change; a lot of people tried OpenFlow, but few adopted it. Five years later, most of the bridges and routers were still working as described by Perlman in her book.

But two revolutions had started:

- A distributed control plane with open API
- A programmable data plane

The second one was not successful because it was too simple and didn't map well to hardware. However, it created the condition for the development of P4 to address those issues (see Chapter 11, "The P4 Domain-Specific Language").

OpenFlow impacted even more host networking, where the SDN concept is used in a plethora of solutions. It also had some traction in specific solutions such as SD-WAN.

The remainder of this chapter discusses these topics in detail.

4.2.1   OpenFlow

OpenFlow is a switching and routing paradigm that was originally proposed by Professor Nick McKeown and others [2]. The project is now managed by the Open Networking Foundation (ONF) [3], a nonprofit operator-led consortium that maintains and develops the OpenFlow specification.

The genesis of OpenFlow is rooted in two separate factors. The first was a profound dissatisfaction of the network managers about how closed and proprietary routers and switches were. The issue was not related to the routing protocols that were standard and interoperable; it was the management experience that was a nightmare. Each different vendor had a different command line interface (CLI), which sometimes also had variations among different models from the same vendor. The only programmatic interface was Simple Network Management Protocol (SNMP) that was only used to collect information, not to configure the boxes. A correct REST API was missing or, when present, it was just a wrap-around of the CLI, returning unstructured data that needed custom text parsing instead of standard format like XML or JSON. Network managers wanted a programmatic interface to configure and provision switches and routers.

The second factor was related to the research community and academia. They also were concerned about how closed and proprietary the routers and switches were, but for a different reason: It was impossible for them to develop and test new routing protocols and forwarding schemes. The abstract of the original OpenFlow paper [2] states: "*We believe that OpenFlow is a pragmatic compromise: on one hand, it allows researchers to run experiments on heterogeneous switches in a uniform way at line-rate and with high port-density, while on the other hand, vendors do not need to expose the internal workings of their switches.*"

OpenFlow gained some popularity among the folks that challenged the conventional wisdom of shortest path first (SPF), the most common style of routing, as they needed to provide custom forwarding and traffic engineering between data centers, based on custom business logic; for example, routing based on time of day.

A lot of people in the networking community thought that OpenFlow could kill two birds with one stone and solve both problems at the same time. But let's not get ahead of ourselves, and let's first understand what OpenFlow is. OpenFlow is an architecture that separates the network control plane (where the routing protocols run) from the data plane (where packets are forwarded). The control plane runs on servers called controller, while the data plane runs on routers and switches that can be either hardware devices or software entities (see Figure 4-1).

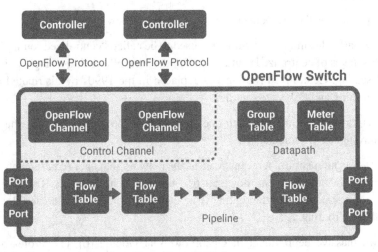

FIGURE 4-1   Main Components of an OpenFlow Switch

The OpenFlow specification [4] defines two types of OpenFlow switches: OpenFlow-only and OpenFlow-hybrid (in this chapter the word *switch* means a combination of a layer 2 switch and a layer 3 router, which is commonly used in SDN/OpenFlow). OpenFlow-only switches forward packets according to the OpenFlow model only. OpenFlow-hybrid switches have a classification mechanism, outside the specification of OpenFlow, that decides whether the packets must be forwarded according to classical layer 2 and layer 3 models, or according to OpenFlow. In the rest of this section, we focus on OpenFlow-only switches and their four basic concepts: ports, flow tables, channels, and the OpenFlow protocol.

The OpenFlow ports are the switch ports passing traffic to and from the network. OpenFlow packets are received on an ingress port and processed by the OpenFlow pipeline, which may forward them to an output port. They can be physical ports, as in the case of the switch front panel ports, or they can be logical ports; for example, a linux netdev interface, which can be a virtual ethernet (vEth) port.

Reserved ports are also available; for example, for forwarding traffic to the controller.

The OpenFlow flow tables are the key components of the OpenFlow pipeline, which is an abstraction of the actual hardware of the switch. The pipeline and the tables are divided into two parts: ingress and egress. Ingress processing is always present, whereas egress processing is optional. A flow table is composed of flow entries, and each packet is matched against the flow entries of one or more tables. Each flow entry has match fields that are compared against packet headers, a priority, a set of counters, and a set of actions to be taken if the entry is matched. This is a simplified view; for full details, see the OpenFlow Switch Specification [4].

The OpenFlow channel is the control channel between the OpenFlow controller and the OpenFlow switch. The OpenFlow controller uses this channel to configure and manage the switch, to receive events and packets, and to send out packets.

The OpenFlow protocol is the protocol spoken over the OpenFlow channel.

OpenFlow has remarkable similarities with what used to be called "centralized routing" [5]. It also has the same disadvantages of centralized routing, mainly the controller being a single point of failure and not capable of scaling. Centralized routing was replaced in the 1990s by distributed routing such as distance vector routing and link state routing.

Although the centralized routing approach does not scale at the Internet level, it has some merit in limited and controlled environments.

OpenFlow has lost its momentum in recent years as the network manager requirements of provisioning and programming network boxes are now satisfied by approaches such as REST API, NETCONF/ YANG, gRPC, and so on, whereas the routing issue continues to be well-addressed by distance vector routing and link state routing.

The only known massive deployment of OpenFlow is at Google [6], [7]. Professor Amin Vahdat explained part of Google's strategy in an interview with NetworkWorld [8]. What emerges is that Google has a substantial investment in wide-area networks, the links are costly, and there is a desire to run them more efficiently, as closely as possible to 100 percent utilization. Google uses OpenFlow for traffic engineering and prioritization, an approach also called SD-WAN and discussed in the next section.

Recently, Google has also started to push for another approach called gRIBI, described in section 4.2.3.

OVS, described in section 4.3.1, also uses OpenFlow as the datapath, and OVS is used by VMware NSX, OpenStack and a few others.

Finally, Professors Nick McKeown and Amin Vahdat are now on the board of the P4 Language Consortium [9]. P4 is a language designed for programming of packet forwarding planes. P4 addresses some shortcomings of OpenFlow by allowing flexible packet header parsing, coupled with the match-action pipeline of OpenFlow. We discuss the P4 approach in Chapter 11.

4.2.2   SD-WAN

Software-defined wide-area network (SD-WAN) is the combination of the SDN and VPN technologies designed to support WAN connectivity to connect enterprise networks, branch offices, data centers, and clouds over vast geographic distances [10]. It is a packaging of many existing technologies in a new creative way. The promises of SD-WAN are many, including its ability to manage multiple types of connections, from MPLS to broadband and LTE; simplified cloud-based management; the capability of provisioning bandwidth on demand; of using different links according to cost or time of day; and so on.

Another attraction of SD-WANs is their ability to consistently manage all policies across all the sites from a common place. Policy management was one of the biggest challenges before SD-WAN, creating security lapses and forcing manual reconciliation of policies.

In a nutshell, it is a lower-cost option, more flexible, and easier to manage than a classical router-based WAN. One practical advantage is the possibility of using lower-cost Internet access from different providers, instead of more expensive MPLS circuits. Another appeal derives from replacing branch routers with virtualized appliances that can implement additional functions, such as application optimization, network overlays, VPNs, encryption, firewall, and so on.

4.2.3 gRIBI

The OpenFlow section presented one possible implementation of SDN through directly programming forwarding plane entries using OpenFlow, or P4Runtime (see section 11.5). These are extreme approaches because they take complete control of the switches and give up all the features provided by standard protocols. Often this is not what is desired.

An alternative approach is to use protocols such as BGP or IS-IS to bring up the network and establish standard functionalities and then inject a few route optimizations using separate means. For example, this may work well for SD-WAN where by default packets follow the shortest path, but an SDN controller could enable other routes.

gRPC Routing Information Base Interface (gRIBI) [11] follows this second model, and the way it plugs into a switch software is shown in Figure 4-2.

gRIBI has a daemon inside the switch software that acts as a routing protocol, but instead of exchanging routing control packets to compute routes, it receives routes from a programming entity via gRPC (see section 3.4.2).

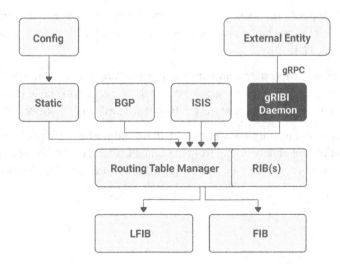

FIGURE 4-2 gRIBI

The support of multiple simultaneous routing protocols on a switch is a standard feature. Routing protocols populate a software data structure called routing information base (RIB), and so does gRIBI. The switch software uses the RIB as the input to program the forwarding information base (FIB) that is the structure used by the switch hardware to forward the data packets in the data plane.

Two other advantages of this architecture are that gRIBI is part of the control plane of the switch, and entries are created as they were learned via a dynamic routing protocol, not treated as device configuration. gRIBI has a transactional semantic that allows the programming entity to learn about the success or failure of the programming operation.

4.2.4   Data Plane Development Kit (DPDK)

DPDK is a technique to bypass the kernel and to process packets in userspace.

DPDK is a set of userspace software libraries and drivers that can be used to accelerate packet processing. DPDK creates a low-latency, high-throughput network data path from the NIC to the user space, bypassing the network stack in the kernel; see Figure 4-3.

DPDK is processor agnostic and currently supported on Intel x86, IBM POWER, and ARM. It is used mainly on Linux and FreeBSD. It utilizes a multicore framework, huge page memory, ring buffers, and poll-mode drivers for networking, crypto, and events.

The kernel still needs to provide access to the memory space of the NIC, and also provide interrupt handling, even though DPDK was designed to use poll-mode drivers. The interrupt handling is usually limited to link up and down events. These tasks are performed using a kernel module known as UIO (user space I/O). The Linux kernel includes a basic UIO module, based on the device file /dev/uioX, which is used to access the address space of the card and handle interrupts. Note: This module does not provide IOMMU protection, which is supported by a similar and more secure module known as VFIO.

When using DPDK, applications need to be rewritten. For example, to run an application that uses TCP, a userspace TCP implementation must be provided, because DPDK bypasses the network portion of the kernel, including TCP.

DPDK has a growing and active user community that appreciates the network performance improvements obtainable through DPDK. Reducing context switching, networking layer processing, interrupts, and so on is particularly relevant for processing Ethernet at speeds of 10Gbps or higher.

A portion of the Linux community does not like DPDK and userspace virtual switches in general, because they remove control of networking from the Linux kernel. This group prefers approaches such as eBPF (see section 4.3.5) and XDP (see section 4.3.6), which are part of the kernel.

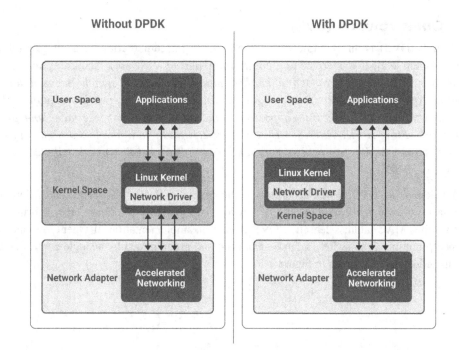

FIGURE 4-3 DPDK

4.3 Virtual Switches

We introduced virtual switches (vSwitches) in section 3.2. We described them as software entities, typically present inside the hypervisors, to switch packets among virtual machines and through the NICs (network interface cards) to the outside world. Hypervisors are not the only users of vSwitches; containers use them, too.

In this section and the following ones, we describe a few vSwitch implementations, and we try to classify them according to criteria such as the following:

- Where the switching is done—in the hardware, the kernel, or the userspace

- Whether all the packets are treated equally or whether the concept of a "first packet" exists

- Whether vSwitches are individual entities or whether a higher level of coordination exists; that is, can a management software manage multiples of them as a single entity?

4.3.1   Open vSwitch (OVS)

Open vSwitch (OVS) is an example of an open-source implementation of a distributed virtual multilayer switch [12]. It was created by Nicira (now part of VMware). According to the official documentation, it is *"... a production quality, multilayer virtual switch licensed under the open source Apache 2.0 license. It is designed to enable massive network automation through programmatic extension, while still supporting standard management interfaces and protocols (e.g., NetFlow, sFlow, IPFIX, RSPAN, CLI, LACP, 802.1ag). In addition, it is designed to support distribution across multiple physical servers similar to VMware's vNetwork distributed vSwitch or Cisco's Nexus 1000V...."*

Figure 4-4 depicts an OVS switch according to the official website [13]. There are different ways of using an OVS switch. By default, an OVS switch is a standard-compliant layer 2 bridge acting alone and doing MAC address learning. OVS is also an implementation of OpenFlow and, in this embodiment, multiple OVS switches can be managed and programmed by a single controller and act as a distributed switch, as shown in Figure 4-5.

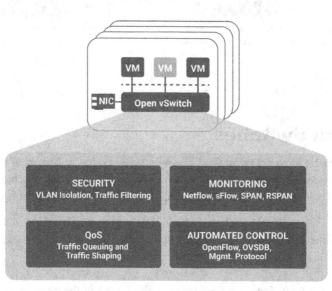

FIGURE 4-4   OVS (Open Virtual Switch)

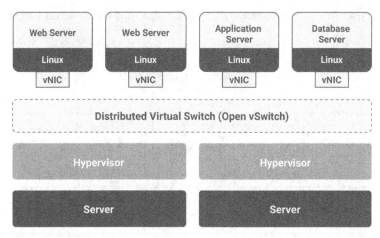

FIGURE 4-5   A Distributed OVS

Figure 4-6 shows the OVS architecture, outlining the kernel component, the user space datapath, the management utilities, and the optional connection to a remote controller.

Let's start our description from the Open vSwitch kernel module ("kmod-openvswitch") that implements multiple datapaths in the kernel. Each datapath can have multiple "vports" (analogous to ports within a bridge), and it has a "flow table." It should be noticed that the OVS datapath in the kernel is a replacement of the standard Linux kernel network datapath. The interfaces associated with OVS use the OVS datapath instead of the Linux datapath.

A flow key is computed each time a packet is received on a vport, and the flowkey is searched in the flow table. If found, the associated action is performed on the packet; otherwise, the flow key and the packet is passed to "ovs-vswitchd," which is the userspace daemon.

The userspace daemon can do a very sophisticated analysis of the packet, consulting multiple OpenFlow-style tables. As part of the processing, the daemon customarily sets up the flow key in the kernel module to handle further packets of the same flow directly in the kernel. This behavior is similar to the one explained in section 2.8 about Cache-based forwarding.

The OVS configuration is permanent across reboots. The "ovs-vswitchd" connects to an "ovsdb-server" and it retrieves its configuration from the database at startup. OVSDB (Open vSwitch Database) is a management protocol to configure OVS [14].

In Figure 4-6 there are a few blocks whose names end in "ctl" (pronounced "cutle"). These blocks are the CLIs used to program the different features.

What has been described up to now is the standard implementation of OVS, mostly done in user space but with a kernel component. OVS can also operate entirely in user space by using DPDK to pass all the packets to the user space. In both cases, OVS is putting a load on the server CPU that can be very relevant.

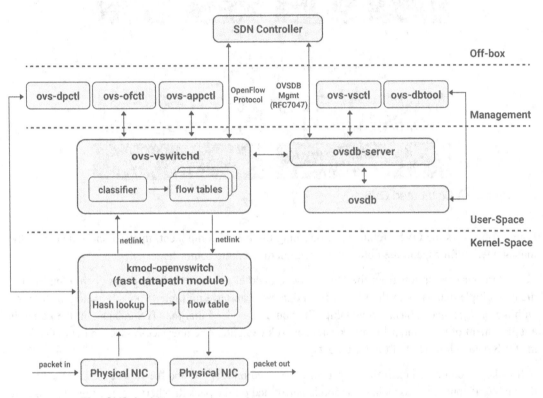

FIGURE 4-6   The OVS Architecture

OVS can also be hardware accelerated; for example, by replacing the kernel module table with a hardware table on a NIC. Figure 4-7 shows a possible implementation of OVS in conjunction with a NIC that has an OVS-compliant hardware flow table and one or more processors onboard to run the OVS daemon and OVSDB. This concept is similar to the one outlined in section 2.8.1 when describing Microsoft GFT and the Azure SmartNIC.

Please notice that the previous solution is feasible because it is totally included in the NIC and therefore transparent to the kernel. The Linux kernel community has refused to *upstream* (a term that means to include in the standard kernel) any OVS hardware offload. To bypass this limitation, some companies have developed the solution described in the next section.

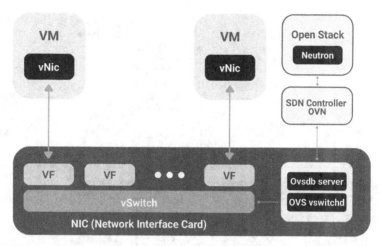

FIGURE 4-7 OVS in a NIC

Figure 4-7 also shows a possible integration with OpenStack (see section 3.5). In OpenStack, both the Neutron node and the compute node (Nova) are running OVS to provide virtualized network services.

OVS is also the default virtual switch for XEN environments (see section 3.2.5).

4.3.2 tc-flower

"tc-flower" is an extension of "tc," the traffic classification subsystem of the Linux kernel. tc-flower allows construction of a match-action datapath.

The match part is used to classify packets on a variety of fields in the L2, L3, and L4 headers, and metadata fields. It uses a subsystem in the kernel called *flow dissector*. tc-flower actions include output, drop, edit packet, and VLAN actions such as push and pop VLAN tags.

tc-flower match-action logic is stateless; that is, each packet is processed independently of the others. There is no possibility to base the decision on the status of a connection usually kept in conntrack.

Also, tc-flower has not been widely adopted due to its relative complexity, which is inherited from tc.

So, why do some companies plan to use tc-flower in conjunction with OVS?

Because from Linux kernel v4.14-rc4, it is possible to offload tc-flower in hardware through a utility called "ndo-setup-tc" [15]. The same service is also used to offload Berkeley Packet Filter (BPF), described in the next section. Figure 4-8 shows this arrangement.

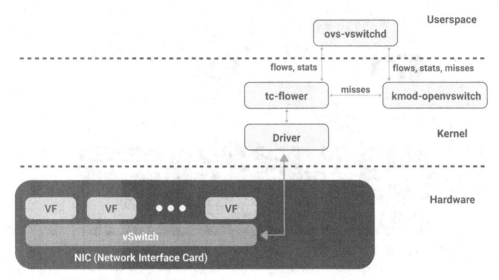

FIGURE 4-8 OVS Offload with tc-flower

The basic idea is to piggyback OVS offload through tc-flower. The NIC maintains the OVS flow table in hardware and, when a packet misses the flow table, it is passed to tc-flower—that is almost an empty shell—by merely redirecting the miss to the OVS kernel module. The kernel module may have a larger flow table compared to the hardware, including flows that are making a limited amount of traffic, also called "mice flows" in contrast to high byte-count "elephant flows." If the miss matches in the OVS kernel module flow table, a reply is returned to tc-flower; otherwise, the userspace module of OVS is activated, as in the normal OVS processing. OVS supports tc-flower integration since OVS 2.8.

As already mentioned, the most significant limitation of this approach is that tc-flower match is stateless; to make it stateful, it requires a combination with conntrack and potentially two passes in tc-flower, one before and one after conntrack. "Stateful security groups" is another name for this missing feature.

4.3.3 DPDK RTE Flow Filtering

The DPDK Generic Flow API [16] provides a way to configure hardware (typically a NIC) to match specific packets, decide their fate, and query related counters. It is yet another match-action API that, being based on DPDK, has no kernel components and therefore requires no kernel upstreaming or nonstandard kernel patches.

DPDK RTE Flow Filtering is another name for the same API since all the calls start with "rte_." (RTE stands for run time environment.)

This approach suffers from the same limitation of the tc-flower approach; it only supports stateless rules, no stateful security groups.

4.3.4 VPP (Vector Packet Processing)

The last of the kernel-bypass approaches covered in this book is Vector Packet Processing (VPP) [17], which was donated by Cisco to the Linux Foundation Project and is now part of FD.io (Fast Data - Input/Output). According to the official documentation: *"The VPP platform is an extensible framework that provides out-of-the-box production quality switch/router functionality."*

VPP uses DPDK to bypass the network stack in the kernel and move packet processing to userspace, but it also implements additional optimization techniques such as batch packet processing, NUMA awareness, CPU isolation, and so on to improve performance.

The packet processing model of VPP is a "packet processing graph," as shown in Figure 4-9.

Packets are processed in batches. At any given time, VPP collects all the packets waiting for processing, batches them together, and applies the graph to the packets. The advantage of this approach is that all packets are processed at the same time by the same code so that the hit ratio in the CPU instruction cache is increased significantly. Another way of thinking about this is that the first packet of the batch warms up the instruction cache for the remaining packets. Because packets are collected through DPDK, there are no interrupts; that is, no context switching. This minimizes overhead and increases performance.

VPP also supports "graph plugins" that can add/remove graph nodes and rearrange the packet graph. Plugins are a very convenient way to upgrade or add new features.

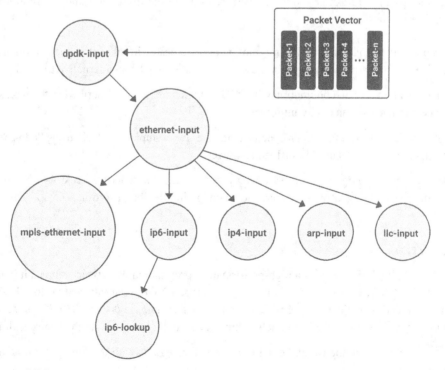

FIGURE 4-9 VPP

4.3.5   BPF and eBPF

All the virtual switch approaches discussed up to now try to avoid the Linux kernel as much as possible and therefore move a significant part of the work to userspace. This section and the next one describe approaches that leverage the Linux kernel to its full extent and are thus supported by the Linux kernel community.

Let's start with the original effort. In 1992, Van Jacobson and Steven McCanne proposed a solution for minimizing unwanted network packet copies to userspace by implementing in Unix an in-kernel packet filter known as Berkeley Packet Filter (BPF) [18].

BPF defined an abstract register-based "filter machine" similar to RISC CPUs.

The BPF machine consists of an accumulator, an index register, a scratch memory, and an implicit program counter. Filters are programs for the BPF machine. When BPF is active, the device driver, on receiving a packet, delivers the packet to BPF for filtering. The resulting action may be to accept or reject the packet.

In 2014, Alexei Starovoitov introduced eBPF (extended BPF) that more closely resembles contemporary processors, broadens the number of registers from two to ten, moves to 64-bit registers, and adds more instructions, making an eBPF machine C-programmable using the LLVM compiler infrastructure [19], [20]. eBPF also provides improved performance compared to BPF.

A reasonable question to ask is, "Why is eBPF relevant in the discussion about virtual switches?" There are four reasons:

- It is possible to code in an eBPF program, not only a basic virtual switch but also other network services such as a firewall, so for some applications, it may be an alternative to OVS.

- When eBPF is used in conjunction with XDP, a kernel technique described in the next section, the performance dramatically improves.

- eBPF can be offloaded to domain-specific hardware; for example, on a NIC, using "ndo-setup-tc," the same utility that is used to offload tc-flower.

- eBPF can perform operations at various layers in a Linux networking stack; for example, before routing, post routing, at socket layer, and so on, giving flexible insertion points.

4.3.6   XDP

eXpress Data Path (XDP) provides a high-performance, programmable network data path in the Linux kernel [20], [21]. The Linux kernel community developed XDP as an alternative to DPDK. David Miller, the primary maintainer of the Linux networking subsystem, says that "*DPDK is not Linux.*" He reasons that DPDK bypasses the Linux networking stack, and it lives outside the Linux realm.

XDP is the mechanism in the Linux kernel to run eBPF programs with the lowest possible overhead; see Figure 4-10 [22].

XDP executes in the receiving side of the driver as soon as the packet is pulled out of the ring. It is the theoretical first opportunity to process a packet. XDP is invoked before the socket buffer (SKB) is attached to the packet. SKB is a large data structure used by the network stack, and there is a significant performance advantage to processing the packet before the SKB is attached. XDP works on a linear buffer that must fit on a single memory page, and the only two pieces of metadata it has are the pointers to the beginning and end of the packet. The buffer is not read-only, and eBPF can modify the packet to implement, for example, routing. One of these four actions results from the eBPF packet processing: drop the packet, abort due to an internal error in eBPF, pass the packet to the Linux networking stack, or transmit the packet on the same interface it was received. In all cases, eBPF may have modified the packet.

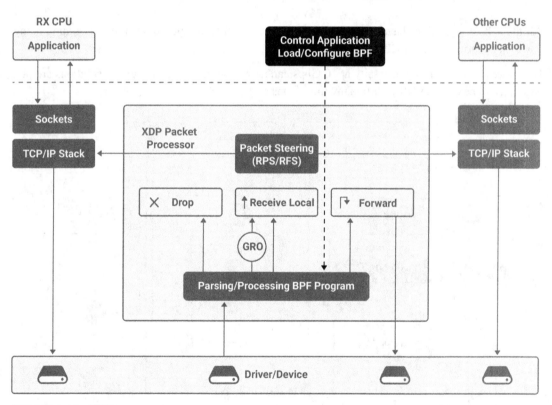

FIGURE 4-10   XDP

In addition to bridging and routing, other use cases for XDP/eBPF are Denial of Service detection [23], load balancing, traffic sampling, and monitoring.

Following the introduction of XDP in the Linux kernel, proposals have been presented to use eBPF/XDP in conjunction with OVS [24]. Two different approaches are possible:

- Rewrite the OVS kernel module (kmod-openvswitch) using eBPF
- use the AF_XDP socket and move flow processing into userspace.

4.3.7   Summary on Virtual Switches

The previous sections have described several different ways of implementing virtual switches. Figure 4-11 is my attempt at summarizing all of them into a single picture.

They differ for the following three main reasons:

- They use a native Linux model or bypass the Linux network stack.
- They run in the kernel or userspace, or a combination of the two.
- They use hardware acceleration.

All the software solutions have real performance issues at 10 Gbps and above, thus consuming many cores on the primary server CPUs.

Hardware acceleration is a necessity at 10 Gbps and above, but many of the current solutions are just additions to the existing NICs with many limitations.

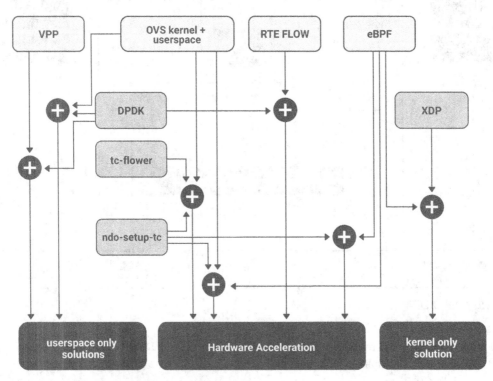

FIGURE 4-11   All Solutions in One Picture

The real solution will come from domain-specific hardware capable of implementing the classical bridging and routing models, in addition to the principal distributed network services, such as NAT, firewall, load balancing, and so on.

The next sections explain these distributed network services that complement routing and bridging.

4.4   Stateful NAT

IP address management remains a sore point, with the never ending transition to IPv6 still in the future. The use of private IPv4 addresses according to RFC 1918 is a common practice, which leads to address duplication in the case of hybrid cloud infrastructure, company merger, and acquisition. In this environment, good support for stateful NAT is a must.

The acronym *NAT* properly means network address translation, and it refers to changing only the IP addresses in an IP packet. In common parlance, NAT is also mixed/confused with PAT (port address translation) that refers to the capability of dynamic mapping/changing TCP/UDP port numbers. For a complete discussion of NAT versus PAT, see RFC 2663 [25].

The NAT also needs to be "stateful" any time it works in a modality, called *IP masquerading*, in which a group of private IP addresses is mapped to a single public IP address by using PAT, a typical case being a home gateway that connects multiple PCs, tablets, and phones to the Internet using a single public IP address. For example, in this case, the first packet generated by a tablet for a particular connection creates the mapping that is needed by the packets traveling in the opposite direction for the same session; hence the name, "stateful NAT."

Fortunately, the number of application protocols that need to cross the NAT has dramatically decreased with most of them being NAT-friendly, such as SSH, HTTP, and HTTPS. Some old protocols require NAT ALGs (application layer gateways) because they carry IP addresses or port numbers inside the payload—one notable example being FTP, which is still widely used even if excellent secure alternatives exist that don't have NAT issues.

4.5   Load Balancing

Another layer 4 service that is becoming ubiquitous is load balancing.

Its main application is to load balance web traffic by distributing HTTP/HTTPS requests to a pool of web servers to increase the number of web pages that can be served in a unit of time [26] (see Figure 4-12).

Load balancers act as proxies as they query the back-end web servers in place of the clients; this helps to secure the back-end servers from attack in conjunction with firewalls and microsegmentation (see sections 5.1 and 5.2).

Requests are received and distributed to a particular server based on a configured algorithm; for example, weighted round robin or least response time. This requires the load balancer to be stateful and keep track of the status of the back-end servers, their load, and, under normal operation, direct all the requests from a particular client to the same back-end server.

A load balancer can also perform caching of static content, compression, SSL/TLS encryption and decryption, and single point of authentication.

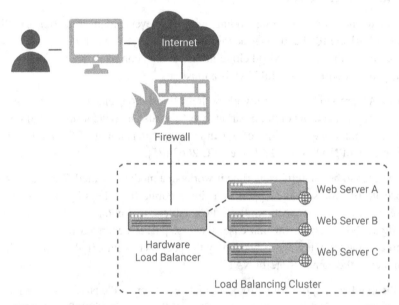

FIGURE 4-12 Web Load Balancing

Historically implemented as discrete appliances, load balancers are now shifting from the centralized model to the distributed-service model, which also guarantees higher performance. Firewalls are undergoing a similar shift toward distributed firewalls: a distributed-service node can implement and integrate both functionalities.

4.6 Troubleshooting and Telemetry

Many of the techniques explained up to this point are essential for building data-center and cloud infra-structures. They also introduce significant complexity and functions that may become bottlenecks and cause slowdowns. Let's consider, for example, I/O consolidation that brings the considerable promise of running everything over a single network for significant cost savings. It also removes a separate storage network that storage managers used to monitor for performance. When an application is slow, this can trigger considerable finger pointing: "Why is my application slow? Is it the network's fault? No, it is the fault of the OS; No, it is the application that is poorly written; No, it is the storage back-end that is slow; No, there is packet loss; No ....." Pick your favorite cause. The only way to understand what is going on is by using telemetry, a word composed of the two Greek words *tele* (remote) and *metron* (measure). We need to measure as much as possible and report the measurements to a remote management station. The reality is that without objective measurement it is impossible to understand what is happening. Here is where telemetry comes into play.

Telemetry is the real-time measurement of a large number of parameters. In itself this is not new; switches and routers have multiple hardware counters that are typically read through Simple Network Management Protocol (SNMP) [27].

SNMP is a "pull" model (often also called a "poll" model) in which a management station periodically pulls data from the network devices. A pull interval of 5 minutes is typical, and SNMP on network devices is known to be inefficient and to use a lot of CPU cycles: sending too many SNMP requests may saturate, for example, a router CPU.

An alternative to pull models are push models in which the network devices periodically push out data, for example, to export flow statistics through NetFlow [28] to a NetFlow collector, and to log events to a remote server through Syslog [29].

Telemetry builds on these existing ideas, but it also adds a few new concepts:

- Usually, the data is modeled through a formal language such as Yang so that applications can consume data easily. Then it is encoded in a structured format such as XML, JSON, or Google's protocol buffer (see section 3.4.2). Another important consideration is a compact encoding scheme, because the volume of data to be streamed is high.

- The protocols used to do the pushing are more modern and derived from the computing world, not from the network world. Google's protocol buffer message format is often used to stream the data.

- Pre-filtering is often used to reduce the enormous amount of data that needs streaming to a data collector. For example, data that shows normal behavior can be streamed less frequently than data associated with abnormal behavior.

- The push can be "cadence-based" or "policy-based"; that is, it can be done periodically, or when a particular policy is triggered; for example, a threshold is exceeded. The policies can also be refined in real time to make the data collection more useful.

Accurate telemetry is an essential tool to perform root cause analysis. In many cases the failures are difficult to locate, especially when intermittent; to identify the primary cause of an application slowdown a sequence of events needs to be analyzed, which is impossible without good telemetry.

In a distributed-service platform telemetry should cover all the different services in order to be effective. In particular, when multiple services are chained together, telemetry should help to identify which service in the chain is causing the problem.

4.7 Summary

In this chapter, we have presented networking distributed services that are extremely valuable in cloud and enterprise networks. Domain-specific hardware can make their implementation extremely performant and scalable. These services can be deployed in different parts of the network and implementing them in devices such as appliances or switches offers additional advantages of also supporting bare-metal servers and the possibility to share the domain-specific hardware across multiple servers, thus reducing the cost of ownership.

4.8 Bibliography

[1] Radia Perlman. 1999. *Interconnections* (2nd Ed.): *Bridges, Routers, Switches, and Internetworking Protocols.* Addison-Wesley Longman Publishing Co., Inc., Boston, MA, USA.

[2] Nick McKeown, Tom Anderson, Hari Balakrishnan, Guru Parulkar, Larry Peterson, Jennifer Rexford, Scott Shenker, and Jonathan Turner. 2008. "OpenFlow: enabling innovation in campus networks." SIGCOMM Comput. Commun. Rev. 38, 2 (March 2008), 69–74. DOI=http://dx.doi.org/10.1145/1355734.1355746

[3] The Open Networking Foundation (ONF), https://www. opennetworking.org

[4] The Open Networking Foundation (ONF), "OpenFlow Switch Specification Version 1.5.1 (Protocol version 0x06)," March 26, 2015, ONF TS-025.

[5] https://en.wikibooks.org/wiki/Routing_protocols_and_architectures/Routing_algorithms

[6] NetworkWorld, "Google Showcases OpenFlow network," https://www.networkworld.com/article/2222173/google-showcases-openflow-network.html

[7] Google, "OpenFlow @ Google," http://www.segment-routing.net/images/hoelzle-tue-openflow.pdf

[8] NetworkWorld, "Google's software-defined/OpenFlow backbone drives WAN links to 100% utilization," https://www.networkworld.com/article/2189197/google-s-software-defined-openflow-backbone-drives-wan-links-to-100--utilization.html

[9] P4 Language Consortium, https://p4.org

[10] NetworkWorld, "SD-WAN: What it is and why you'll use it one day," 2016-02-10, https://www.networkworld.com/article/3031279/sd-wan-what-it-is-and-why-you-ll-use-it-one-day.html

[11] gRIBI, https://github.com/openconfig/gribi

[12] T. Koponen, K. Amidon, P. Balland, M. Casado, A. Chanda, B. Fulton, I. Ganichev, J. Gross, N. Gude, P. Ingram, E. Jackson, A. Lambeth, R. Lenglet, S.-H. Li, A. Padmanabhan, J. Pettit, B. Pfaff, R. Ramanathan, S. Shenker, A. Shieh, J. Stribling, P. Thakkar. Network virtualization in multi-tenant data centers, USENIX NSDI, 2014.

[13] Linux Foundation Collaborative Projects, "OVS: Open vSwitch," http:// www.openvswitch.org

[14] Pfaff, B. and B. Davie, Ed., "The Open vSwitch Database Management Protocol," RFC 7047, DOI 10.17487/RFC7047, December 2013.

[15] Simon Horman, "TC Flower Offload," Netdev 2.2, The Technical Conference on Linux Networking, November 2017.

[16] DPDK, "Generic Flow API," https://doc.dpdk.org/guides/prog_guide/rte_flow.html

[17] The Linux Foundation Projects, "Vector Packet Processing (VPP)," https://fd.io/technology

[18] Steven McCanne, Van Jacobson, "The BSD Packet Filter: A New Architecture for User-level Packet Capture," USENIX Winter 1993: 259–270.

[19] Gianluca Borello, "The art of writing eBPF programs: a primer," February 2019, https://sysdig.com/blog/the-art-of-writing-ebpf-programs-a-primer

[20] Diego Pino García, "A brief introduction to XDP and eBPF," January 2019, https://blogs.igalia.com/dpino/2019/01/07/introduction-to-xdp-and-ebpf

[21] Fulvio Risso, "Toward Flexible and Efficient In-Kernel Network Function Chaining with IO Visor," HPSR 2018, Bucharest, June 2018, http://fulvio.frisso.net/files/18HPSR%20-%20 eBPF.pdf

[22] The Linux Foundation Projects, "IO Visor Project: XDP eXpress Data Path," https://www.iovisor.org/technology/xdp

[23] Gilberto Bertin, "XDP in practice: integrating XDP in our DDoS mitigation pipeline," 2017, InNetDev 2.1—The Technical Conference on Linux Networking. https://netdevconf.org/2.1/ session.html?bertin

[24] William Tu, Joe Stringer, Yifeng Sun, and Yi-HungWei, "Bringing The Power of eBPF to Open vSwitch," In Linux Plumbers Conference 2018 Networking Track.

[25] Srisuresh, P. and M. Holdrege, "IP Network Address Translator (NAT) Terminology and Considerations," RFC 2663, DOI 10.17487/RFC2663, August 1999.

[26] Nginx, "What is load balancing," https://www.nginx.com/resources/glossary/load-balancing

[27] Harrington, D., Presuhn, R., and B. Wijnen, "An Architecture for Describing Simple Network Management Protocol (SNMP) Management Frameworks," STD 62, RFC 3411, DOI 10.17487/RFC3411, December 2002.

[28] Claise, B., Ed., "Cisco Systems NetFlow Services Export Version 9," RFC 3954, DOI 10.17487/RFC3954, October 2004.

[29] Gerhards, R., "The Syslog Protocol," RFC 5424, DOI 10.17487/RFC5424, March 2009.

Chapter | 5

Security Services

This chapter describes important security services required in cloud and data center networks to combat the continuously evolving security threats and to comply with regulatory issues.

Security threats can be external (coming from the network) or internal (from compromised applications). Today's solutions either assume that application/hypervisor/OS can't be compromised, or network-based security models consider the network trusted and locate the enforcement points only at the periphery.

Both approaches need scrutiny; for example, in the wake of Spectre and Meltdown [1], we can't trust a compromised host, OS or hypervisor. Similarly, it is crucial to limit the ability to move laterally (in East-West direction) to prevent damage in case of a compromise.

Initially, security architectures were based on the idea of a "perimeter" and of securing the "North-South" traffic entering and exiting the data center (see Figure 5-1). The East-West traffic inside the datacenter was trusted, considered secure, and immune from attacks. In other words, the "bad guys" were outside the perimeter, and the "good guys" were inside.

Over time this model has shown its limitations because the perimeter has become much more fragmented with the necessity of having B2B (business to business) connections to support remote offices and remote and mobile workers.

The virtual private network (VPN) technology has helped tremendously (see section 5.12), but the attacks have evolved, requiring increased attention to secure the East-West traffic inside the data center.

According to the 2017 Phishing Trends Report of Keepnet Labs [2] "Over 91% of system breaches have been caused by a phishing attack." Phishing attacks are a type of attack in which someone inside the secure perimeter clicks on a bogus link received by email that, as a result, compromises a system inside the boundary.

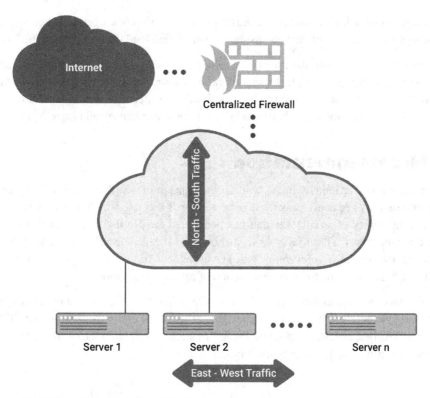

FIGURE 5-1   North-South versus East-West

A solution to this problem is composed of a combination of security services including firewall, microsegmentation, encryption, key management, and VPNs.

5.1   Distributed Firewalls

Distributed firewalls are becoming a necessity due to the multitenancy requirement and the change in the type of security attacks described earlier. When a system inside the firewall is compromised, traditional security measures based on encryption, while in general a good idea, may not help because the malware can spread through encrypted channels.

Containment of infected systems is the next line of defense, and it is achieved through firewalls. For considerations similar to the one discussed in the NAT section (see section 4.4), firewalls also need to be stateful; for example, the traffic flowing in one direction may create a state to permit traffic in the opposite direction that would otherwise be dropped.

Created for perimeter protection, discrete firewalls can also be used to protect and separate the East-West traffic, typically in combination with VLANs. The technique is called trombone or tromboning (see section 2.7.1), and it consists of sending the traffic that needs to go from one VLAN to another through a firewall. Of course, the centralized firewall becomes a performance bottleneck, and all the routing and forwarding of packets inside the datacenter/cloud becomes suboptimal.

A better solution is to distribute the firewall functionality as closely as possible to the final user in a distributed-service node; for example, by incorporating the firewall functionality in a ToR/leaf switch or in an SR-IOV capable NIC (see section 8.4). Both solutions decouple routing and forwarding from firewalling, remove the performance bottlenecks, and offer lower latency and jitter.

5.2 Microsegmentation

Microsegmentation is a technique that is built on the concept of distributed firewalls by dividing the datacenter into security segments associated with workloads that, by default, cannot talk to each other. This restricts the ability of an attacker that has penetrated the North-South firewall to move in the East-West direction freely. These security segments are also called security zones, and they decrease the network attack surface by preventing attacker movement from one compromised application to another. Figure 5-2 shows a pictorial representation of microsegmentation.

Microsegmentation associates fine-grained security policies to datacenter applications, which are enforced by distributed firewalls. These policies are not restricted to the IP addresses or VLAN tags of the underlying network, and they can act on the information contained in the overlay network packets, being specific to virtual machines or containers.

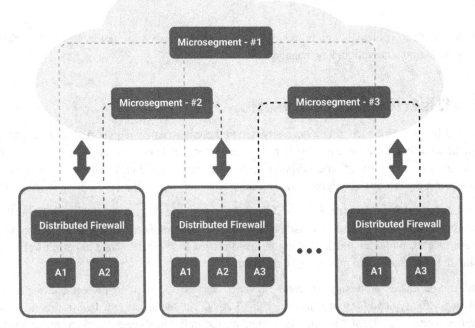

FIGURE 5-2   Microsegmentation

The concept of "zero-trust" is also a part of microsegmentation: "never trust, always verify." This means that only the necessary connections are enabled, blocking anything else by default. For example, it is possible to create a segment that contains all the IoT (Internet of Things) devices of a particular laboratory and create a policy that allows them to talk to each other and a gateway. If an IoT device moves, its security policies follow it.

The term *zero-trust security* in this context implies that having network access doesn't mean access to all applications in the network. It is an extension of the white list concept: don't allow anything unless it's asked for.

Low throughput and complex policy management are two significant operational barriers to microsegmentation. Low throughput is the result of tromboning into centralized firewalls. Even if these firewalls are upgraded (an operation that could be extremely expensive), they still create a performance bottleneck resulting in high latency, jitter, and potentially packet loss. The solution to this issue is a distributed firewall architecture, with firewalls located as closely as possible to the applications. Once again, these firewalls need to be stateful for the reasons explained in Chapter 4, "Network Virtualization Services" (for example, NAT, IP masquerading). Any time there is state, there is a potential scaling problem: How fast can we update the flow database (connections per second)? How many entries can we support? A distributed solution naturally scales with the size of the problem. This also implies that firewalls for microsegmentation cannot be discrete appliances. However, distributing the firewalls very granularly also creates a policy management issue that brings us to the next point.

Policy management complexity increases exponentially with the number of workloads, the number of firewalls, and the need to support mobility in rapidly changing environments. Manually programming the firewalls for microsegmentation is, at best, impractical, and, at worst, impossible. Microsegmentation requires a capable policy manager where security policies are formulated independently of network topology or enforcement point location. This policy manager is in charge of communicating with all the distributed firewalls through a programmatic API such as a REST API or gRPC. This API is used to pass the appropriate subset of policies to each firewall and to modify them as users and applications move or change their policies.

For more information, we recommend the book *Micro-Segmentation For Dummies*, where author Matt De Vincentis analyzes in greater detail the advantages and limitations of microsegmentation [3].

5.3   TLS Everywhere

Transport Layer Security (TLS) is a modern security standard to secure communications inside and outside the datacenter. Initially developed to secure web traffic, TLS can be used to secure any traffic. Sections 5.11.2 and 5.11.3 discuss the encapsulation aspect of TLS; here the focus is on its security aspects.

Before starting our discussion, let's understand the differences between HTTP, HTTPS, SSL, and TLS.

- **HTTP** (Hypertext Transfer Protocol) is an application layer protocol used to communicate between two machines and mostly used for web traffic. HTTP in itself does not provide any security. Original HTTP suffered from some performance issues, but the latest HTTP/2 is very efficient. Usually, web servers bind HTTP on TCP port 80.

- **HTTPS** (HTTP Secure) is a secure version of HTTP. Security is added by running HTTP on top of SSL or TLS. For this reason, it is also referred to as HTTP over SSL or HTTP over TLS. Usually, web servers bind HTTPS to TCP port 443.

- **SSL** (Secure Sockets Layer) is a cryptographic protocol that provides authentication and data encryption. SSL 2.0 was introduced in 1995 and evolved into SSL 3.0. All SSL versions have been deprecated due to security flaws.

- **TLS** (Transport Layer Security) is a successor to SSL. TLS 1.1 was introduced in 2006 and is now deprecated. The current versions of TLS are 1.2 (launched in 2008) [4] and 1.3 (introduced in 2018) [5]. Figure 5-3 shows the TLS protocol stack.

SSL/TLS Handshake	SSL/TLS Change Cipher Spec	SSL/TLS Alert	HTTP
SSL/TLS Record Protocol			
TCP			
IP			

FIGURE 5-3   TLS Protocol Stack

When TLS is implemented with perfect forward secrecy (PFS), it provides a good security solution. PFS generates a unique key for every user-initiated session to protect against future compromises of secret keys or passwords.

The simple reason that all major companies have moved the transport of their web pages from HTTP to HTTPS to improve security makes TLS a crucial protocol, but TLS can be used for other applications as well; for example, in a new type of virtual private network (VPN).

Proper implementations of TLS require many different pieces:

- Symmetric encryption used to protect user data

- Asymmetric encryption used during session creation

- Digital certificates

- Hashing algorithms

- Secure storage for keys, certificates, and so on

- A mechanism to generate a private key

- An appropriate implementation of TCP, because TLS runs over TCP

The following sections describe these aspects in more detail.

5.4 Symmetric Encryption

Symmetric encryption is a type of encryption that uses the same key for encrypting and decrypting the message. The symmetric algorithm universally used is Advanced Encryption Standard (AES) established by the National Institute of Standards and Technology (NIST) in 2001 [6].

AES is a block cipher and can be used with keys of different length, usually 128, 192, or 256 bits. It can also be used in different modes, the most common being GCM (Galois Counter Mode), a hardware-friendly implementation widely used for web traffic; and XTS ("Xor-encrypt-xor"-based, tweaked-codebook mode with ciphertext stealing), widely used to encrypt data-at-rest in storage applications.

Even if AES 128-bit GCM is probably the most commonly used symmetric encryption in TLS, TLS supports other encryption algorithms, including stream ciphers, such as ChaCha20-Poly1305 [7].

Today, symmetric encryption is widely supported in a variety of devices and processors. Moving it to domain-specific hardware still has performance and latency advantages over processors, but the performance gap is much wider in asymmetric encryption, discussed in the next section.

5.5 Asymmetric Encryption

Asymmetric encryption, also known as public key cryptography, is a form of encryption in which there are two separate keys, one to encrypt and one to decrypt the message, and it is computationally infeasible to derive one key from the other (the original idea is attributed to Whitfield Diffie and Martin Hellman [8]). The two keys are also referred to as the private and the public key. Anyone who wants to receive messages using asymmetric encryption will generate the two keys, publish the public key, and keep secret the private one. As an example, Linux provides the openssl utility for key generation. The sender will encrypt the message using the public key, and only the owner of the private key will be able to decode the message.

Asymmetric encryption is computationally much heavier than symmetric encryption, and, for this reason, TLS only uses it at the connection setup phase.

TLS 1.2 supported approximately 20 different schemes of key exchange, agreement, and authentication, but TLS 1.3 reduced them to three. They are based on a combination of the original idea from Diffie-Hellman, RSA (Rivest-Shamir-Adleman) [9], and Elliptic Curves [10], [11].

The concept behind RSA is the difficulty of the factorization of the product of two large prime numbers.

An elliptic curve is the set of points that satisfy a specific mathematical equation that looks like $y^2 = x^3 + ax + b$. Computing the private key from the public key in elliptic curve requires solving a logarithm problem over finite fields, a very difficult problem. Elliptic curves require a smaller key, compared to RSA, for the same level of security. For example, the NSA recommends using either a 3072-bit RSA key or 256-bit Elliptic Curves key [12] for a security level comparable to a 128-bit AES symmetric key.

Today, CPUs do not support asymmetric encryption adequately and, for this reason, domain-specific hardware provides a significant improvement in TLS connection setup per second.

5.6   Digital Certificates

Before encrypting a message with a public key, it is essential to be sure that the public key belongs to the organization we want to send the data to. Certification authorities guarantee ownership of public keys through digital certificates. Besides establishing ownership, a digital certificate also indicates expected usages of that key, expiration date, and other parameters.

5.7   Hashing

A cryptographically secure hash is a unidirectional function that is hard to invert and computes a short signature of a much larger number of bits. It is usually applied and appended to a message to verify that the message has not been altered. The hard-to-invert property of the hash function prevents attacks, because it is hard for an adversary to find an alternative message with the same hash. Famous hashing algorithms are MD5, which produces a 128-bit hash value, and SHA, a family of hashing algorithms. MD5 is not considered good enough for security applications, and even SHA-1 (160-bit hash value) is deprecated. The current state of the art is SHA-256 that not only extends the signature to 256-bits but is also a significant redesign compared to SHA-1. Any security solution needs to implement hashing algorithms in hardware for performance reasons.

5.8   Secure Key Storage

The security of any solution fundamentally depends on the capability to keep the private keys secret, but at the same time to not lose them.

The well-publicized Spectre, Meltdown, and Zombieload exploits, where data can leak from one CPU process to another, show that the server cannot guarantee security. Therefore, encryption keys need to be stored securely in a dedicated hardware structure named hardware security module (HSM). HSMs are typically certified to the FIPS 140 [13] standard to provide users with independent assurance that the design and implementation of the product and cryptographic algorithms are sound. HSMs can be separate appliances or hardware modules that are integrated into cards or ASICs. HSMs must also be protected against tampering, by either being tamper resistant, tamper evident, or tamper responsive (for example, by being capable of automatically erasing the keys in the case of a tamper attempt).

An HSM may also be capable of generating the keys onboard so that the private keys never leave the HSM.

5.9   PUF

The physical unclonable function (PUF) is a hardware structure that serves as a unique identity for a semiconductor device. PUF is used to generate a strong cryptographic key unique to each ASIC. PUF is based on natural variations that occur during semiconductor manufacturing. For example, PUF can create cryptographic keys that are unique to individual smartcards. A special characteristic of PUF is that it is repeatable across power-cycles: It always produces the same key, which therefore does not need to be saved on nonvolatile memory. Although various types of PUFs exist today, RAM-based PUFs are the most commonly used in large ASICs [14] [15], and they are based on the observation that RAM cells initialize to random but repeatable values at startup time. Previous solutions based on EEPROM or flash memory were much less secure.

5.10   TCP/TLS/HTTP Implementation

To provide pervasive encryption in the data center, excellent implementation of TCP, TLS and HTTP are required. The relation among these three protocols is more complex than may appear at first glance.

In HTTP/2 [16] a single TCP connection is shared by multiple HTTP requests and responses. Each request has a unique stream ID that is used to associate the response with the request. Responses and requests are divided into frames and marked with the stream ID. Frames are multiplexed over a single TCP connection. There is no relation between frames and IP packets: A frame may span multiple IP packets, and many frames may be contained in a single IP packet. Add TLS to all this, and you realize that the only way to process HTTPS properly is to terminate TCP, decrypt the TLS, pass the payload to HTTP/2, and let HTTP/2 delineate the frames and reconstruct the streams.

This complexity is not difficult to handle in software for a general-purpose processor, but it can be a challenge when implemented in domain-specific hardware. For example, in the past, there have been several attempts to implement TCP in the NIC with limited success, a practice called TCP offload. TCP in hardware has also been opposed by the software community, in particular by the Linux community.

For domain-specific hardware, implementing a generic TCP termination externally to the server to offload the termination of all TCP flows is not particularly attractive. On the other hand, an example of an interesting application is TCP termination used in conjunction with TLS termination to inspect encrypted traffic flows. It has applications in server load balancing, identification of traffic belonging to a particular user or application, routing different HTTP requests to different servers according to their URLs, and implementing sophisticated IDS (intrusion detection) features.

5.11   Secure Tunnels

In Chapter 2, "Network Design," we presented multiple encapsulation and overlay schemes to solve addressing issues, layer 2 domain propagation, multicast and broadcast propagation, multiprotocol support, and so on. These schemes do not deal with the privacy of the data. In fact, even when the data undergoes encapsulation, it is still in the clear and can be read by an eavesdropper. This lack of security may be acceptable inside the datacenter, but it is not tolerable when the transmission happens on a public network, in particular on the Internet.

The conventional way to secure tunnels is with the addition of encryption.

5.11.1   IPsec

IPsec is a widely used architecture that has been around since 1995 to secure IP communications [17]. Figure 5-4 shows a simplified view of the two encapsulation schemes supported by IPsec: transport mode and tunnel mode.

The IPsec header may provide just data authentication (the data is still in the clear, but the sender cryptographically signs it) or authentication plus encryption (an eavesdropper cannot decode the information).

In transport mode, the original IP header is used to route the packet in the network, and the IPsec header protects only the data part of the packet. In tunnel mode, the whole packet (including the IP header) is protected by the IPsec header, and a new IP header is added to route the packet through the network.

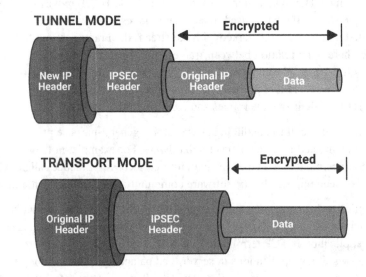

TUNNEL MODE

Encrypted

| New IP Header | IPSEC Header | Original IP Header | Data |

TRANSPORT MODE

Encrypted

| Original IP Header | IPSEC Header | Data |

FIGURE 5-4   IPsec Encapsulations

In both cases, the presence of the IPsec header is identified by the value 51 (for encryption) or 50 (for authentication only) in the protocol type of the IP header; there is no TCP or UDP header after the IP header. For this reason, IPsec is not a modern encapsulation scheme (see section 2.3.3) because routers cannot use the TCP/UDP header to load balance the IPsec traffic across multiple ECMP links. Sentences such as "lack of overlay entropy" or "lack of network entropy" are often used to describe this phenomenon, where the term entropy is used as a measure of the randomness of the information content.

The next two secure tunneling schemes (TLS and DTLS) are more modern and provide overlay entropy, although IPsec remains an active player in the VPN arena.

5.11.2 TLS

Transport Layer Security (TLS) [18] is the evolution of Secure Sockets Layer (SSL), and it is a vital component of any modern security architecture. The broad adoption and large install base of SSL and TLS is attributed to the use of these protocols to secure the traffic on the Web. Used to protect the most sensitive data, TLS has been scrutinized in all of its details, an essential factor in hardening its implementations. TLS is also a standard with a high degree of interoperability among different implementations, and it supports all the latest symmetric and asymmetric encryption schemes.

Typically, TLS is implemented on top of TCP for HTTPS-based traffic with an encapsulation like the one shown in Figure 5-5.

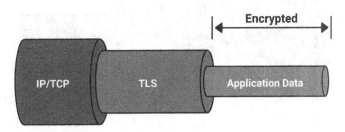

FIGURE 5-5　TLS Encapsulation

Because the external encapsulation of TLS is IP/TCP, TLS provides network entropy, allowing load balancing of TLS traffic in the core of the network, based on classical 5-tuples, a feature that is missing in IPsec. The same applies to DTLS (see the next section) where an IP/UDP header replaces the IP/TCP header.

TLS traffic suffers from reduced performance if the data that is encapsulated is another TCP packet, as discussed in section 2.3.3.

To avoid this double TCP, it is theoretically possible to terminate the unencrypted TCP session, add the TLS header, and then regenerate a new TCP session and do the opposite in the reverse direction. This operation, also called "proxy," requires terminating two TCP sessions, which is computationally expensive and may require a significant amount of buffering. Moreover, the processing cannot be done on a packet by packet basis because the TCP and TLS application data needs reconstruction before being re-encapsulated. Web traffic load balancers support the proxy feature by terminating the HTTPS sessions coming from the Internet (encrypted with TLS), decrypting them, and generating clear-text HTTP sessions toward the internal web servers. This scheme works well for web traffic, but it is not used for VPN because DTLS offers a better solution.

5.11.3 DTLS

Datagram TLS (DTLS) [19], [20] is particularly desirable for tunneling schemes because it avoids running TCP over TCP, and there is no need for TCP terminations at tunnel endpoints. DTLS not only allows TCP to run end-to-end but, when combined with VXLAN, it also supports any L2 protocol inside VXLAN, while providing the same security as TLS. DTLS works packet by packet; it is fast, low latency, and low jitter. Figure 5-6 shows the DTLS encapsulation.

DTLS was invented because TLS cannot be used directly in a UDP environment because packets may be lost or reordered. TLS has no internal facilities to handle this kind of unreliability because it relies on TCP. DTLS makes only minimal changes to TLS to fix this problem. DTLS uses a simple retransmission timer to handle packet loss and a sequence number to handle packet reordering.

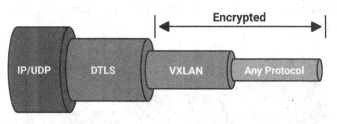

FIGURE 5-6 DTLS Encapsulation

5.12 VPNs

The term *virtual private network* (VPN) is a very generic one, and it is a common umbrella for multiple technologies. In general, VPN network technologies can be classified according to three main parameters:

- Type of encapsulation used
- Presence or absence of encryption
- Control protocol used to create tunnels, if any

5.12 VPNs   95

In section 2.3, we discussed overlay networks and covered several encapsulation schemes. In this section, we focus on the security aspect of VPNs and therefore on the kind of encryption used.

There are a few applications of VPNs that do not use encryption, two examples being EVPNs and MPLS VPNs.

EVPNs (described in section 2.3.4) are usually confined inside a datacenter where eavesdropping is considered unlikely due to the need to physically access the datacenter and the difficulty of tapping fiber links.

MPLS VPNs were one of the first ways for Telcos to provide virtual circuits to connect different sites of the same company. The trust to guarantee the privacy of the transmission was placed on the Telco. MPLS VPNs have been declining in popularity, mostly due to their cost, and replaced by VPNs that use the Internet to create the virtual circuits (see Figure 5-7).

In this case, the use of encryption is mandatory, especially when Wi-Fi is present. With a significant part of the workforce either telecommuting, working from home, or merely using their cellular devices, encrypted VPNs have become mandatory. One can reasonably ask, "Why do we need encrypted VPNs if we have HTTPS?" The answer is, "To protect all the traffic, not just the web." In the case of HTTPS, even if the pages are encrypted, the IP addresses of the sites are not. There is a lot that a hacker can learn about you and your business just by looking at your traffic by eavesdropping at a coffee shop Wi-Fi. If in doubt, read *The Art of Invisibility* [21] for some eye-opening information.

Figure 5-7 shows both site-to-site or host-to-site VPNs.

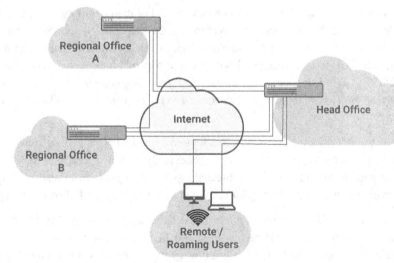

FIGURE 5-7 Example of a VPN

Site-to-site VPNs are a convenient way to interconnect multiple offices by using the Internet, often in conjunction with a technology such as SD-WAN (described in section 4.2.2). Historically, site-to-site VPNs used the IPsec protocol [22], but there is a trend to shift them toward TLS. These employ the same TLS security architecture used by HTTPS; in this case, to encrypt all your traffic. Usually, site-to-site VPNs are data intensive due to the need to transfer and back up data from one site to another, and therefore they often require hardware acceleration for encryption. For example, this is the case in a hybrid cloud where different parts of the cloud are interconnected using site-to-site VPNs, normally IPsec-based.

The host-to-site VPNs usually adopt a software client on the host (often a laptop, tablet, or phone in today's world) and hardware-based termination on the network side, generally in the form of a VPN gateway. In this kind of VPN, OpenVPN [23] is becoming the dominant standard, replacing the two old approaches PPTP and L2TP/IPsec.

OpenVPN is an open-source project, published under the GPL license and offered as a product by several different commercial companies. OpenVPN employs TLS to create the session, which, once initialized and authenticated, is used to exchange random key material for the bidirectional cipher and HMAC (Hash-based Message Authentication Code) keys used to secure the actual tunnel.

OpenVPN is NAT and firewall friendly, an important characteristic to use it on public Wi-Fi. It can be configured to use both TCP and UDP and is often set to use TCP on port 443 so that its traffic is indistinguishable from HTTPS traffic, and therefore not deliberately blocked.

OpenVPN heavily reuses OpenSSL code and has a vast code footprint.

Wireguard [24] is emerging as an alternative to OpenVPN. It has the goal of having a tiny code base, being easily understandable, being much more performant than OpenVPN, and using state-of-the-art encryption algorithms, such as ChaCha20 and Poly1305, which are more efficient and thus mobile friendly. There is a high hope that Wireguard will become part of Linux Kernel 5.0. Linus Torvalds himself wrote [25]: "... *Can I just once again state my love for it and hope it gets merged soon? Maybe the code isn't perfect, but I've skimmed it, and compared to the horrors that are OpenVPN and IPSec, it's a work of art....*"

Independent of the technology choice, the need to adopt encrypted VPNs is getting more critical every day. Even technologies such as EVPN that do not necessarily require encryption may benefit from encryption if they need to extend outside a protected environment such as a datacenter. EVPN in a hybrid cloud is an excellent example of a technology that may require the addition of encryption.

The bottom line is, *any distributed-services platform needs to support encryption.* Having to choose only two schemes, the preference would be for IPsec and TLS. Availability of hardware acceleration for both symmetric and asymmetric encryption is a must, complemented by the availability of modern stream ciphers such as ChaCha/Poly, in addition to the classical AES in GCM mode.

5.13   Secure Boot

We have seen that the DSN is responsible for implementing policies, but these policies can be trusted only as far as the DSN can be trusted. To trust the DSN device, whether it is in a NIC or a switch and so on, we must first be sure that is has not been compromised. The standard solution for this is known as *secure boot*, which ensures that the device is running authentic and trusted firmware. In addition, if the DSN is directly attached to the host (via PCIe, for example), we must ensure that access from the host is restricted to only certain allowed regions. This PCIe filtering (see section 9.1.10) should also be configured by the secure boot process.

A secure boot system begins with two implicitly trusted items:

- A source of immutable, trusted boot code; for example a boot ROM

- An immutable root of trust public key (ROTPK), either in ROM or programmed at manufacturing into a one-time-programmable (OTP) memory

The CPU boot sequence begins execution in the trusted ROM. It loads new runtime software from untrusted media, such as a flash disk, into secure memory and then verifies that the software image has come from a trusted source. This verification is via a digital signature that accompanies the image. The signature for the image is verified using the ROTPK. If the check fails, then the image is rejected. If the check passes then the image is authentic and may be executed. The new image continues the boot process similarly, further loading new code and verifying its digital signature, until the device is fully operational.

In addition to loading code images, a secure boot sequence may also load public key certificates. These certificates hold subordinate public keys that can be used to authenticate further objects. The certificates themselves are authenticated by previously loaded certificates, or the ROTPK.

Each step along the secure boot path extends trust to the newly authenticated object, and similarly the authenticity of every loaded object can be traced back along a sequence of certificates back to the ROTPK.

5.14   Summary

In this chapter, we have presented distributed services that are important to increase the security in cloud and enterprise infrastructure. In particular, we have covered segregation services such as firewall and microsegmentation, privacy services such as encryption, and infrastructural services such as PUF, HSM, and secure boot. We have seen that encryption comes paired with encapsulation, and we've discussed IPsec, the first widely implemented encryption tunnel, and TLS/DTLS, a more modern, growing solution. Encryption is at the basis of VPN deployments, which are essential for today's mobile workforce and geographically spread corporations.

The next chapter presents two network services that are best suited to be hosted directly on the server: Storage and RDMA.

5.15   Bibliography

[1]   Wired, "The Elite Intel Team Still Fighting Meltdown and Spectre," https://www.wired.com/story/intel-meltdown-spectre-storm/, 01/03/2019.

[2]   Keepnet, "2017 Phishing Trends Report," https://www.keepnetlabs.com/phishing-trends-report

[3]   Matt De Vincentis, *Micro-Segmentation For Dummies*, 2nd VMware special edition, John Wiley & Sons, Inc, 2017.

[4]   Dierks, T. and E. Rescorla, "The Transport Layer Security (TLS) Protocol Version 1.2," RFC 5246, August 2008.

[5]   Rescorla, E., "The Transport Layer Security (TLS) Protocol Version 1.3," RFC 8446, DOI 10.17487/RFC8446, August 2018.

[6]   "Announcing the ADVANCED ENCRYPTION STANDARD (AES)," Federal Information Processing Standards Publication 197. United States National Institute of Standards and Technology (NIST). November 26, 2001.

[7]   Langley, A., Chang, W., Mavrogiannopoulos, N., Strombergson, J., and S. Josefsson, "ChaCha20-Poly1305 Cipher Suites for Transport Layer Security (TLS)," RFC 7905, DOI 10.17487/RFC7905, June 2016.

[8]   Whitfield Diffie; Martin Hellman (1976). "New directions in cryptography." IEEE Transactions on Information Theory. 22 (6): 644.

[9]   Rivest, R.; Shamir, A.; Adleman, L. (February 1978). "A Method for Obtaining Digital Signatures and Public-Key Cryptosystems" (PDF). Communications of the ACM. 21 (2): 120–126.

[10]   Koblitz, N. "Elliptic curve cryptosystems." Mathematics of Computation, 1987, 48 (177): 203–209.

[11]   Miller, V. "Use of elliptic curves in cryptography. CRYPTO," 1985, Lecture Notes in Computer Science. 85. pp. 417–426.

[12]   "The Case for Elliptic Curve Cryptography." NSA.

[13]   "FIPS 140-3 PUB Development." NIST. 2013-04-30.

[14]   Tehranipoor, F., Karimian, N., Xiao, K., and J. Chandy , "DRAM based intrinsic physical unclonable functions for system-level security," In Proceedings of the 25th edition on Great Lakes Symposium on VLSI, (pp. 15–20). ACM, 2015.

[15]   40 Intrinsic ID, "White paper: Flexible Key Provisioning with SRAM PUF," 2017, www.intrinsic-id.com

[16] Belshe, M., Peon, R., and M. Thomson, Ed., "Hypertext Transfer Protocol Version 2 (HTTP/2)," RFC 7540, DOI 10.17487/RFC7540, May 2015.

[17] Kent, S. and K. Seo, "Security Architecture for the Internet Protocol," RFC 4301, December 2005.

[18] Rescorla, E., "The Transport Layer Security (TLS) Protocol Version 1.3," RFC 8446, August 2018.

[19] Modadugu, Nagendra and Eric Rescorla. "The Design and Implementation of Datagram TLS." NDSS (2004).

[20] Rescorla, E. and N. Modadugu, "Datagram Transport Layer Security Version 1.2," RFC 6347, January 2012.

[21] Mitnick, Kevin and Mikko Hypponen, *The Art of Invisibility: The World's Most Famous Hacker Teaches You How to Be Safe in the Age of Big Brother and Big Data*, Little, Brown, and Company.

[22] Kent, S. and K. Seo, "Security Architecture for the Internet Protocol," RFC 4301, DOI 10.17487/RFC4301, December 2005.

[23] OpenVPN, https://openvpn.net

[24] Wireguard: Fast, Modern, Secure VPN Tunnel, https://www.wireguard.com

[25] Linus Torvalds, "Re: [GIT] Networking," 2 Aug 2018, https://lkml.org/lkml/2018/8/2/663

Chapter 6

Distributed Storage and RDMA Services

In previous chapters, we have discussed distributed application services that can be placed almost anywhere on the network. In this chapter, we focus on infrastructure services that require access to server memory, typically through a PCIe interface.

In the not-so-distant past, the typical server included up to three types of communication interfaces, each connected to a dedicated infrastructure network (see Figure 6-1):

- A network interface card (NIC) connecting the server to the LAN and the outside world

- A storage interface that could attach to local disks or a dedicated storage area network (SAN)

- A clustering interface for high-performance communication across servers in distributed application environments

Over the past two decades, the communication substrate for these infrastructure services has been mostly unified. The opportunity to significantly reduce costs has driven this convergence. Cloud deployments with their massive scales have dramatically accelerated this trend. Today, networking, distributed storage, and RDMA clustering all ride the ubiquitous Ethernet; see Figure 6-2.

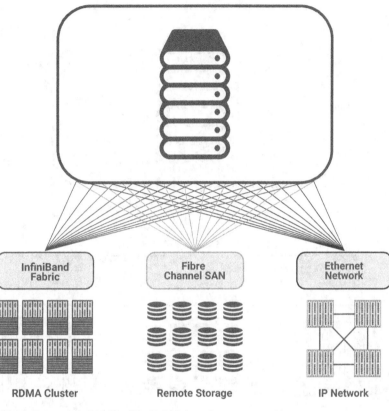

FIGURE 6-1   Host Connected to Dedicated Networks

In spite of the physical network consolidation, the three discussed infrastructure services remain individually exposed to the host operating systems through distinct software interfaces; see Figure 6-3. In all cases, these interfaces rely on direct memory access (DMA) to and from memory by the I/O adapter, most typically through PCIe.

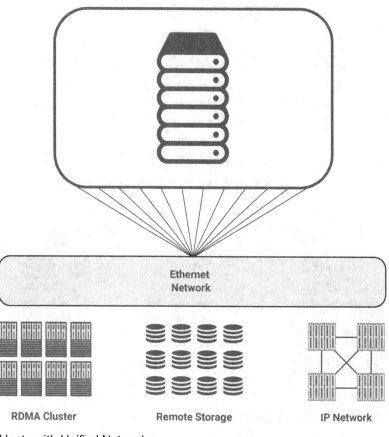

RDMA Cluster   Remote Storage   IP Network

FIGURE 6-2   Hosts with Unified Networks

RDMA Verbs   Block Storage Interface   Sockets API

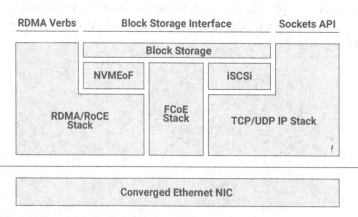

FIGURE 6-3   Unified Network Software Stack

6.1 RDMA and RoCE

Computer clusters have been around for many decades with successful commercial products since the 1980s by Digital Equipment Corporation [1], Tandem Computers [2], Compaq, Sun, HP, and IBM.

In a world where individual CPUs could no longer evolve at the pace of Moore's law, scaling out became the most viable way to satisfy the growing demand for compute-intensive applications. Over time, the move toward cloud services motivated the deployment of racks of standard servers at very large scale. Clusters of commodity servers have become the standard for the modern datacenter ranging from on-premise enterprise deployments all the way to public clouds.

In contrast to CPUs, communication technology continued to evolve at a steady pace and allowed bigger and better clusters. With faster networks came the demand for a more efficient I/O software interface that would address the communication bottleneck for high-performance distributed applications. In this context, the industry defined the Virtual Interface Architecture (VIA), intending to increase communication performance by eliminating host processing software overheads [3]. The objective: high bandwidth, low latency, and low CPU utilization.

These ideas were picked up in 1999 by two initially competing industry groups: NGIO and FutureIO. In the NGIO camp were Intel and Sun Microsystems, while IBM, HP, and Compaq led FutureIO. The head-to-head race to specify the new I/O standard was settled as both groups joined forces and created the InfiniBand Trade Association (IBTA), which in 2000 produced the first (InfiniBand) RDMA Specification [4], [5].

InfiniBand RDMA (Remote Direct Memory Access) was originally conceived as a vertically integrated protocol stack (see Figure 6-4) covering switches, routers, and network adapters and including from a physical layer up to software and management interfaces.

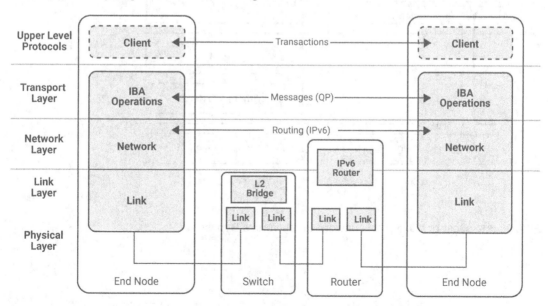

FIGURE 6-4   InfiniBand Protocol Stack and Fabric Diagram

The value proposition of RDMA is mainly derived from the following four characteristics:

- **Kernel bypass:** A mechanism that allows secure and direct access to I/O services from user-space processes without having to go through the OS kernel; see Figure 6-5. It eliminates a significant latency component and reduces CPU utilization.

- **Zero-copy:** The ability for the I/O device to directly read from and write to userspace memory buffers, thereby eliminating multiple copies of I/O data that is common with the OS-based software stack of traditional network protocols; see Figure 6-6.

- **Protocol offload:** Message segmentation and reassembly, delivery guarantees, access checks, and all aspects of a reliable transport are offloaded to the NIC, eliminating the consumption of CPU resources for network protocol processing; see Figure 6-7.

- **One-sided operations:** RDMA Read, Write and Atomic operations are executed without any intervention of the target-side CPU, with the obvious benefit of not spending valuable compute cycles on the target system; see Figure 6-8. This asynchronous processing approach results in a significant increase in message rates and a drastic reduction in message completion jitter, as the processing completely decouples I/O execution from the scheduling of the receiver's I/O stack software.

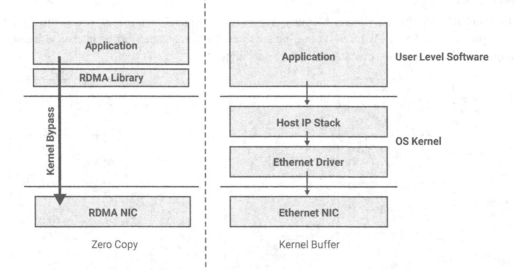

FIGURE 6-5   Cost of I/O, Kernel Network Stack versus Bypass

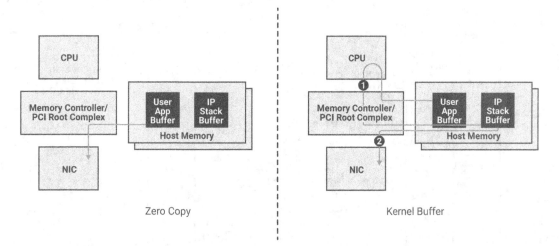

FIGURE 6-6 Kernel Buffer versus Zero-Copy

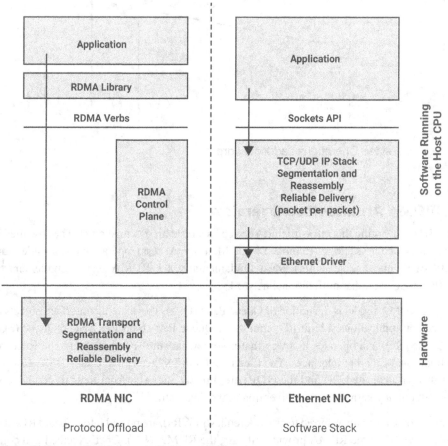

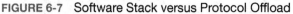

FIGURE 6-7 Software Stack versus Protocol Offload

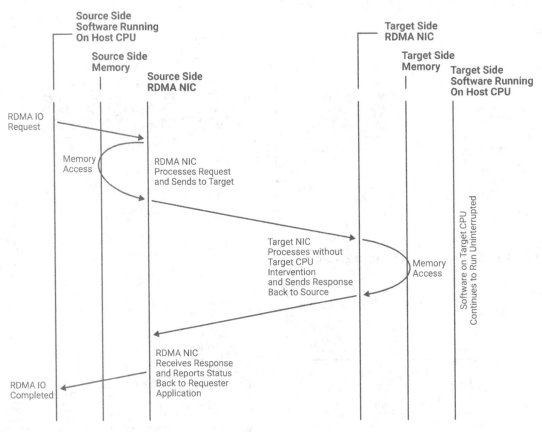

FIGURE 6-8 One-sided Operations Ladder Diagram

6.1.1   RDMA Architecture Overview

The term *RDMA*, denoting this infrastructure service, is a little bit of a misnomer. The so-called RDMA service includes actual RDMA (Remote Direct Memory Access) operations alongside traditional SEND/RECEIVE message semantics. Most fundamentally, the RDMA service implements a quite different I/O model than that of traditional networks.

Central to the RDMA model is the notion of Queue Pairs (QPs). These are the interface objects through which consumer applications submit I/O requests. A Queue Pair comprises a Send Queue (SQ) and a Receive Queue (RQ) and operates in a way that is somewhat similar to how Send and Receive Rings work on traditional Ethernet interfaces. The fundamental difference is that each RDMA flow operates on top of its own dedicated QP, and these QPs are directly accessed from their respective consumer processes without any kernel driver intervention in the data path.

RDMA operations, normally referred to as work requests (WRs), are posted into SQs and RQs and asynchronously serviced by the RDMA provider (that is, the RDMA NIC). Once executed and completed, the provider notifies the consumer process through Completion Queues (CQs); see Figure 6-9. Consumer processes may have one or more CQs that can be flexibly associated with their QPs.

The RDMA provider guarantees QP access protection across multiple consumers via a combination of regular host virtual memory and the mapping of I/O space into each process's own space. In this manner, user processes can exclusively access their respective RDMA resources. Typically, each process is assigned a dedicated page in the I/O address space of the RDMA NIC that is mapped to the process's virtual memory. The process can then directly interact with the RDMA NIC using regular userspace memory access to these mapped addresses. The NIC, in turn, can validate legitimate use of the corresponding RDMA resources and act upon the I/O requests without the intervention of the OS kernel.

As a corollary to the direct access model and the individual flow interfaces (that is, QPs) being visible to the NIC, fine-grained QoS is a natural characteristic of RDMA. Most typically, RDMA NICs implement a scheduler that picks pending jobs from QPs with outstanding WRs following sophisticated programmable policies.

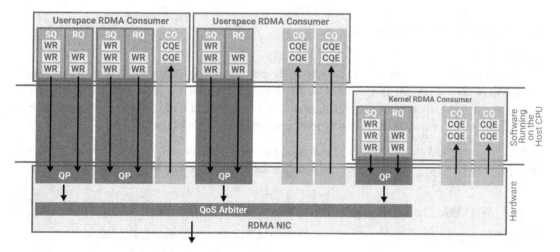

FIGURE 6-9   QPs, WRs, CQs, and Scheduler/QoS Arbiter

To allow direct I/O access to/from user-level process buffers, the RDMA model includes a mechanism called *memory registration*. This facility is used to pin into physical memory the user memory ranges that are meant to be used as the source or target of RDMA operations. In addition to pinning, during memory registration, the RDMA provider updates its memory mapping table with the physical addresses of the registered buffers and returns a memory key to the RDMA consumer process. Once registered, consumer processes can then refer to these memory regions in their submitted work requests, and the RDMA NIC can directly access these buffers during execution (that is, zero-copy).

6.1.2   RDMA Transport Services

The RDMA protocol standard originally defined two connection-oriented transport services: Reliable Connected (RC), Unreliable Connected (UC); and two datagram services: Reliable Datagram (RD) and Unreliable Datagram (UD); see Figure 6-10. The most commonly used ones are RC and UD. UC is rarely used and RD was never implemented.

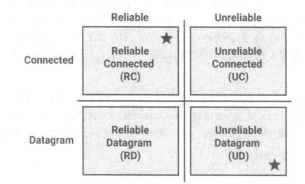

FIGURE 6-10   RDMA Transport Services

As far as reliability and connection characteristics are concerned, RC could be seen as the logical equivalent of the well-known TCP. A lot of the RDMA value proposition requires this transport service, and hence most RDMA consumer applications use it. Meanwhile, the UD transport service resembles UDP, and RDMA consumers use it mostly for management and control operations.

Over time, a new XRC transport service was added to the specification. It is a variation on RC that is mostly relevant for reducing the number of connections in scenarios with lots of processes per node.

6.1.3   RDMA Operations

The RDMA protocol includes Send/Receive semantics, RDMA Read/Writes, and Atomics.

Even though Send/Receives are semantically similar to their traditional network counterparts, the RDMA version leverages the kernel-bypass, the zero copy, and the reliable transport protocol offload of RDMA. In this way, consumer applications can attain low latency, high bandwidth, and low CPU utilization without significant changes to their communication model.

The Remote Direct Memory Access (RDMA) operations, RDMA Read and RDMA Write, give their name to the protocol. The main difference between these and Send/Receive is the one-sided nature of the execution. RDMA accesses complete with no intervention of the target-side CPU. Consumer applications can asynchronously read and write from and to remote node memory locations, subject to strict access right checks. Applications that have been coded for the explicit use of RDMA services typically exploit the full value proposition via RDMA Reads and Writes.

RDMA Atomic operations allow one-sided atomic remote memory accesses. The InfiniBand RDMA standard defines 64-bit CompareAndSwap and FetchAndAdd operations, but over time vendors have extended the support to longer data fields and other variants such as the support for masked versions of the operations. Among others, RDMA Atomics are widely used by distributed lock applications and clustered database systems.

6.1.4   RDMA Scalability

The InfiniBand RDMA architecture follows very strict protocol layering and was designed with a hardware implementation in mind. However, not all RDMA implementations are created equal. One challenge is that of delivering RDMA services at scale. The offloaded nature of the RDMA model mandates per-flow context structures of considerable size. Reasonably, the more RDMA flows, the more state the RDMA NIC needs to maintain. It's not rare for consumer applications to demand tens and hundreds of thousands of RDMA flows with some even reaching the millions. One possible approach is that of caching context structures on the RDMA device itself while maintaining the complete state tables in host memory. When there is significant locality in RDMA flow usage, this type of solution can deliver adequate performance. However, for several deployment scenarios, context cache replacement may introduce significant performance jitter. With these use cases in mind, high-scale RDMA NICs have been designed with onboard dedicated context memory that can fit the entire RDMA protocol state.

6.1.5   RoCE

In addition to the software interface advantages of the RDMA model, InfiniBand dominated the high-performance clustering space, thanks to the performance advantage of its dedicated L1 and L2 that was at that time faster than that of the much more established Ethernet. A few years later, as 10Gig and 40Gig Ethernet turned out to be more common, it became apparent that the same benefits of RDMA could be obtained over the ubiquitous Ethernet network. Two standards emerged to address this approach, iWARP and RoCE. iWARP defined RDMA semantics on top of TCP as the underlying transport protocol [6]. Meanwhile, the IBTA defined RoCE by merely replacing the lower two layers of its vertical protocol stack with those of Ethernet [7].

The first version of RoCE did not have an IP layer and hence wasn't routable. This happened at pretty much the same time as FCoE was being defined under the similar vision of flat L2-based networks. Eventually, it became clear that Routable RoCE was required, and the spec further evolved to become RoCEv2, defining the encapsulation of RDMA on top of UDP/IP [8]. In addition to making RoCE routable, RoCEv2 leverages all the advantages of the IP protocol, including QoS marking (DSCP) and congestion management signaling (ECN).

The resulting architecture is depicted in Figure 6-11. The first column from the left represents the classical implementation of InfiniBand RDMA. The middle column is ROCEv1 (no IP header, directly over Ethernet), and the third column is RoCEv2 in which the InfiniBand transport layer is encapsulated in IP/UDP.

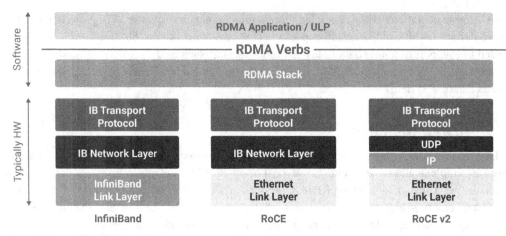

FIGURE 6-11   RDMA over Ethernet Protocol Stack Evolution

6.1.6 RoCE vs iWARP

iWARP and RoCE are functionally similar but not identical in terms of the RDMA services that they offer. There are some semantic differences between the two protocols and a few functional aspects of RoCE that were not covered by the iWARP specification. In practice, iWARP didn't attain a wide adoption in the market, due in part to the fact that the RoCE specification is much more suitable for efficient hardware implementations. Figure 6-12 illustrates the protocol stack differences between the two.

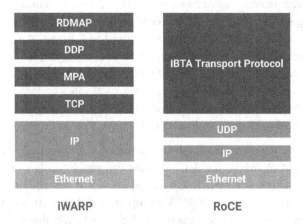

FIGURE 6-12   RoCE versus iWARP

6.1.7 RDMA Deployments

RDMA was initially deployed in high-performance computing (HPC) where ultra-low latency and high bandwidth dominate the requirements. The cost/performance advantages were so drastic that in a few years InfiniBand debunked well-established proprietary networks and became the de facto standard for top-end HPC clusters; see Figure 6-13. This broad adoption in the HPC space fueled the development of high-end RDMA and made it a more mature technology [9].

Embedded platforms were also among the early adopters of RDMA technology. Examples included data replication in storage appliances, media distribution, and others. The unrivaled performance of RDMA and the fact that it was an open standard with a visible roadmap into the future made the solution very attractive to this market that traditionally aims for long-term investments in technology.

One other major milestone in the growth of RDMA was the adoption of the technology at the core of Oracle's flagship clustered database [10]. This use case was instrumental in bringing RDMA into the enterprise network.

Another wave of early adoption came when the financial market identified a significant edge for market data delivery systems in the ultra-low latency of InfiniBand.

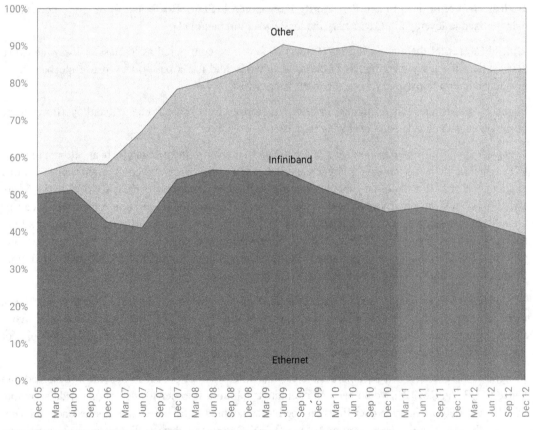

FIGURE 6-13   InfiniBand and Ethernet Shares (Data courtesy of top500.org)

Currently, RoCEv2 offers the RDMA value proposition on Ethernet networks with applications covering remote storage protocols, database clustering, nonvolatile memory, artificial intelligence, scientific computing, and others.

Mellanox Technologies has been one of the most significant contributors to the InfiniBand technology; Figure 9-6 shows a Mellanox ConnectX-5 Dual-Port Adapter Supporting RoCEv2 over two 100Gb/s Ethernet ports.

6.1.8   RoCEv2 and Lossy Networks

Due to the simplicity of its transport protocol, RDMA performance is quite sensitive to packet losses. Very much like FCoE, the RDMA protocol was designed with the assumption of an underlying lossless network. The network was indeed lossless when RDMA was running on InfiniBand Fabrics and, when RoCE was defined, the IEEE 802.1 was in the process of standardizing a set of Ethernet specs usually referred to as Data Center Bridging (DCB), which, among other things, offered non-drop (also known as "lossless") priorities through Per-Priority Flow Control (PFC). RoCE and FCoE were both originally defined to leverage PFC to satisfy the lossless requirement [11].

With PFC, each of the eight priorities (from 0 to 7) can be configured as lossless or lossy. Network devices treat the lossy priorities as in classical Ethernet and use a per-priority pause mechanism to guarantee that no frames are lost on the lossless priorities.

Figure 6-14 illustrates this technique: Priority 2 is stopped by a pause frame to avoid overflowing the queue on the switch side and thus losing packets.

Alongside PFC, IEEE has standardized DCBX (Data Center Bridging eXchange) in an attempt to make I/O consolidation deployable on a larger scale. DCBX is a discovery and configuration protocol that guarantees that both ends of an Ethernet link are configured consistently. DCBX works to configure switch-to-switch links and switch-to-host links correctly to avoid configuration errors, which can be very difficult to troubleshoot. DCBX discovers the capabilities of the two peers at each end of a link: It can check for consistency, notify the device manager in the case of configuration mismatches, and provide a basic configuration in case one of the two peers is not configured. DCBX can be configured to send conflict alarms to the appropriate management stations.

While these DCB techniques can be appropriately deployed and do not present any conceptual flaws, there has consistently been significant concerns from the IT community that prevented their mainstream deployment. Criticism has been fueled by some unfortunate experiences, lack of tools for consistency checks and troubleshooting, and distance limitation both in terms of miles and hops.

In light of the preceding, it became quite clear that PFC was not poised to become widespread and hence FCoE and RoCEv2 would need an alternative solution. In other words, to gain wide adoption, RDMA and Remote Storage over Ethernet need to be adapted to tolerate a non-lossless network. For storage, the real solution comes from NVMe and NVMe over Fabrics (NVMe-oF), which runs on top of RDMA or TCP and leverages their respective transport protocol characteristics as described in section 6.2.2. For RoCEv2, modifications to the protocol have been implemented as described in the following section.

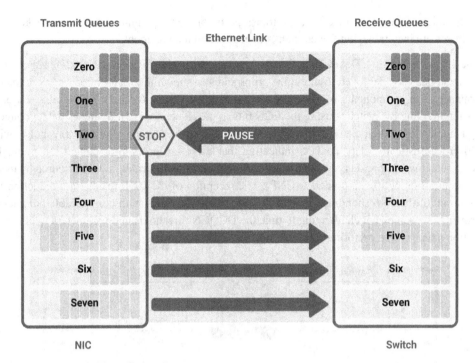

FIGURE 6-14 Priority Flow Control

To properly understand the scope of the problem, it's crucial to establish what defines a *lossy network*. In a nutshell, in modern Ethernet networks, there are two leading causes for packet losses.

The first type of packet drops is literally produced by the forces of nature (for example, alpha particles) that every once in a while cause a bit flip on a packet while it's being transmitted or stored in a network device. This data corruption will be detected by CRCs and will result in the packet's being dropped. In modern data centers and enterprise networks, the probability for these events is very low. This kind of packet loss does occur on the so-called lossless networks; but given the low occurrence rate and the fact that it typically affects a single packet, simple retransmission schemes can effectively overcome it.

The second type of loss comes as a result of congestion. When there is contention on the output port of a network device and this contention lasts until its buffers fill up, the device will have no choice but to start dropping packets. This congestion-induced loss is much more severe and is the actual cause for significant reductions in performance. As described earlier, in a "lossless" network, this problem is addressed with link layer flow control that effectively prevents packets from arriving at a device unless there is enough buffer space to store them.

The strategy to solve the second problem, without using any link-layer flow control, centers around two complementary approaches. First, reduce contention by applying congestion management. With this technique, upon buffer buildup, a closed loop scheme controls injection at the source, thereby reducing the contention and minimizing the cases of packet drop. With congestion reduced to a minimum, the second technique focuses on the efficient retransmission of the few remaining dropped packets. These packet losses are inevitable, but fewer, thanks to congestion management.

Specifically, with RoCEv2, Data Center Quantized Congestion Notification (DCQCN) [12] congestion management has been deployed to minimize drops and was shown to greatly improve overall network performance. The components of DCQCN are depicted in Figure 6-15. DCQCN relies on explicit congestion marking by switches using the ECN bits in the IP header [13]. Switches detect congestion through monitoring of their queue sizes. When a queue size crosses a programmable threshold, switches start to probabilistically mark packets indicating that these are crossing a congestion point. Upon receiving such marked packets, the destination node reflects this information to the source by using an explicit congestion notification packet (CNP). The reception of the CNP results in a reduction in the injection rate of the corresponding flow using a specified algorithm with configurable parameters. It has proven to be somewhat challenging to tune the DCQCN thresholds and parameters to obtain good congestion management performance under a wide variety of flows.

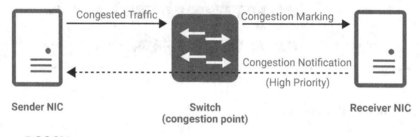

FIGURE 6-15   DCQCN

A newer approach under development utilizes a different congestion signaling scheme that is based on measuring latencies at the end nodes and reacts to queue buildup by detecting a latency change or spike; see Figure 6-16. This new scheme has faster response times than DCQCN and offers the additional benefit of not requiring the tuning of queue thresholds in the switches or other parameters. This mechanism is completely implemented at the end nodes without any reliance on switches.

Congestion management will significantly improve the performance of RDMA in lossy networks by minimizing congestion-induced packet loss. However, in practice it's impossible (actually, extremely inefficient) to guarantee absolutely no drops under all possible conditions, no matter how good the congestion management scheme is. The reaction time for congestion management extends from the moment congestion is detected, through the point where the source reduces the injection rate, and until the reduced rate arrives back at the congested point. During this period, packets continue to accumulate at the higher rate, and it could so happen that buffers overflow and packets are dropped. This delayed reaction characteristic is typical of closed-loop control systems. The congestion management algorithm could be tuned for more aggressive injection rate changes, thereby inducing a quicker reaction, to mitigate the impact of control loop delay. However, an over-aggressive scheme would generally create a prolonged underutilization of the available bandwidth. In essence, there is a tradeoff between the possibility of some packet drops versus utilization of all available bandwidth, and in general it's best to tune for minimal (but non-zero) drops.

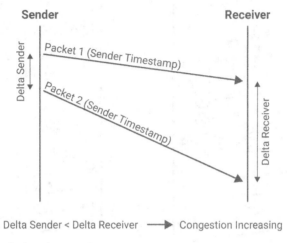

FIGURE 6-16   One-way Latencies

Even with very effective and adequately tuned congestion management, some packets may be dropped. At that point, it's the job of the communication protocol to deal with recovery. The transport layer of the RDMA protocol, as currently defined in the RoCEv2 standard, utilizes a very simplistic approach for this task. Upon detection of a missing packet, the receiver sends a NAK code back to the sender indicating the sequence number of the missed packet. The sender rolls back its state and resends everything from that point on. This "Go Back N" approach was conceived with the assumption of an underlying lossless fabric, and it's not ideal in the presence of congestion-induced drops.

To address this limitation, modern RoCEv2 implementations introduced a selective retransmission scheme that is much better at recovering from losses; see Figure 6-17. The main goal is to recover faster and conserve network bandwidth by resending only the lost packets.

Selective retransmission has been implemented in TCP for quite some time. The resending of individual packets from the source is quite straightforward. The challenge in RDMA networks is mainly at the receiver and has to do with the protocol requirement for in-order processing of inbound packets. For example, a multipacket RDMA Write message only carries the destination address in its first packet. If that packet is lost, subsequent ones can't be placed into their intended memory destinations. Attempts have been discussed to modify the message semantics to allow for out-of-order processing of inbound packets. However, such an approach would have a significant impact on existing RDMA protocol semantics that would be visible to consumer applications. A much more friendly approach (see Figure 6-18) completely preserves existing semantics and is implemented with the help of a staging buffer that is used to temporarily store subsequent packets until the lost ones arrive after being resent. RDMA NIC architectures that support efficient on-NIC memory are particularly suitable for this type of solution.

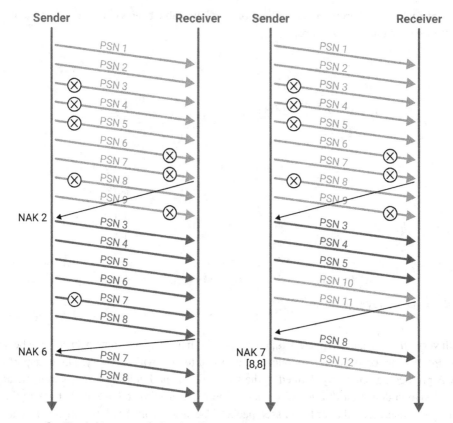

FIGURE 6-17   Go Back N versus Selective Retransmission

As described earlier, the RDMA transport protocol detects missing packets at the target and utilizes explicit NAKs to trigger immediate resends. With selective retransmission, this scheme is efficient except for the case when the lost packets are the last in the message (also known as tail drops), as there are no subsequent packets to detect the loss and trigger the NAK. For this case, the transport protocol relies on a timeout at the sender that kicks in when there are outstanding unacknowledged packets for much longer than expected. However, to prevent unnecessary retransmissions due to latency variations, this timeout is intended to be set to a value that is much higher than the typical network round trip. The effect is that, in case of a tail drop, the completion time of the message is severely impacted. Some RDMA implementations send an unsolicited ACK from the target back to the source, when no further packets are being received on an active flow, to improve the recovery time in the presence of a tail drop; see Figure 6-19. The receiver is in a much better position to eagerly detect the potential loss of a tail in a way that is entirely independent of the fabric round trip latency.

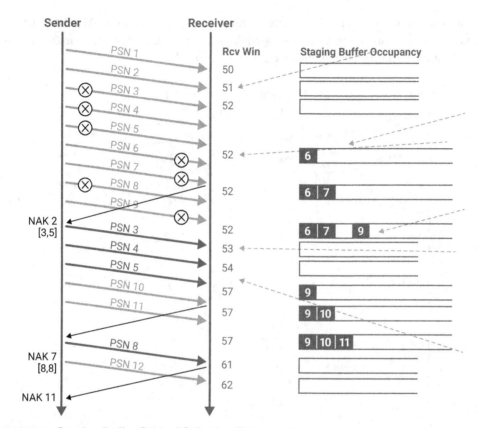

FIGURE 6-18 Staging Buffer Cost of Selective Retransmission

6.1.9 Continued Evolution of RDMA

As it usually happens with technology, RDMA deployment experiences prompted further evolution of the protocol. In this context, the vendor's innovation sets the pace. When adopted by the market, some of the new extensions become candidates for standardization at the IBTA, which has remained active for more than 20 years. Recent areas of activities are discussed next.

Control Plane Acceleration

We have described the mainstream data plane of the RDMA protocol that has been heavily optimized and tuned for maximum performance. Meanwhile, the control plane has been pointed out as a limiting factor for some real-life applications. In particular, with the one-connection-per-flow model that is common with RDMA, the cost of connection setup can become a burden. It is especially true for large deployments or those with very dynamic connection characteristics. Another aspect of RoCE that has been a consistent complaint is the cost of memory registration. This operation involves a mandatory interaction with the OS and typically requires careful synchronization of RDMA NIC state. Some new RDMA implementations optimize these operations, and near-data-plane-performance versions of memory registration and connection setup have become available.

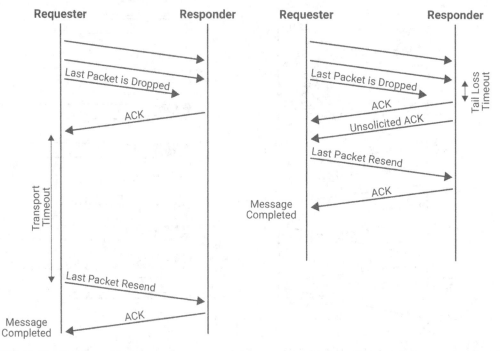

FIGURE 6-19   Tail Drop Recovery

Support for Remote Nonvolatile Memory Accesses

The recent proliferation of new nonvolatile memory technologies has opened up opportunities for a new range of applications and changed the paradigm for many others. NVDIMMs with Load/Store access semantics are adopting the form of a new storage tier. The SNIA has been working to define programming models for these new technologies [14], and the IBTA is extending the RDMA protocol with explicit support for the unique characteristics of explicit nonvolatile memory accesses across the network. Specifically, new RDMA operations will allow remote NVM commits that, once completed at the source, will virtually guarantee that data has been safely delivered to the persistence domain on the target side while maintaining the one-sided execution that is crucial to the RDMA model.

Data Security

Concerning data security, the RDMA protocol covers all aspects of interprocess protection and memory access checks at the end nodes. However, as far as data in transit is concerned, the standard doesn't define data encryption or cryptographic authentication schemes. Still, by being a layered protocol that runs on UDP/IP, there are several ways to implement encrypted RDMA, such as IPSec or DTLS.

Modern RDMA implementations using domain-specific hardware are particularly efficient at this kind of task and can achieve wire rate encryption/decryption for 100GE links.

6.2 Storage

Introduced in 1986, SCSI (Small Computer System Interface) became the dominant storage protocol for servers. SCSI offered a variety of physical layers, from parallel to serial, mostly limited to very short distances.

The demand for longer reach, as well as the opportunity to disaggregate storage, motivated the creation of Fibre Channel [15], a dedicated storage network designed to carry SCSI across a switched fabric and connect to dedicated appliances providing storage services to many clients.

Over time, the network consolidation trend prompted the definition of further remote storage solutions for carrying SCSI across nondedicated networks. iSCSI [16] and FCoE [17] are attempts to converge storage and networking over Ethernet, whereas SRP [18] and iSER [19] are designed to carry SCSI over RDMA; see Figure 6-20. In all cases, the goal is to eliminate the requirement for a dedicated storage network (for example, Fibre Channel). Additionally, storage consolidation has further redefined and disrupted the storage landscape through "hyper-converged infrastructure" (HCI) and "hyper-converged storage" offerings. These are typically proprietary solutions defined and implemented by the top-tier cloud providers [20].

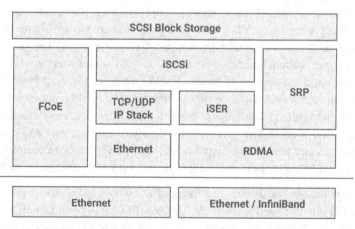

FIGURE 6-20   Remote SCSI Storage Protocols

6.2.1   The Advent of SSDs

Since 2010, solid state drives (SSDs) started to become economically viable. They provide superior performance compared to rotating media hard disks. To fully exploit SSD capabilities, a new standard called Non-Volatile Memory express (NVMe) has been created as a more modern alternative to SCSI.

NVMe [21] is an open logical device interface specification for accessing nonvolatile storage media attached via a PCIe. NVMe has been designed to take advantage of the low latency and high internal parallelism of flash-based storage devices. As a result, NVMe reduces I/O overhead and brings various performance improvements relative to previous logical-device interfaces, including multiple, long command queues and reduced latency. NVMe can be used for SSD, but also for new technologies such as 3D Xpoint [22] and NVDIMMs [23].

6.2.2   NVMe over Fabrics

As was the case with SCSI, a remote storage flavor of NVMe was also defined [24]. NVMe over Fabrics (NVMe-oF) defines extensions to NVMe that allow remote storage access over RDMA and Fibre Channel. Most recently, NVMe/ TCP was also included in the standard (see Figure 6-21).

It seems that the Fibre Channel flavor of NVMe-oF will not be particularly relevant, because it requires maintaining a separate FC network or running over FCoE. Given the benefits already explored in previous sections, the highest performant solution appears to be NVMe over RDMA. The NVMe/TCP approach will likely gain wide acceptance, given the ubiquity of TCP and the opportunity to leverage most of the value proposition of NVMeoF with minimal impact to the datacenter network.

6.2.3   Data Plane Model of Storage Protocols

Remote storage has been in place for a couple of decades. As one looks in more detail, there is a common pattern in the data plane of most remote storage protocols. I/O operations start with a request from the storage client, which is typically delivered to the remote storage server in the payload of a network message. The storage server usually manages the outstanding I/O requests in a queue from which it schedules for execution. Execution entails the actual data transfer between the client and the server and the actual access to the storage media. For I/O reads (that is, read from storage), the server will read from the storage media and then deliver the data through the network into buffers on the client side that were set aside for that purpose when the I/O operation was requested. For I/O writes, the server will access the client buffers to retrieve the data across the network and store it in the storage media when it arrives (a pull model); see Figure 6-22. After the I/O has been completed, the server will typically deliver a completion status to the client in the payload of a message through the network.

Some remote storage protocols also include a flavor of I/O writes where data is pushed into the server directly with the I/O request; see Figure 6-23. The benefit of this optimization is the saving of the data delivery roundtrip. However, this scheme poses a challenge to the storage server as it needs to provision queues for the actual incoming data and, hence, when available, this push model is only permitted for short I/O writes.

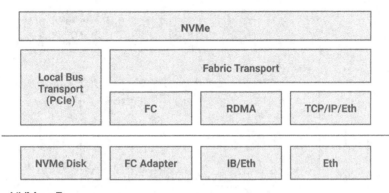

FIGURE 6-21 NVMe-oF

RDMA operations present clear benefits when applied towards data access and I/O requests. With RDMA, the client-side CPU need not be involved in the actual delivery of data. The server asynchronously executes storage requests, and the status is reported back to the client, after the requests are completed. This natural alignment prompted the development of RDMA-based remote storage protocols that would work over SCSI. Initially, the SCSI RDMA Protocol (SRP) [18] was defined, followed sometime later by the IETF standardized iSCSI Extensions for RDMA (iSER) [19], which preserves the iSCSI model by replacing the underlying TCP with RDMA. Finally, NVMe-oF was defined to leverage the NVMe model on RDMA fabrics, given the current momentum and the maturity of RDMA technologies. NVMe-oF seems poised to gain a much broader adoption than either SRP or iSER.

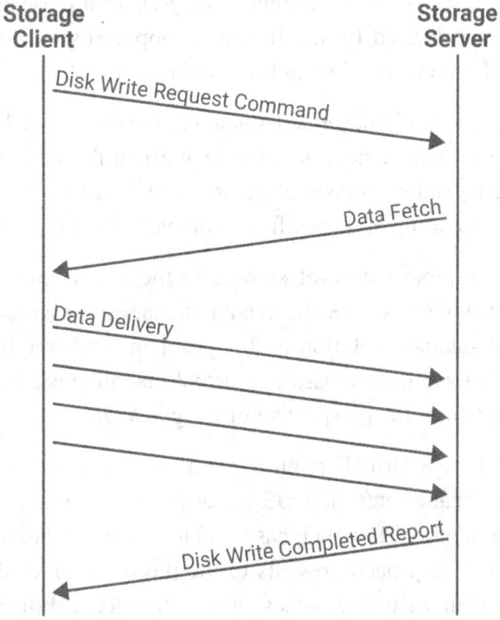

FIGURE 6-22 Example of Storage Write

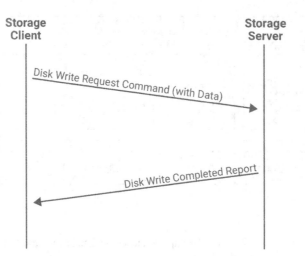

FIGURE 6-23   Push Model

6.2.4   Remote Storage Meets Virtualization

Economies of scale motivated large compute cluster operators to look at server disaggregation. Among server components, storage is possibly the most natural candidate for disaggregation, mainly because the average latency of storage media access could tolerate a network traversal. Even though the new prevalent SSD media drastically reduces these latencies, network performance evolution accompanies that improvement. As a result, the trend for storage disaggregation that started with the inception of Fibre Channel was sharply accelerated by the increased popularity of high-volume clouds, as this created an ideal opportunity for consolidation and cost reduction.

Remote storage is sometimes explicitly presented as such to the client; see Figure 6-24. This mandates the deployment of new storage management practices that affect the way storage services are offered to the host, because host management infrastructure needs to deal with the remote aspects of storage (remote access permissions, mounting of a specific remote volume, and so on).

In some cases, exposing the remote nature of storage to the client could present some challenges, notably in virtualized environments where the tenant manages the guest OS, which assumes the presence of local disks. One standard solution to this problem is for the hypervisor to virtualize the remote storage and emulate a local disk toward the virtual machine; see Figure 6-25. This emulation abstracts the paradigm change from the perspective of the guest OS.

However, hypervisor-based storage virtualization is not a suitable solution in all cases. For example, in bare-metal environments, tenant-controlled OS images run on the actual physical machines with no hypervisor to create the emulation. For such cases, a hardware emulation model is becoming more common; see Figure 6-26. This approach presents to the physical server the illusion of a local hard disk. The emulation system then virtualizes access across the network using standard or proprietary remote storage protocols. One typical approach is to emulate a local NVMe disk and use NVMe-oF to access the remote storage.

One proposed way to implement the data plane for disk emulation is by using so-called "Smart NICs"; see section 8.6. These devices typically include multiple programmable cores combined with a NIC data plane. For example, Mellanox BlueField and Broadcom Stingray products fall into this category.

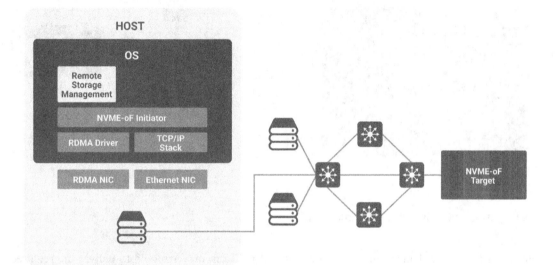

FIGURE 6-24 Explicit Remote Storage

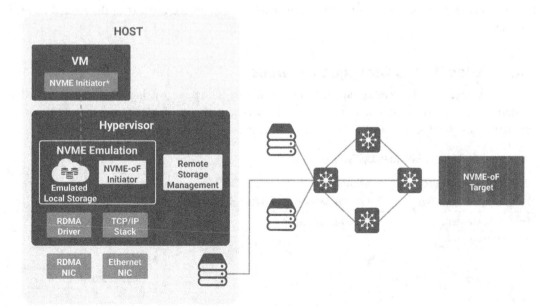

FIGURE 6-25 Hypervisor Emulates Local Disk Towards Guest OS

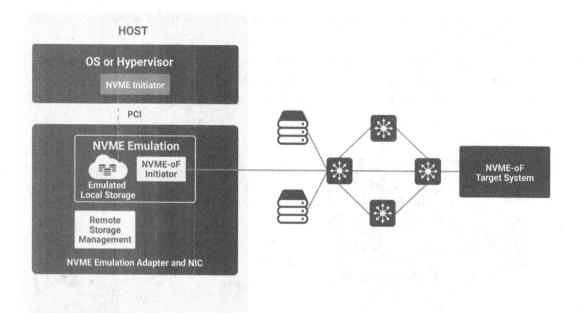

FIGURE 6-26   NIC-Based NVMe Emulation

However, as the I/O demand increases, this kind of platform may struggle to deliver the required performance and latency, and the scalability of the solution, especially in terms of heat and power, may become a challenge. An alternative approach favors the use of domain-specific hardware instead of off-the-shelf programmable cores. We discuss this further in the context of distributed storage services.

6.2.5   Distributed Storages Services

It has been quite a while since storage was merely about reading and writing from persistent media. Modern storage solutions offer multiple additional associated services. Table 6-1 summarizes the more prevalent ones. We discuss some of them in the following sections.

TABLE 6-1   Storage Services by Type

Security and Integrity	Efficiency	Reliability & Availability
■ Encryption and Decryption	■ Compression and Decompression	■ Replication
■ Key Management	■ Deduplication	■ Mirroring
■ Checksum		■ Erasure Coding
		■ Striping
		■ Snapshotting

6.2.6 Storage Security

In today's world, encryption of data is of primary importance. Multiple encryption schemes have been devised over the years for the encryption of data at rest. The recently approved IEEE standard 1619-2018 defines Cryptographic Protection on Block Storage Devices. The algorithm specified is a variant of the Advanced Encryption Standard, AES-XTS (XOR–Encrypt–XOR, tweaked-codebook mode with ciphertext stealing). The AES-XTS block size is 16 bytes, but with ciphertext stealing, any length, not necessarily a multiple of 16 bytes, is supported. AES-XTS considers each storage data block as the data unit. Popular storage block sizes are 512B, 4KB, and 8KB. Each block can also include metadata/Protection Info (PI) and thus be larger than the aforementioned sizes by anywhere from 8 to 32 bytes.

6.2.7 Storage Efficiency

A crucial service of modern storage technology that directly ties to IT costs is data compression. Every day, vast amounts of data are generated and stored—logs, web history, transactions, and so on. Most of this data is in a human-consumable form and is significantly compressible; therefore, doing so allows for better utilization of storage resources. With the advent of SSDs, which offer tremendous performance but have a higher cost per GB than HDDs, data compression becomes even more compelling.

Most of the data compression techniques used in practice today are variants of the Lempel-Ziv (LZ) compression scheme with or without Huffman Coding. These techniques inevitably trade off compression ratio for compression and decompression speed and complexity. For example, deflate compression, the most popular and open source compression in use, implements nine levels, progressively going from speed-optimized (level 1) to ratio-optimized (level 9).

Compression speed, compression ratio, and decompression speed of various algorithms are compared in [25]:

- Fast compression techniques such as LZ4 and Snappy focus on speed optimization by eliminating Huffman Coding.

- The fastest software-based compression algorithm (LZ4) offers a compression ratio of 2 on Silesia benchmark.

- The highest compression ratio of 3 comes from deflate (level 6).

Data deduplication is another data-reduction technique that has become popular in storage platforms. The benefit stems from the reality that it's extremely common for multiple copies of the same data to be stored in the same system. Consider, for example, the OS images for instances of multiple VMs; a large presentation emailed to a work team or multimedia files delivered to social media groups. The explicit goal is to store a single copy of the common data and avoid the waste of storage space on copies.

Data deduplication involves comparing a new data block against all previously stored ones in an attempt to discover a potential copy. Byte-by-byte comparison is not an efficient solution. The most common technique relies on calculating a short digest of the data block and comparing it against the other block's digests. Cryptographic hashes are used as digests thanks to their very low collision probability. For example, a Secure Hash Algorithm 2 (SHA2) 512-bit digest of a 4KB data block is just 64B long but has a collision probability of 2.2×10^{-132}! Different storage systems have chosen different cryptographic hashes, but the most common is the NIST-approved SHA family: SHA1, SHA2, SHA3. SHA2 and SHA3 offer digest sizes of 256, 384, or 512 bits.

6.2.8   Storage Reliability

Resiliency to media failure is among the essential features of a storage system. In its simplest form, this can be achieved by storing two copies of each block on two different disks, and consequently duplicating the cost of the media. By calculating a parity block over N data blocks and then storing the N data blocks and the one parity block on N+1 different drives, the cost can be reduced while tolerating a single drive failure (including a failure to the parity drive). The Redundant Array of Independent Disks standard 5 (RAID5) implements this scheme, but it is less popular these days due to vulnerabilities during rebuild times and the increased size of the individual disks. Similarly, RAID-6 calculates two different parity blocks and can tolerate two drive failures. This approach, known as erasure coding, can be generalized. A scheme to tolerate K drive failures requires calculating K parity blocks over N data blocks and storing N+K blocks on N+K drives. Reed-Solomon [25] is a widespread erasure coding scheme used by many storage systems.

6.2.9   Offloading and Distributing Storage Services

Traditionally, most storage services, like the ones described previously, were provided by the monolithic storage platform. The disaggregation of storage using local disk emulation presents an opportunity for further innovations. Storage services can now be implemented in three different components of the platform: the disk emulation adapter at the host, the front-end controller of the storage server, or the storage backend; see Figure 6-27.

Deployment of storage services using domain-specific hardware within the host platform aligns well with the benefits of other distributed services discussed in previous chapters. Storage compression, for example, appears to be an excellent candidate for this approach. Implementation at the end node versus an appliance offers the benefit of scalability, and, in addition, the advantage of reduced network bandwidth as the storage data is delivered in compressed form.

However, not all services are equally suitable for this approach. In particular, client-side offloads are more efficient when context information is unchanging per flow, which is often the case for compression. In contrast, reliability services that involve persistent metadata schemes are a better fit for the storage server side. Some services could benefit from mixed approaches. For example, deduplication would be naturally implemented by the storage system because it requires the digest of all stored blocks. However, digest calculation, which is a compute-intensive task, could be very well offloaded to the host adapter, attaining a benefit in scalability.

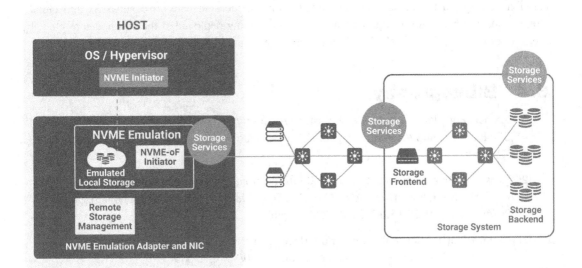

FIGURE 6-27 Distributed Storage Services

With regard to security, distributed storage presents the additional need to protect data in transit. For this purpose, there is no choice but to involve the end node. In cases where the remote storage server implements encryption of data at rest, data in transit can be secured using traditional network packet encryption schemes (for example, IPSec, DTLS). Alternatively, AES-XTS encryption for data-at-rest could be implemented directly at the host adapter, thereby covering the protection of data in transit and relieving the storage platform from the work of encryption/decryption. The AES-XTS scheme is hardware-friendly and particularly suitable for offload to the disk emulation controller on the host side. Encryption of data at rest performed by the end node offers the additional benefit of total data protection under the complete control of the data owner. With encryption performed at the source, services such as compression that require visibility of the data must also be implemented at the endnode.

6.2.10 Persistent Memory as a New Storage Tier

The emergence of nonvolatile memory devices also created the notion of a new storage tier. These new devices, some of which are packaged in DIMM form factors, have performance characteristics that are closer to that of DRAM with capacities and persistency that is more typical of storage. This trend promoted the development of new APIs for efficient utilization of these devices. The Storage Networking Industry Association (SNIA) developed a programming model [26] that covers local access and is now being extended to support remote NVM devices in line with the RDMA protocol extensions discussed in section 6.1.9.

6.3 Summary

As with application services, the demand for cost-efficient scalability and flexibility requires a paradigm change in the deployment of infrastructure services in enterprise networks and clouds. Domain-specific hardware for distributed services processing deployed at the end nodes or close by seems to offer a promising, scalable solution that strikes a good balance of flexibility and cost.

6.4 Bibliography

[1] Kronenberg, Nancy P. et al. "VAXclusters: A Closely-Coupled Distributed System (Abstract)." SOSP (1985), http://citeseerx.ist.psu.edu/viewdoc/download?doi=10.1.1.74.727&rep=rep1&type=pdf

[2] Horst and Diego José Díaz García. "1.0 Introduction, 2.0 ServerNet Overview, 2.1 ServerNet I, ServerNet SAN I/O Architecture." https://pdfs.semanticscholar.org/e00f/9c7dfa6e2345b9a58a082a2a2c13ef27d4a9.pdf

[3] Compaq, Intel, Microsoft, "Virtual Interface Architecture Specification, Version 1.0," December 1997, http://www.cs.uml.edu/~bill/cs560/VI_spec.pdf

[4] InfiniBand Trade Association, http://www.infinibandta.org

[5] InfiniBand Architecture Specification, Volume 1, Release 1.3, https://cw.infinibandta.org/document/dl/7859

[6] RDMA Consortium, http://rdmaconsortium.org

[7] Supplement to InfiniBand Architecture Specification, Volume 1, Release 1.2.1, Annex A16, RDMA over Converged Ethernet (RoCE) https://cw.infinibandta.org/document/dl/7148

[8] Supplement to InfiniBand Architecture Specification, Volume 1, Release 1.2.1, Annex A17, RoCEv2 https://cw.infinibandta.org/document/dl/7781

[9] Top 500, Development over time, https://www.top500.org/statistics/overtime

[10] Paul Tsien, "Update: InfiniBand for Oracle RAC Clusters," Oracle, https://downloads.openfabrics.org/Media/IB_LowLatencyForum_2007/IB_2007_04_Oracle.pdf

[11] IEEE 802.1 Data Center Bridging, https://1.ieee802.org/dcb

[12] Yibo Zhu, Haggai Eran, Daniel Firestone, Chuanxiong Guo, Marina Lipshteyn, Yehonatan Liron, Jitendra Padhye, Shachar Raindel, Mohamad Haj Yahia, and Ming Zhang. 2015. Congestion Control for Large-Scale RDMA Deployments. SIGCOMM Comput. Commun. Rev. 45, 4 (August 2015), 523–536. DOI: https://doi.org/10.1145/2829988.2787484, https://conferences.sigcomm.org/sigcomm/2015/pdf/papers/p523.pdf

[13]   Ramakrishnan, K., Floyd, S., and D. Black, "The Addition of Explicit Congestion Notification (ECN) to IP," RFC 3168, DOI 10.17487/RFC3168, September 2001, https://www.rfc-editor.org/info/rfc3168

[14]   SNIA, "NVM Programming Model (NPM)," https://www.snia.org/tech_activities/standards/curr_standards/npm

[15]   FCIA, Fibre Channel Industry Association, https://fibrechannel.org

[16]   Chadalapaka, M., Satran, J., Meth, K., and D. Black, "Internet Small Computer System Interface (iSCSI) Protocol (Consolidated)," RFC 7143, DOI 10.17487/RFC7143, April 2014, https://www.rfc-editor.org/info/rfc7143

[17]   Incits, "T11 - Fibre Channel Interfaces," http://www.t11.org

[18]   Incits "T10, SCSI RDMA Protocol (SRP)," http://www.t10.org/cgi-bin/ac.pl?t=f&f=srp-r16a.pdf

[19]   Ko, M. and A. Nezhinsky, "Internet Small Computer System Interface (iSCSI) Extensions for the Remote Direct Memory Access (RDMA) Specification," RFC 7145, DOI 10.17487/RFC7145, April 2014, https://www.rfc-editor.org/info/rfc7145

[20]   Google, "Colossus," http://www.pdsw.org/pdsw-discs17/slides/PDSW-DISCS-Google-Keynote.pdf

[21]   NVM Express, http://nvmexpress.org

[22]   Rick Coulson, "3D XPoint Technology Drives System Architecture," https:// www.snia.org/sites/default/files/NVM/2016/presentations/RickCoulson_All_the_Ways_3D_XPoint_Impacts.pdf

[23]   Jeff Chang, "NVDIMM-N Cookbook: A Soup-to-Nuts Primer on Using NVDIMM-Ns to Improve Your Storage Performance," http://www.snia.org/sites/default/files/SDC15_presentations/persistant_mem/Jeff Chang-ArthurSainio_NVDIMM_Cookbook.pdf, Sep. 2015

[24]   NVM Express, "NVMExpress over Fabrics," Revision 1.0, June 5, 2016, https://nvmexpress.org/wp-content/uploads/NVMe_over_Fabrics_1_0_Gold_20160605-1.pdf

[25]   GitHib, "Extremely Fast Compression algorithm," https://github.com/lz4/lz4

[26]   SNIA, "NVM Programming Model (NPM)," Version 1.2, https://www.snia.org/sites/default/files/technical_work/final/NVMProgrammingModel_v1.2.pdf

Chapter | 7

CPUs and Domain-Specific Hardware

In Chapter 1, "Introduction to Distributed Platforms," you saw that a distributed services platform requires distributed services nodes (DSNs) to be present as close as possible to the user applications. The services provided by these DSNs may require substantial processing capabilities, especially when features such as encryption and compression are required.

DSNs can be implemented with domain-specific hardware or general-purpose CPUs. It is essential to have a historical perspective on this topic because the pendulum has swung in both directions a couple of times.[1] Back in the 1970s–1980s, at the time of mainframes, the central CPUs were not fast enough to do both computing and I/O. Coprocessors and I/O offloads were the norm [1]. The period of the 1990s and 2000s were dominated by the rapid growth of processor performance associated with significant innovation in the processor microarchitecture. For example, from an Intel x86 perspective, the Intel 386 was the first processor with an integrated cache, the 486 was the first pipelined processor, the Pentium was the first superscalar processor, the Pentium Pro/II was the first with speculative execution and integrated L2 cache, and the Pentium 4 was the first SMT x86 processor with virtualization extensions for speeding up hypervisors. Integrated caches played a big part in this performance boost as well, because processor speeds grew super-linearly as compared to DRAM speeds.

All this evolution happened thanks to the capability to shrink the transistor size. In the 2000s, with transistor channel-length becoming sub-micron, it became challenging to continue to increase the frequency because wires were becoming the dominant delay element. The only effective way to utilize the growing number of transistors was with a multicore architecture; that is, putting multiple CPUs on the same chip. In a multicore architecture, the speed-up is achieved by task-level parallelism, but this requires numerous software tasks that can run independently of each other. These architectures were based on the seminal paper on the Raw Architecture Workstation (RAW) multicore architecture written by Agarwal at MIT in the late '90s [2].

---

1. The author would like to thank Francis Matus for his significant contribution to this chapter.

Multicore architectures provided sufficient numbers of cores such that coprocessors were no longer required. Even as the processor technology continued to advance, in 2010 the pendulum started to swing back.

Multicore started to be coupled with virtualization technology, allowing a CPU with multiple cores to be shared across many virtual machines.

Then the "cloud" arrived, and cloud providers began to realize that the amount of I/O traffic was growing extremely fast due to the explosion of East-West traffic, storage networking, and applications that are I/O intensive. Implementing network, storage, and security services in the server CPU was consuming too many CPU cycles. These precious CPU cycles needed to be used and billed to users, not to services.

The historical period that was dominated by the mindset: "*... we don't need specialized hardware since CPU speeds continue increasing, CPUs are general purpose, the software is easy to write ...*" came to an end with a renewed interest in domain-specific hardware.

Another relevant question is, "What does *general-purpose CPU* mean in the era of Internet and cloud characterized by high volumes of data I/O and relatively low compute requirements?" Desktop CPUs are only "general purpose" in the realm of single-user applications. All the CPU resources, the cache hierarchy, out-of-order issue, branch prediction, and so on, are designed to accelerate a single thread of execution. A lot of computation is wasted, and some of the resources are expensive in terms of power and area. If you're more concerned with average throughput over multiple tasks at the lowest cost and power, a pure CPU-based solution may not be the best answer.

Starting in 2018, single-thread CPU speed has only grown approximately 4 percent per year, mainly due to the slowdown in Moore's law, the end of Dennard scaling, and other technical issues related to the difficulty of further reducing the size of the transistors.

The slowing rate of CPU performance growth opens the door to domain-specific hardware for DSNs because user applications require these precious CPU cycles that should not be used by taxing network services. Using domain-specific devices also has a significant benefit in terms of network latency and jitter.

But before we get ahead of ourselves, let's start analyzing the causes mentioned earlier.

7.1   42 Years of Microprocessor Trend Data

The analysis of objective data is essential to understand microprocessor evolution. M. Horowitz, F. Labonte, O. Shacham, K. Olukotun, L. Hammond, and C. Batten did one of the first significant data collections [3], but it lacks more recent data. Karl Rupp [4], [5] added the data of the more recent years and published it on GitHub with a Gnu plotting script. The result of this work is shown in Figure 7-1.

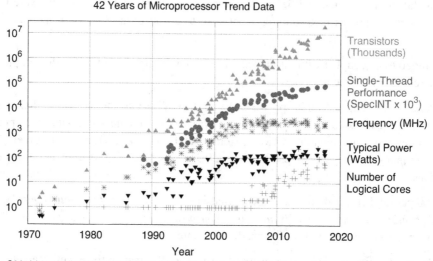

FIGURE 7-1   42 Years of Microprocessor Trend Data

This figure contains five curves:

- The transistor count curve is usually known as Moore's law and is described in more detail in the next section.

- The single-thread performance curve shows the combined effect of all the factors described in this chapter and is discussed in detail in section 7.6. At first glance, it is evident that this curve is flattening out; that is, single-thread performance is not growing linearly any longer.

- Frequency is another curve that has flattened out mainly due to technological factors such as Dennard scaling, described in sections 7.3 and 7.5.

- The typical power curve shows a trend similar to the frequency curve.

- Finally, the curve "number of logical cores" shows the role of the multicore architecture introduced around 2005 and presents significant implications when coupled with Amdahl's law described in section 7.4.

7.2 Moore's Law

One of the typical statements used to justify the adoption of domain-specific hardware is, "Moore's Law is dead." Is this sentence correct?

Gordon Moore, the co-founder of Fairchild Semiconductor and longtime CEO and Chairman of Intel, formulated the original Moore's Law in 1965. There are different formulations, but the one commonly accepted is the 1975 formulation that states that "transistor count doubles approximately every two years." This is not really a law; it is more an "ambition."

Figure 7-2 contains a plot of the transistor count on integrated circuit chips courtesy of Our World in Data [6].

At first glance, Figure 7-2 seems to confirm that Moore's Law is still on track. It also correlates well with the transistor count curve of Figure 7-1. A more specific analysis of Intel processors, which are the dominant processors in large data centers and the cloud, is shown in Figure 7-3 and presents a different reality. In 2015 Intel itself acknowledged a slowdown of Moore's Law from 2 to 2.5 years [7], [8].

Gordon Moore recently estimated that his law would reach the end of applicability by 2025 because transistors would ultimately reach the limits of miniaturization at the atomic level.

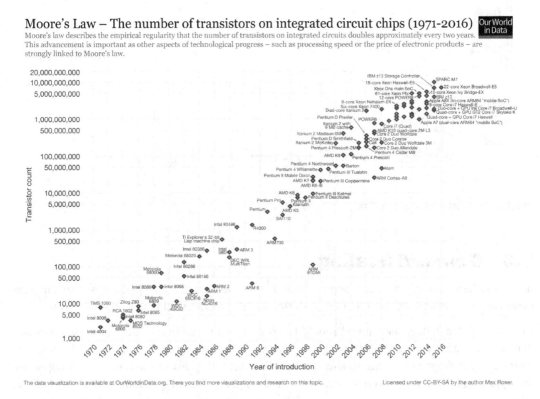

FIGURE 7-2 Transistor Count as a Function of Years

To show the slowdown of CPUs in terms of the SPEC Integer benchmark (used for comparing the performance of a computer when dealing with a single task, such as the time to complete a single task), you need to add other factors from the Hennessy and Patterson Turing Award lecture [9], [10]:

- The end of Dennard scaling
- The restricted power budgets for microprocessors

- The replacement of the single power-hungry processor with several energy-efficient processors
- The limits to multiprocessing due to Amdahl's Law

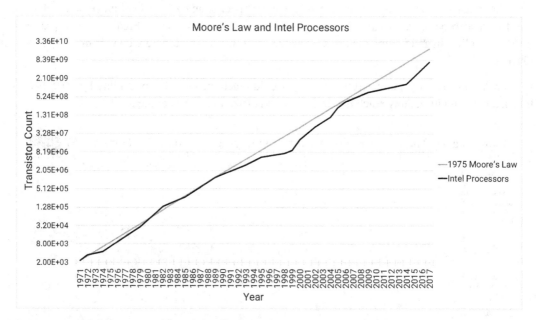

FIGURE 7-3   Intel Processor Transistor Count

7.3 Dennard Scaling

In 1974, Robert Dennard observed that power density remained constant for a given area of silicon (nanometers square) when the dimension of the transistor shrank, thanks to technology improvements [11].

He observed that voltage and current should be proportional to the linear dimensions of a transistor; thus, as transistors shrank, so did voltage and current. Because power is the product of voltage and current, power dropped with the square. On the other hand, the area of the transistors dropped with the square, and the transistor count increased with the square. The two phenomena compensated each other.

Dennard scaling ended around 2004 because current and voltage couldn't keep dropping while still maintaining the dependability of integrated circuits.

Moreover, Dennard scaling ignored the leakage current and threshold voltage, which establish a baseline of power per transistor. With the end of Dennard scaling, with each new transistor generation, power density increased. Figure 7-4 shows the transistor size and the power increase as a function of the years.

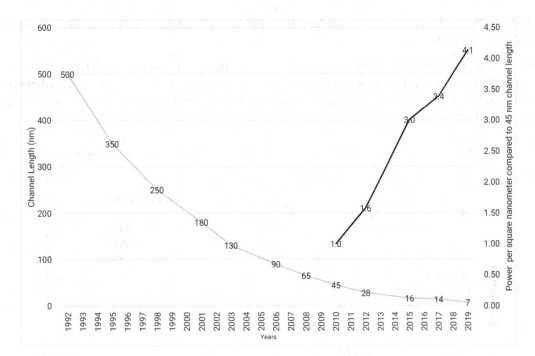

FIGURE 7-4 Dennard Scaling

The power data is estimated using the International Technology Roadmap for Semiconductors (ITRS) data from Hadi Esmaeilzadeh, et al. [12]. All these data are approximated and should be used only to obtain a qualitative idea of the phenomena.

The increase in power density also started to pose a limitation to the increase in clock frequencies and, as a consequence, to the performance increase of a single CPU core.

Dennard scaling is the dominant factor in the slowdown of the growth of a single CPU core.

Starting in 2005, CPU manufacturers focused on multicore architecture as a way to continue to increase performance, and here is where Amdahl's law comes into play.

7.4 Amdahl's Law

In 1967, computer scientist Gene Amdahl formulated his law that is used to predict the theoretical speedup when using multiple processors [13]. It has three parameters:

- "Speedup" is the theoretical speedup of the execution of the whole task.

- "N" is the number of cores.

- "p" is the proportion of the program that can be parallelized; if N approaches infinity then Speedup = 1 / (1 − p).

For example, if 10% of the task is serial (p = 0.9), then the maximum performance benefit from using multiple cores is 10.

Figure 7-5 shows possible speedups when the parallel portion of the code is 50%, 75%, 90%, and 95%. At 95% the maximum achievable speedup is 20 with 4096 cores, but the difference between 256 cores and 4096 is minimal. Continuing to increase the number of cores produces a diminished return.

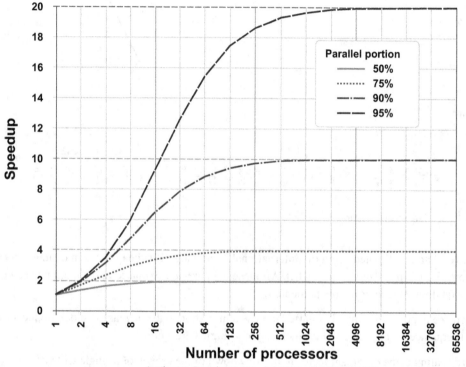

Attribution: Daniels220 at English Wikipedia [CC BY-SA 3.0]

FIGURE 7-5   Amdahl's Law

7.5 Other Technical Factors

All modern processors are built using MOSFETs (metal-oxide-semiconductor field-effect transistors). Shrinking the size of these transistors is very desirable because it allows us to pack more functions on a single chip and reduces the cost and power per feature. We have already discussed a few reasons why shrinking the size of MOSFET is difficult, but here are a few others:

- Shrinking the size of the transistor also implies shrinking the size of the metal traces that interconnect them, and this results in an increased electrical resistance, which, in turn, limits the frequency of operations.

- Reducing the voltage at which circuits operate can be done up to a point. However, there are minimum threshold voltages; for example, for memory circuits, which cannot be exceeded. Reducing voltage below a certain level also causes transistors not to switch on and off completely and, therefore, consume power due to subthreshold conduction.

- There is an intrinsic power dissipation related to distributing the clock along the clock tree.

- Other leakages become important when reducing channel length; for example, gate-oxide leakage and reverse-biased junction leakage. These were ignored in the past but now can account for more than half of the total power consumption of an application specific integrated circuits (ASIC).

- Associated with power consumption are heat production and heat dissipation. Maintaining the transistor below a specific temperature is mandatory for device reliability.

- Process variations also become more critical. It is more difficult to precisely align the fabrication masks and control the dopant numbers and placement.

All these factors, plus Amdahl's Law and Dennard Scaling discussed in the previous sections, explain why in Figure 7-1 the frequency and power curves have flattened out in recent years. Economic factors are also important; for example, the adoption of esoteric, expensive technology to cool a chip is not practical.

7.6 Putting It All Together

As of today, the transistor count still follows the exponential growth line predicted by Gordon Moore. The AMD Epyc processor and the NVIDIA CP100 GPU are two recent devices that track Moore's law.

Single-thread performance growth is now only increasing slightly year over year, mainly thanks to further improvements in instructions per clock cycle.

The availability of additional transistors translates into an increase in the number of cores.

Combining the effects described in the three preceding sections produces the result shown in Figure 7-6.

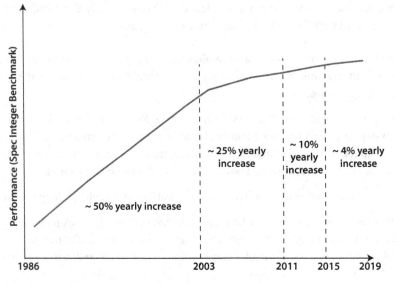

FIGURE 7-6   Combined effect on single-thread performance

The vertical axis is the performance of a processor according to the SPEC Integer benchmark, a standard benchmarking technique from spec.org; the horizontal axis is a timeline. Data is qualitative and obtained by linearizing the "single-thread performance points" of Figure 7-1.

The important datum the graph shows is that since 2015, the SPEC Integer speed of the processors has only grown 4 percent per year. If this trend continues, it will take 20 years for the single-thread performance to double!

7.7   Is Moore's Law Dead or Not?

Moore's law, in its 1975 formulation, says that "transistor count doubles approximately every two years." We have seen that this still holds in general, even if the steadily reducing transistor channel-length is approaching the size of atoms; this is a primary barrier. Gordon Moore and other analysts expect Moore's law to end around 2025.

We have also seen that Intel processors, today the most deployed in data centers and clouds, have had difficulty tracking Moore's law since 2015.

The most important conclusion is the fact that single-thread performance will take 20 years to double if it continues to grow at the current pace.

This last factor is what makes most analysts claim that Moore's law is dead [14].

7.8   Domain-specific Hardware

Domain-specific hardware is optimized for certain types of data processing tasks, allowing it to perform those tasks way faster and more efficiently than general-purpose CPUs.

For example, graphics processing units (GPUs) were created to support advanced graphics interfaces, but today they are also extensively used for artificial intelligence and machine learning. The key to GPUs' success is the highly parallel structure that makes them more efficient than CPUs for algorithms that process large blocks of data in parallel and rely on extensive floating-point math computations. This is an example in which the sea of processor architecture cannot compete. For example, Intel's Larrabee project was an attempt to contrast GPUs with a sea of processor cores, but it was cancelled due to delays and disappointing early performance figures [15], mainly because the sea of core structure was not a good match for the graphic problem.

In the enforcement of network services, some operations are not well suited for CPUs, but they can take advantage of domain-specific hardware. Let's consider the longest prefix match and access control lists. Both can be implemented effectively in ternary content addressable memory (TCAM), but are not supported natively by CPUs and, therefore, must be implemented in software using tree-like data structures. The same is partially correct for encryption. Modern CPUs have added support for symmetric encryption algorithms, but they typically lack significant optimizations for asymmetric encryption algorithms (for example, RSA, Diffie-Hellman) that are used when new secure connections need to be set up. Also, lossless data compression and data deduplication are standard in storage applications, and CPUs don't have native instructions for these functions.

Another critical point is that CPUs are not designed to process packets with low delay and minimal jitter, whereas network devices are generally designed with these specific attributes. CPUs typically run an operating system with a scheduler in charge of sharing the CPU across different processes. This scheduler is not designed to minimize jitter and latency, but rather to optimize overall CPU utilization. Jitter and delay are two fundamental parameters when processing network packets. Therefore, there is a mismatch between network services and CPUs that is not present between network services and domain-specific hardware.

7.9   Economics of the Server

The fundamental question that we need to ask ourselves is, "Where do we put our dollars to obtain maximum system performance—in other words, is there a business case for domain-specific hardware in distributed services platforms?"

Let's start by analyzing what makes a server: CPU, RAM, peripherals, and motherboard. The motherboard is a commodity component in which there is minimal differentiation. Intel mainly controls the CPU market. The RAM market has a few vendors with little price differentiation. Among the different peripherals, an important one for distributed services is the network interface card (NIC).

We have seen that the current trend is to load the CPU with tasks such as security, management, storage, and control functions. Reversing this trend and pushing these auxiliary functions to domain-specific hardware in network devices frees up CPU cycles for real applications. For example, security and network functions are computation-intensive and better implemented in domain-specific, power-efficient hardware.

Also, the refreshment period of domain-specific hardware tends to be faster than the one of CPUs (typically two years, compared to four years for a new CPU complex), allowing the distributed services improvements to happen at a quicker pace.

All these points indicate that there is a business case for domain-specific hardware for distributed services platforms and that we will see a growing number of such platforms in the next few years.

7.10   Summary

In this chapter, we have shown that the availability of domain-specific hardware is key to an efficient implementation of a distributed services platform.

The next chapter presents the evolution of NICs and discusses whether they can be used to host the hardware required by the DSN, or if a better placement of this hardware is in other network devices.

7.11   Bibliography

[1] Wikipedia, "Coprocessors," https://en.wikipedia.org/wiki/Coprocessor

[2] Anant Agarwal, "Raw Computation," *Scientific American*, vol. 281, no. 2, 1999, pp. 60–63. JSTOR, www.jstor.org/stable/26058367

[3] W. Harrod, "A Journey to Exascale Computing," slide 12, https://science.energy.gov/~/media/ascr/ascac/pdf/reports/2013/SC12_Harrod.pdf

[4] Karl Rupp, "42 Years of Microprocessor Trend Data," https://www.karl-rupp.net/2018/02/42-years-of-microprocessor-trend-data

[5] Karl Rupp, "Microprocessor Trend Data," https://github.com/karlrupp/microprocessor-trend-data

[6] Our World in Data, "Moore's Law - The number of transistors on integrated circuit chips (1971–2016)," https://ourworldindata.org

[7] https://www.technologyreview.com/s/601102/intel-puts-the-brakes-on-moores-law

[8] https://www.businessinsider.com/intel-acknowledges-slowdown-to-moores-law-2016-3

[9] John L. Hennessy and David A. Patterson, 2019. A new golden age for computer architecture. Commun. ACM 62, 2 (January 2019), 48–60. DOI: https://doi.org/10.1145/3282307

[10]   John Hennessy, "The End of Moore's Law & Faster General Purpose Computing, and a Road Forward," Stanford University, March 2019, https://p4.org/assets/P4WS_2019/Speaker_Slides/9_2.05pm_John_Hennessey.pdf

[11]   R. H. Dennard, F. H. Gaensslen, V. L. Rideout, E. Bassous, and A. R. LeBlanc, "Design of ion-implanted MOSFETs with very small physical dimensions," in IEEE *Journal of Solid-State Circuits*, vol. 9, no. 5, pp. 256–268, Oct. 1974.

[12]   Hadi Esmaeilzadeh, et al. "Dark silicon and the end of multicore scaling." 2011 38th Annual International Symposium on Computer Architecture (ISCA) (2011): 365–376.

[13]   Gene M. Amdahl, 1967. Validity of the single processor approach to achieving large scale computing capabilities. In Proceedings of the April 18–20, 1967, Spring Joint Computer Conference (AFIPS '67 (Spring)). ACM, New York, NY, USA, 483–485.

[14]   Tekla S. Perry, "David Patterson Says It's Time for New Computer Architectures and Software Languages," IEEE Spectrum, 17 Sep 2018, https:// spectrum.ieee.org/view-from-the-valley/computing/hardware/david-patterson-says-its-time-for-new-computer-architectures-and-software-langauges

[15]   Wikipedia, "Larrabee (microarchitecture)," https://en.wikipedia.org/wiki/Larrabee_(microarchitecture)

Chapter | **8**

NIC Evolution

Previous chapters presented the importance of domain-specific hardware in a distributed services platform. One of the places where this domain-specific hardware can be located on is the network interface card (NIC).

Historically the NIC was designed to satisfy the server's need to communicate over one or more Ethernet networks effectively. In its purest form, a NIC is a device receiving packets arriving from the network and sending them on the server bus and vice versa.

This chapter discusses the NIC evolution from a primitive packet-passing widget of the 1990s to today's SmartNIC—a sophisticated device capable of hosting domain-specific hardware either in the form of an additional ASIC or on the NIC ASIC itself.

An example of additional ASIC implementation is the Microsoft Azure SmartNIC described in section 2.8.1 that has a field programmable gate array (FPGA) on board next to a regular NIC ASIC. An example of extra hardware on the NIC ASIC is the Broadcom BCM58800 that includes, among other things, several ARM cores.

Also, memory considerations are essential because a distributed services platform needs memory to store its multiple tables.

We have seen in Chapter 6, "Distributed Storage and RDMA Services," that locating the domain-specific hardware on the NIC is the preferred embodiment for storage and RDMA services because they are tied to the server memory subsystem and PCIe bus semantics.

When appropriately implemented, the addition of domain-specific hardware to a NIC can reduce the server CPU load caused by network, storage, and security services and, therefore, return precious server CPU cycles to user applications.

8.1 Understanding Server Buses

Server buses are in constant evolution, but all modern servers use PCI Express (Peripheral Component Interconnect Express), officially abbreviated as PCIe or PCI-e, a high-speed serial computer expansion bus.

Whereas PCI and PCI-X were bus topologies, PCIe is a point-to-point standard that supports bridges. The resulting topology is a tree structure with a single root complex, as illustrated in Figure 8-1.

The PCIe root complex is responsible for enumeration of PCIe resources and system configuration; it also manages interrupts and errors for the PCIe tree. Historically, the root complex functionality was located in the South Bridge (also known as ICH or I/O Controller Hub), whereas today processors often integrate it onboard.

PCIe is composed of a variable number of "lanes," whose allowed values are 1, 2, 4, 8, 12, 16, or 32 [1]. The notation used is in the form "x4," which means four lanes. Each lane is composed of two differential signaling pairs: one RX pair and one TX pair. Therefore, each lane supports full-duplex operation.

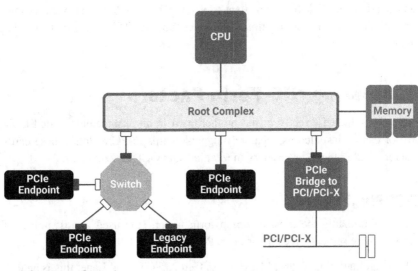

FIGURE 8-1 PCIe Root Complex

PCIe exists in different "generations" or "versions." Currently, the most commonly used is PCIe Gen 3, and the industry is getting ready to adopt Gen 4. Table 8-1 summarizes the differences. For each version, the throughput is expressed in Giga transfers per second (GT/s), in GB/s (Gigabyte/s), and Gb/s (Gigabit/s). The number of transfers also includes the overhead encoding bits that are excluded in GB/s and Gb/s.

TABLE 8-1   PCIe Performance

PCIe Version	Year	Line Code	Transfer Rate	Throughput				
				x1	x2	x4	x8	x16
1.0	2003	8b/10b	2.5 GT/s	250 MB/s 2 Gb/s	0.5 GB/s 4 Gb/s	1.0 GB/s 8 Gb/s	2.0 GB/s 16 Gb/s	4.0 GB/s 32 Gb/s
2.0	2007	8b/10b	5.0 GT/s	500 MB/s 4 Gb/s	1.0 GB/s 8 Gb/s	2.0 GB/s 16 Gb/s	4.0 GB/s 32 Gb/s	8.0 GB/s 64 Gb/s
3.0	2010	128b/130b	8.0 GT/s	985 MB/s 7/88 Gb/s	1.97 GB/s 15.76 Gb/s	3.94 GB/s 31.52 Gb/s	7.88 GB/s 63.04 Gb/s	15.8 GB/s 126.08 Gb/s
4.0	2017	128b/130b	16.0 GT/s	1969 MB/s 15.76 Gb/s	3.94 GB/s 31.52 Gb/s	7.88 GB/s 63.04 Gb/s	15.75 GB/s 126.08 Gb/s	31.5 GB/s 252.16 Gb/s
5.0	2019	128b/130b	32.0 GT/s	3938 MB/s 31.52 Gb/s	7.88 GB/s 63.04 Gb/s	15.75 GB/s 126.08 Gb/s	31.51 GB/s 252.16 Gb/s	63.0 GB/s 54.32 Gb/s

An error-correcting code protects data transfers. For example, in Gen 3 each lane is capable of transferring 8 Gb/s but, because the encoding requires a transfer of 130 bits to get 128 bits of data, the effective transfer rate is 7,877 Mb/s, equivalent to 984.6 MB/s. Table 8-1 also shows that four Gen 3 lanes support a 25 Gb/s Ethernet connection, eight lanes support 50 Gb/s Ethernet, and sixteen support 100 Gb/s Ethernet.

8.2   Comparing NIC Form Factors

NICs can either be soldered directly in the motherboard in an arrangement called LOM (LAN On Motherboard) or can be installed as separate pluggable cards in PCIe slots. These cards have three main form factors: PCIe plugin, proprietary mezzanine, and OCP mezzanine.

8.2.1   PCI Plugin Cards

The plugin card is probably the most common form factor. It is used almost universally on rack-mounted servers. These servers have one or more PCIe slots for PCIe cards.

Figure 8-2 shows an Intel plugin card, PCI Express Gen 2, 5 GT/s, x4 Lane; this is an old card shown for historical reasons with 2 x 1 Gbps ports. Intel now makes much faster state-of-the-art cards. Note the absence of a heatsink or fan.

Figure 8-3 shows a Broadcom BCM957454A4540C NeXtreme E-Series Single-Port 1/10/25/40/50/100 Gb/s Ethernet PCI Express Gen 3 x16.

FIGURE 8-2   Intel I350-T2 Intel Ethernet Server Adapter

FIGURE 8-3   Broadcom NeXtreme E-Series

PCIe slots have a standard power and cooling limitation of 25 Watts per slot [2], and this limits the amount of hardware that can be installed on a PCIe board. Some NIC manufacturers are not able to comply with this strict budget requirement and use two adjacent slots for a single card. Some server vendors offer more power per slot, but all the power consumed must be dissipated, increasing operation cost.

In general, the design of domain-specific hardware must take into significant consideration that power is limited and, therefore, use all possible design techniques to reduce power consumption.

8.2.2   Proprietary Mezzanine Cards

Many enterprise datacenters use Blade servers as a way to optimize cabling and power efficiency when compared to rack-mounted servers. The form factors of these servers vary with the manufacturer, and they are proprietary.

Blade servers cannot host generic PCIe plugin cards but require "mezzanine daughter cards" that also have proprietary form factors and proprietary connectors. The daughter card is parallel to the main board in a stacking configuration.

Although the connector is proprietary, the protocol spoken on the connector is always PCIe.

Figure 8-4 shows a NC532m 10GbE 2-port adapter for a Hewlett-Packard Enterprise BladeSystem c-Class.

FIGURE 8-4   HPE Card in a Mezzanine Form Factor (Courtesy of Hewlett Packard Enterprise)

8.2.3 OCP Mezzanine Cards

The Open Compute Project (OCP) [3] is a community of engineers whose mission is to standardize hardware designs for server, storage, and datacenter hardware.

Particularly relevant for our discussion is the OCP NIC subgroup currently working on a follow-on to the OCP Mezzanine 2.0 design specification called OCP NIC 3.0, a new specification that supports small form factor cards and large form factor cards. The small card allows for up to 16 PCIe lanes, and the large card supports up to 32 PCIe lanes.

Figure 8-5 shows a pictorial representation of these two cards.

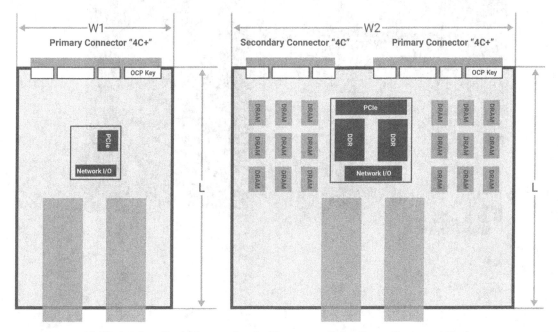

FIGURE 8-5   OCP 3.0 Small and Large Cards (Courtesy of the Open Compute Project Foundation)

OCP 3.0 cards support up to 80 Watts in a small form factor and up to 150 Watts in large form factor. However, the limiting factor is not current delivery but thermal dissipation. Each platform will limit the power consumption based on its thermal capabilities, and a typical range will be 15 to 25 watts, as in the case of PCIe plugin cards, with some platforms trying to push it somewhere around 35 watts.

Figure 8-6 shows a Mellanox ConnectX-5 Dual Port 100GbE in OCP 3.0 form factor for an OCP server.

FIGURE 8-6   Mellanox ConnectX-5 in OCP 3.0 Form Factor (Courtesy of the Open Compute Project Foundation)

8.2.4   Lan On Motherboard

It is pretty standard for some class of servers to have a LAN On Motherboard (LOM); that is, to solder on the motherboard the same ASIC used on a NIC card, sometimes also in conjunction with some other chips, such as NIC memories.

LOMs are very important on cost-sensitive servers where the cost of the slot, the connector, and the NIC card are difficult to justify.

Figure 8-7 shows a LOM on a Cisco UCS C220 M5 Server, with two ports at 10 Gbps.

FIGURE 8-7 LOM on a Cisco UCS

8.3 Looking at the NIC Evolution

If we look at the evolution of NICs until 2005, the focus has been to increase the speed of ports, increase the number of ports, support new faster buses (PCI, PCI-X, PCIe), and adapt to new form factors, including reducing power consumption to fit in server expansion slots.

Until that time, NIC architecture had remained pretty constant, mostly based on a simple state machine in charge of processing packets in order: one packet in, one packet out.

Starting around 2005, NICs have gained new functionalities, such as:

- **Multiple queues:** To add Quality of Service (QoS) features, the NIC introduced multiple queues to process different kinds of packets with different priorities. With queues also came a scheduler based on an algorithm such as Deficit Weighted Round Robin (DWRR). There has been a continuous trend towards increasing the number of queues to better support multicore CPUs and application-based queueing. The NIC can assign different network flows to different queues and different queues to different CPUs and cores in the system, thus enabling the system to process the network traffic in parallel, achieving greater network throughput.

- **Traffic shaping:** Traffic shaping is a feature related to QoS to shape the outgoing traffic according to a predefined profile.

- **Multicast handling:** With the increased utilization of multicast applications, in particular in the financial sector, the NIC introduced the capability to support multiple multicast groups and to use protocols such as IGMP to join and leave such multicast groups.

- **Support for TCP/UDP/IP stateless offloads:** These should not be confused with TCP Termination, Stateful Offload, or Proxy that are much more complex features. The three common stateless offloads are:

  - *Checksum offload,* a technique that delegates the computation of checksums to the NIC.

  - *Large send offload (LSO),* a technique for reducing CPU utilization while at the same time increasing egress network throughput. It works by passing a large buffer to the NIC, which splits this buffer into separate packets. This technique is also called TCP segmentation offload (TSO) when applied to TCP, or generic segmentation offload (GSO). For example, a CPU may pass a 64KB buffer and a TCP protocol header template to the NIC. The NIC segments the payload, for example, into 45 segments of 1460 bytes each, and appends the proper Ethernet/IP/TCP header to each segment before sending them out.

  - *Large receive offload (LRO),* the companion technique of LSO on the receiving side. It aggregates multiple incoming packets from a single flow into a single buffer that is passed higher up the networking stack to reduce the number of packets that have to be processed by the OS. Linux implementations generally use LRO in conjunction with the New API (NAPI), an interface that provides interrupt mitigation techniques for networking devices in the Linux kernel. This feature is also called Receive Side Coalescing (RSC).

- **Receive Side Scaling (RSS):** In multicore processors, before this feature, all the packets/interrupts from a NIC went to the same CPU/core, and this created a bottleneck on that CPU/core. RSS enables the spreading of the packets received among all the CPUs/cores in the system. This spreading is typically done using a hashing function on the five-tuples (IP addresses, protocol type, TCP/UDP ports) so that all the packets belonging to the same flow go to the same CPU/core.

- **Message Signaled Interrupts-Extended (MSI-X):** Before MSI-X, the NIC was asserting interrupts to the CPU using dedicated interrupt lines, requiring separate pins on the NIC, on the processors, and all the connectors. With MSI-X, interrupts are signaled using in-band messages. MSI-X is the sole mechanism to signal interrupts on PCIe. MSI-X was introduced in PCIe 3.0 and supports up to 2048 interrupts. MSI-X allows the spreading of interrupts to multiple CPUs and cores.

- **Interrupt moderation:** The idea behind interrupt moderation is that in a high traffic environment, it is counterproductive to interrupt the CPU per each packet. A single interrupt can serve multiple packets. With interrupt moderation, the NIC hardware will not generate an interrupt immediately after it receives a packet—it will wait for more packets to arrive or until a timeout expires.

- **VLAN tagging support:** Virtual LANs (VLANs) are a well-established reality in modern networks. IEEE standardized them as IEEE 802.1Q and, for this reason, the tag in the Ethernet frame is also called "dot 1Q Tag." Modern NICs support one or multiple levels of VLAN tags.

- **Overlay support:** This is an extension of the VLAN tagging support, and it refers to the capability to insert an overlay header in the frame to create a tunnel. For example, in VXLAN the NIC may act as a VTEP (see section 2.3.4).

- **Packet filtering and replication:** To better support virtualization, most NICs added packet filtering and replication. Examples of filtering and replication modes are:

  - By VLAN tag

  - By Ethernet unicast, multicast, or broadcast addresses

  - By replicating a packet to multiple VMs

  - By various mirroring modes

- **Support for DCB:** The term *data center bridging* (DCB) is used by IEEE to collectively indicate Priority-based Flow Control (PFC), Data Center Bridging eXchange (DCBX), and bandwidth management (Enhanced Transmission Selection [ETS]). In the past, these techniques have also been called CEE (Converged Enhanced Ethernet) and Data Center Ethernet (DCE). The most important and controversial of the three is clearly PFC, also known as Per Priority Pause (PPP). With PFC, a physical link can be partitioned into multiple logical connections (by extending the IEEE 802.1Q priority concept), and each priority can be configured to have either lossless or lossy behavior (lossy being the Ethernet default).

- **Support for unified/converged fabric:** The primary motivation for DCB is to support a unified and converged fabric. This term indicates using the same Ethernet infrastructure not only for "native" network traffic (mainly the IP protocol), but also for storage and RDMA traffic. Storage and RDMA traffic don't tolerate packet loss as TCP/IP does. The idea behind DCB was to create logical links that do not lose packets for this kind of traffic. See section 6.1.8 for more details.

- **Support for time synchronization:** Server time synchronization is becoming more important every day to track and correlate what happens on the networks. Initially, the NTP protocol run on the server CPU was precise enough and easy to implement, but the requirement to reach microsecond precision and even 100 nanosecond precision makes NTP inadequate. The next step is to use Precision Time Protocol (PTP), which is part of IEEE 1588. PTP is a protocol used to synchronize clocks throughout a local area network where it achieves clock accuracy in the submicrosecond range. For this to be true, the NIC needs to provide support for it.

- **Support for SR-IOV:** SR-IOV (Single Root I/O Virtualization), discussed in detail in the next section, is based on the idea to integrate a network switch into the NIC to do the functions that are generally done in software by a virtual switch; for example, in a hypervisor.

8.4   Using Single Root Input/Output Virtualization

Single Root Input/Output Virtualization (SR-IOV) is a standard developed by PCI-SIG and used in conjunction with virtual machines and hypervisors [4]. It has been around for more than ten years, and it is gaining ground in the cloud offering. SR-IOV allows different virtual machines running on the same hypervisor/server (single root complex) to share a single piece of PCI Express hardware without requiring the hypervisor to implement a software network switch.

SR-IOV defines physical functions (PFs) and virtual functions (VFs). PFs are full-featured PCIe functions, and they are discovered, managed, and manipulated like any other PCIe device. VFs are simpler, and they only provide input/output functionality. An SR-IOV device can have a few PFs (for example, sixteen) and multiple VFs per PF (for instance, 256 VFs/PF). A total limit on the number of VFs is also present, usually 1024.

Figure 8-8 shows the SR-IOV architecture and the relation between the physical NIC, one PF associated with the hypervisor network driver, and two VFs associated with two virtual NICs inside two VMs. This is a hardware alternative to the hypervisor virtual switch: In SR-IOV the switch is in the NIC, in contrast to being in the hypervisor.

The SR-IOV architecture specifies a simple layer 2 switch, and as Chapter 2, "Network Design," discussed, this is easy to implement because it requires only a binary matching engine. Nothing prevents implementing a more sophisticated layer 3 or layer 4 forwarding in the SR-IOV switch. From a data plane perspective, an approach such as LPM forwarding or flow table forwarding can be used. From a control and management plane perspective, the switch can be programmed; for example; using a RESTful API or using an OpenFlow controller (for example, the Faucet controller [5]). Another alternative is to use OVSDB to program the switch inside SR-IOV (see section 4.3.1).

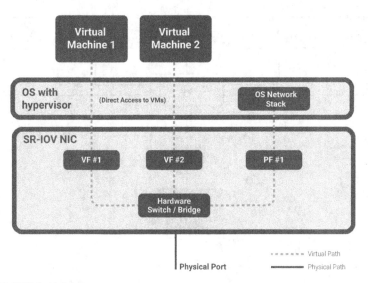

FIGURE 8-8   SR-IOV Architecture

The control and management planes may run on the server CPUs, or they can run on a core embedded in the NIC. The same is true for the first packet processing, in the case of the flow table approach.

Again, the level of server CPU offload obtained will depend on these choices.

8.5 Using Virtual I/O

Virtual I/O (VirtIO) [6], [7] is an OASIS project [8] to simplify virtual devices, making them more extensible, recognizable, and supported across multiple operating systems. It was introduced in section 3.2.4. VirtIO PCI devices are very similar to physical PCI devices, and, therefore, they can be used both by physical NICs and virtual NICs. Standard drivers for them have been upstreamed in the major operating systems. Two popular VirtIO devices are virtio-blk (for block storage) and virtio-net (for network communications). The other three are PCI emulation, a balloon driver (for dynamically managing guest memory usage), and a console driver. Figure 8-9 shows the VirtIO architecture.

At the top are the front-end drivers implemented, for example, in the VM operating system. At the bottom there are the back-end drivers implemented, for example, in the hypervisor. Each front-end driver has a corresponding back-end driver. Two additional layers in between implement queueing among other services.

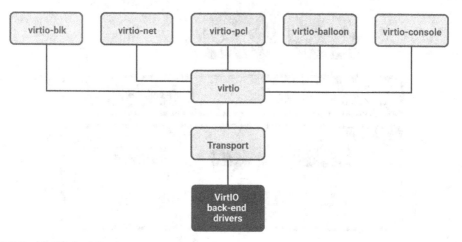

FIGURE 8-9   VirtIO Architecture

When the front-end drivers are used in conjunction with a virtualization environment, they are aware that they are running in a virtual environment and cooperate with the hypervisor to improve performance.

8.6   Defining "SmartNIC"

Up to now, we have discussed the evolution of classical NICs. Around 2016, the term *SmartNIC* was introduced, although there is no clear and broadly accepted definition of that term. One of the best and simpler definitions is "a NIC that offloads processing tasks that the system CPU would normally handle."

To achieve this goal, a SmartNIC typically includes some of these features:

- **Processors:** These are generally in the form of ARM cores and usually run control and management protocols.

- **L2/L3 switching, regularly using SR-IOV:** The goal is to offload switching in hardware, but the level of offload obtained varies significantly with implementations.

- **Support for SDN flow tables:** Similarly to the previous point, flow tables can be used to offload switching from the host to the NIC.

- **Network overlays (for example, IP in IP, VXLANs):** These are particularly relevant in cloud environments, where almost all the packets need to transit through an overlay network.

- **RDMA:** This is relevant for machine learning, high-performance computing (HPC), and other tasks that require distributing large datasets, and for remote NVMe storage.

- **Storage protocols with I/O consolidation:** The NIC exposes NVMe interfaces to the host and supports directly attached disks or remote (virtual) disks.

Even if these features should be independent of the speed of the links, due to their recent introduction on the market, SmartNICs typically are 100 Gbps devices with a few 100 GE ports, also configurable as 25GE and 50GE.

Examples of 100 Gbps SmartNIC are:

- The Broadcom BCM58800 - Stingray SmartNIC and Storage Controller IC that includes eight ARMv8 Cortex-A72 CPUs at 3.0 GHz and three memory channels DDR4-2400 [9]

- The Mellanox BlueField Multicore System-on-Chip (SoC) that includes 16 ARMv8 A72 cores and two DDR4 memory channels [10]

8.7 Summary

In this chapter, we have discussed the evolution of the NIC from a simple packet-passing device to domain-specific hardware that can implement features of a distributed-services platform. We have explained that one of the main issues is power consumption, which is limited by thermal dissipation.

In the next chapter, we compare the advantages and disadvantages of implementing features in the NIC or another part of the network.

8.8 Bibliography

[1] Ravi Budruk, "PCI Express Basics," PCI-SIG presentation, 2007-08-21, archived on Wikipedia, https://en.wikipedia.org/wiki/PCI_Express

[2] Zale Schoenborn, "Board Design Guidelines for PCI Express Architecture," 2004, PCI-SIG, pp. 19–21, archived on Wikipedia, https://en.wikipedia.org/wiki/PCI_Express

[3] Open Compute Project, http://www.opencompute.org

[4] Single Root I/O Virtualization and Sharing, PCI-SIG.

[5] "Faucet: Open source SDN Controller for production networks," https://faucet.nz

[6] VirtIO, https://wiki.libvirt.org/page/Virtio

[7] libvirt, libvirt. https://libvirt.org

[8] Oasis, Open Standards, Open Source, https://www.oasis-open.org

[9] Broadcom, "Stingray SmartNIC Adapters and IC," https://www.broadcom.com/products/ethernet-connectivity/smartnic

[10] Mellanox, "BlueField SmartNIC for Ethernet" https://www.mellanox.com/related-docs/prod_adapter_cards/PB_BlueField_Smart_NIC_ETH.pdf

Chapter | 9

Implementing a DS Platform

In Chapter 1, "Introduction to Distributed Platforms," we introduced the concept of a distributed services platform. Figure 1-1 (reproduced here as Figure 9-1) depicts a high-level view of the components required to implement a distributed services platform. Key components are the distributed services nodes (DSNs) placed in servers, switches, and appliances that need to be managed by a policy manager.

In this chapter, we detail the goal of a distributed services platform. We also describe the constraints that derive from the server architectures (for example, virtual machines versus bare-metal servers) and from the need to fit into existing installation or the possibility of designing the architecture from scratch. We compare the Enterprise data center architecture with one of the public clouds, and we analyze where to best locate the DSNs.

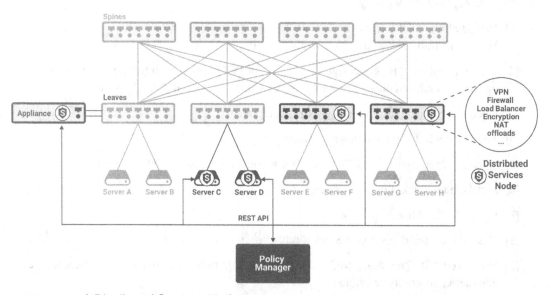

FIGURE 9-1   A Distributed Services Platform

9.1 Analyzing the Goals for a Distributed Services Platform

Let's first analyze the goals for a distributed services platform. In previous chapters we saw that we want to distribute services at the periphery of the network by installing DSNs as close as possible to the applications, to make the network as simple as possible, and to adopt for services the same scale-out model adopted for computing. Moreover, we want to be able to chain together multiple services inside the DSN, avoiding useless network crossing.

In this section, we analyze more specific requirements for this distributed services architecture. Let's first analyze the goals for a distributed services platform.

9.1.1 Services Everywhere

Today, one of the complexities of service implementation is that different services are implemented by various appliances in different parts of the network. Because several services need to be chained together to build a complete application, this results in unnecessary complexity and packets having to travel multiple times over the network with various overlay encapsulations—a phenomenon known as *tromboning* (see section 2.7.1).

An ideal distributed services platform makes all the services available in all the DSNs so that service chaining can happen inside the DSN and does not require redirecting packets between boxes to chain multiple services, such as a firewall and load balancing.

A real distributed services platform approximates the ideal one by taking into consideration several other aspects described in the remainder of this chapter.

9.1.2 Scaling

With the introduction of cloud architectures, scaling has become a primary requirement because of multi-tenancy. A cloud provider, be it private, public, or hybrid, needs to run IP routing for the underlying network and all the overlay networks associated with each tenant. Moreover, protection between different tenants is put in place in terms of Access Control Lists (ACLs), even if each tenant does not explicitly require it. Also, if each tenant uses a moderate number of routes and ACLs (let's say up to one thousand), a DSN located in a server with 100 tenants requires the simultaneous presence of 100,000 routes and 100,000 ACLs for both IPv4 and IPv6. The situation can be more extreme if the DSN is located in a switch or an appliance that processes the traffic aggregated by, let's say, 40 servers: 4 million routes and ACLs can be required in this case. The same is true for the scaling of other services such as firewall, load balancing, and network address translation (NAT). In this case, to support stateful services the DSN needs to keep a flow table that can accommodate tens of millions of flows in addition to the number of routes and rules quoted previously. A similar consideration applies to encryption, both in terms of the number of keys and the number of encrypted tunnels, with the additional complication that keys need to be stored in a secure place, such as a hardware security module (HSM) (see section 5.8).

9.1.3   Speed

Speed requirements vary between enterprises and cloud providers. At the time of writing, most enterprise servers are connected at 10 Gbps, and the transition to 25 Gbps is starting. Cloud provider servers are mostly 40 Gbps to 50 Gbps, moving to 100 Gbps. Backbone links vary from 100 Gbps to 400 Gbps.

Let's consider in greater detail what 100 Gbps means. With an average packet length of approximately 400 bytes, a 100-Gbps DSN needs to be capable of processing about 30 million packets/second. This processing must at least include the chaining of the most common services; for example, receiving an encrypted overlay tunnel, decrypting it and decapsulating it, applying firewall rules, routing the packets, and delivering them to the layer 2 destination. We will see in the next chapter that a performance of this order of magnitude strictly limits the architectural choices at the hardware level. Another consideration is that an average flow length is approximately 1 Mbit, and this implies that at 100 Gbps there are 100,000 new flows every second. Stateful flow tables and all the telemetry apparatus must be designed to be capable of supporting this number of new flows per second. Once again, this can be challenging from a hardware perspective.

9.1.4   Low Latency

The need to provide services with low latency is essential. At today's 100 Gbps transmission speeds, a 1500-byte Ethernet frame has a serialization delay of 120 nanoseconds. The speed of light in fiber is 200,000 Km/s; that is, a 100 meters (328 feet) link has a delay of 500 nanoseconds. Overall, the delay associated with transmission should be less than 2 microseconds. The majority of the delay is associated with packet processing related to services and routing/bridging. When multiple services need to be applied to a packet, and the services are implemented in different appliances, the delay is caused by the packet having to cross the network artificially multiple times to chain the services and by the bottleneck caused by tromboning into the appliances.

Of course, the lower the latency is, the better the overall performance will be but, in practice, a good goal is to try to implement a service chain with a latency below 10 microseconds.

9.1.5   Low Jitter

In the previous section, we discussed the importance of limiting "average" delay, but different packets experience different delays. This delay variation is called *jitter*, and it is as crucial as delay, especially for applications that require real-time communications such as IP telephony and video conferencing. If jitter is high, packets can be reordered or dropped, and this shows up as a malfunction at the application layer.

The makers of network equipment have been aware of this issue for a long time, and their hardware designs limit jitter as much as possible and don't reorder frames. Frame reordering is terrible even for a protocol like TCP that will associate packet reordering with congestion and, therefore, reduce its throughput.

The same level of awareness is not present in software implementation. Techniques discussed in section 6.3 such as interrupt moderation and coalescing sacrifice jitter while trying to increase overall throughput. Packet processing in software requires activities to be scheduled by the operating system, whose goal is to create fairness among all the processes, not to minimize jitter. It is not uncommon in software implementation to see jitter exceeding 100 microseconds, and this becomes the dominant factor of poor performance.

9.1.6 Minimal CPU Load

In the previous chapter, we have seen that single-thread performance is now growing very slowly and that CPU cycles must be saved for user applications and not used for distributed services. An ideal distributed services platform has a zero footprint in the host, allowing all the CPU cycles to be dedicated to user applications.

An additional consideration is that general-purpose CPUs are not designed for packet processing, and their hardware architecture is not a good fit for operations commonly used in packet processing.

For this reason, a software implementation of a DSN, even though it is extraordinarily flexible and potentially scalable with a lot of memory, has low performance, high delay, and high jitter.

The term *offloading* is often used to indicate attempts to move part of the processing to a domain-specific hardware structure, but offloading still leaves a footprint on the host software that can be extremely significant.

It is the author's opinion that a successful DSN implementation should be self-contained and have no footprint on the server software. This provides greater security, better control of noisy neighbors, and allows separate administration domains.

"No footprint" on the server software is also a mandatory requirement for bare-metal servers, where no assumption can be made about the software run on the server.

9.1.7 Observability and Troubleshooting Capability

With billions of packets being exchanged every second over a network, it is challenging to troubleshoot when something goes wrong. The historical approach has been to have a management station that pulls information from network devices, using a protocol such as SNMP, and SSH to connect to the CLI of network devices. This approach is now inadequate.

A more modern approach is telemetry-based and includes the following parts:

■ **Measure and collect in the data path:** With a link at 100 Gbps passing 30 million packets per second, measurement and collection cannot rely on a management processor outside the data path; they must be built as an integral part of the data path from day one.

- **Timestamp accurately:** The data path needs to timestamp packets with a very accurate time-stamp; let's remind ourselves that at 100 Gbps a packet lasts less than 500 nanoseconds, and without a timestamp synchronized network-wide with tens of nanosecond precision, it is impossible to understand what happened first. The Precision Time Protocol (PTP) [1] is the standard solution to this problem, but it is complicated to set up. A more modern approach [2] developed at Stanford University and at Google is looking promising.

- **Stream out:** After telemetry is collected and timestamped, it needs to be streamed out toward a collection station. Due to the sheer volume of data, filtering may be used to stream out only data that is associated with potential issues; for example, when predefined thresholds are exceeded.

- **Collect:** A telemetry collection station must store all this information, typically in a time-series database [3] where it can be retrieved and analyzed later on.

- **Correlate and analyze**: This step is the last one, and it correlates all the information to help the network manager understand what is happening in the network and identify possible bottle-necks and malfunctions.

9.1.8   Manageability

The best distributed services platform will fall short without excellent management. It must be model-based; that is, all the management tools, interfaces, and protocols must be derived from a common model. Commonly used modeling languages are Swagger [4], OpenAPI [5], and Yang [6]. From them, it is possible to generate in an algorithmic way a RESTful API [7] and gRPC [8]/protobuff [9] (see sections 3.4.1 and 3.4.2). The model must come first, APIs second, and all the remaining tools such as CLI, SNMP, and so on must be layered over the APIs.

Using a microservices architecture to build a distributed management system can offer better scale, composability, and high availability.

The scope of the management system is to define policies in a central location and enact them on the DSNs. In a simple situation, all policies can be pushed everywhere, but with the growth of the number of DSNs, partitioning policies may become a necessity, both at the policy definition and enforcement level. For example, policies that are specific to one site can be defined locally and do not need to be propagated to other locations. For this reason, it is essential that the management system supports the concept of "federation." In a federated system, multiple policy managers work together to enforce a combination of global and local policies.

9.1.9   Host Mode versus Network Mode

The next management consideration is where is the entry point into the DSN for the management protocol. Two main modes exist: host mode and network mode.

In host mode, the DSN is managed through the PCIe interface of the NIC (Network Interface Card). This mode is not the most desirable for the DSN, because a compromised host may compromise the DSN and nullify its security features.

A more desirable mode is the network mode in which the DSN is managed through a secure network connection—either in-band or out-of-band—by a trusted policy manager. This mode is more secure and in general all implementations of DSNs can use it, even the ones that do not rely on the presence of a PCIe interface.

9.1.10 PCIe Firewall

To increase security, a NIC must not only support the previously described network mode but must also implement a PCIe firewall, a hardware structure similar to a Memory Management Unit (MMU) that controls the access to internal NIC resources through the PCIe bus. This additional security measure is particularly relevant in the presence of SR-IOV to guarantee that each vNIC in a VM accesses only the resources associated with its virtual function (VF; see section 8.4). With this protection in place, rogue software running on a compromised VM cannot access the network resources of other VMs.

9.2 Understanding Constraints

In designing a distributed services platform, we need to keep considering not only the goals listed in the previous sections, but also the constraints listed in the following subsections. The combination of the two will often result in the decision of where to best locate the DSN.

9.2.1 Virtualized versus Bare-metal Servers

Usually, virtualized servers are provisioned to users in terms of VMs. The virtualization/cloud provider has full control over the hypervisor, including the vSwitch that can be used to host a DSN. Also, a VM on the same server may be used to run distributed services management and control protocols. Some of these features may also be offloaded to hardware, minimizing the footprint on the server CPUs. One may question the overall performance of a DSN implemented in software, but today this is a deployed solution.

The situation is different in bare-metal servers; that is, in servers that are provisioned without making any assumption about the operating system or applications that will be running on them. In bare-metal servers, the server provider cannot assume anything, including the presence of a hypervisor, and cannot run a DSN or a service VM on the server. In this case, the software implementation of a DSN is unfeasible, and it is necessary to provide distributed services with a DSN that has a zero footprint on the host; for example, in a NIC or a switch.

9.2.2   Greenfield versus Brownfield Deployment

A standard definition of the term *greenfield project* is, "a project that lacks any constraints imposed by prior work."

In a greenfield installation of a cloud infrastructure, each component is chosen carefully, and it is possible, for example, to install the more desirable server configuration, including a NIC capable of supporting a DSN. In general, a greenfield installation offers the highest level of flexibility on where to locate the DSNs.

When servers are deployed in production, they become brownfield, and their hardware configuration is usually kept unchanged until the server is decommissioned. Therefore, if a server was installed with a NIC that is incapable of supporting a DSN, the NIC is not upgraded.

In brownfield projects, the retrofitting of a distributed services platform is done by adding or replacing network boxes with new ones capable of supporting DSNs.

9.2.3   The Drivers

Software drivers for NIC cards need to be installed in the kernel of the operating system or the hypervisor. Although all NIC vendors provide drivers for their NICs for a variety of operating systems and hypervisors, sometimes users prefer to install NIC cards for which the driver is already present in the distribution of the operating system and does not need to be installed manually.

To be included in an operating system distribution—that is, to be an in-box driver—a driver needs to be "upstreamed" (i.e., a driver is merged and becomes part of a standard operating system distribution), a process that may easily take one year. Usually, upstreamed drivers are available only for the latest versions of the OS. This is an issue with legacy bare-metal servers that run applications certified with old or customized kernels.

The availability of drivers may limit the choice of which NIC to install and, therefore, where to place the DSNs.

9.2.4   PCIe-only Services

In Chapter 4, "Network Virtualization Services," and Chapter 5, "Security Services," we analyzed several network and security services that conceptually can be located anywhere in the cloud or data center network. Placing them as closely as possible to the user applications is always the best choice, but because these distributed services work on network packets, they can be placed outside the servers.

A different situation exists for the services described in Chapter 6, "Distributed Storage and RDMA Services"; namely RDMA and storage. These services are strictly coupled with a server PCIe interface, and, therefore, should be implemented in a NIC. For example, RDMA accesses the memory of the server through PCIe without the intervention of the server CPU, which is not possible without a direct PCIe connection.

The situation is slightly more flexible for storage services, in which some value-added features, such as encryption and compression, are not strictly tied to the PCIe interface.

In general, for PCI-based services, the optimal location of the DSN is in the NIC.

Although security can be implemented in multiple places, it is ideal when implemented in the NIC: the traffic can be encrypted and decrypted at the edge of the network (or as close as possible to the application), so no plain text is exposed at any portion of the network.

9.2.5 Power Budget

The power budget is probably the single most significant constraint for a DSN. The next chapter presents a few hardware alternatives for implementing a DSN. Power consumption and the associated cooling considerations are critical parameters for comparing them.

Chapter 8, "NIC Evolution," contains a discussion of the power budget for NICs. In a standard PCIe slot, power must be limited to 25 watts, and some adapters use two adjacent PCIe slots to be able to draw between 25 and 50 watts, but this is a suboptimal solution, not available in the case of other form factors, such as the Open Compute Project (OCP).

9.3 Determining the Target User

A distributed services platform has applicability for different classes of users: cloud providers, enterprises, and service providers. Their use cases and requirements have significant overlaps, but also differences, as discussed in the following sections.

9.3.1 Enterprise Data Centers

Enterprise data centers, while potentially extremely large, don't have the level of scale of public clouds. A distributed services platform is appealing to them for the following reasons:

- It increases the East-West security by deploying more firewalling and opportunistic encryption everywhere (if encryption is a free service, let's use it).

- It simplifies the network infrastructure by eliminating traffic trombone and the associated overlay encapsulation.

- A cloud-like infrastructure plays well with public clouds and can lend itself to become a hybrid cloud.

- Enterprises are interested in a turnkey solution that includes a policy manager and all the telemetry tools required for troubleshooting and performance analysis.

- It eliminates the need for costly discrete appliances such as the firewall and load balancer to achieve a lower total cost of ownership. This requirement is real in large data centers, but it is extreme in small satellite data centers, where the cost of discrete appliances is shared across a limited number of servers and, therefore, becomes the dominating factor.

The amount of traffic an enterprise solution should support, although high, is not comparable to that of public cloud providers.

9.3.2 Cloud Providers and Service Providers

Cloud and service providers have scaling issues that are second to none. They need a solution that pushes the boundaries in terms of the number of routes, ACLs, flows, firewall rules, security association, and so on.

They are not interested in a turnkey solution because they have huge investments in the management infrastructures. They require DSNs that are easy to integrate through the availability of programmatic APIs, such as REST API and gRPC.

Often these APIs are not enough for them as they want to be able to port their management agent software directly on the DSN and interface it with a low-level hardware API for deeper integration. For this reason, the availability on the DSN of a standard processor that runs a Linux OS distribution is desirable.

Once again, telemetry is critical, and cloud providers already have some telemetry infrastructure in place where they want to feed the telemetry data coming from the DSNs.

9.4 Understanding DSN Implementations

This section describes five possible ways to implement a DSN, starting from the one "inside" the server and moving into the network progressively farther away from the server.

9.4.1 DSN in Software

One of the possibilities is to implement the DSN in software on the main server CPU. At the time of writing this option is deployed in some enterprise data centers, but it doesn't scale for cloud providers.

The software solution requires the presence of a hypervisor and a virtual switch, a non-starter for bare-metal servers where the entire server is dedicated to a user, and there is no place to run the DSN.

Different solutions exist depending on whether the hypervisor is public domain or proprietary.

For example, for a proprietary hypervisor like ESXi, VMware sells a software solution called NSX that includes switching, routing, firewalling, and microsegmentation, with the availability of SSL and IPsec VPNs for site-to-site communications.

For open-source hypervisors, it is possible to extend the functionality of the virtual switch to implement a DSN, but this can get complicated quickly, often requiring programming and debugging in the kernel space.

Most of the available solutions move the programming into userspace, implementing the DSN in software in a virtual machine or container. Of course, these solutions rely on the main server CPU to run the DSN.

Figure 9-2 shows a possible arrangement. A standard NIC sends all the incoming packets to a virtual machine or to a container that implements the DSN and, after the appropriate processing, the packets are delivered to the final destination (another virtual machine or container). Similar processing happens on the reverse path.

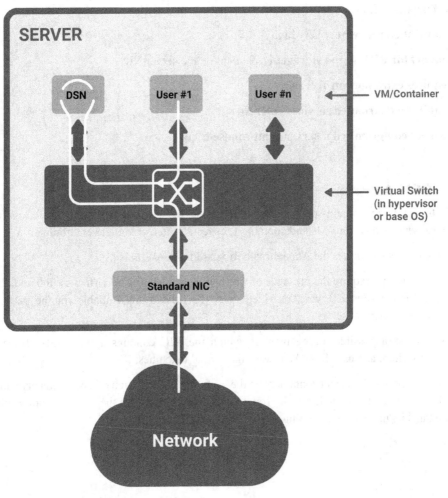

FIGURE 9-2 Server with a Classical NIC

Offload techniques have been attempted to improve performance, but the results are not great, especially in terms of latency and jitter.

The software option can be used in greenfield and brownfield deployments for both VMs and containers, and it does protect VMs and containers on the same server from each other but, from a security perspective, if the server is compromised, the DSN is also potentially compromised.

The following summarizes the characteristics of this solution for comparison with the other four proposed in this chapter:

- **Applicability:** Greenfield and brownfield
- **Bare-metal:** No support
- **Performance:** Low
- **Footprint on the server:** Very high
- **Support for RDMA and storage:** Dependent on the server NIC
- **Requires extra port on ToR:** No
- **Requires a distributed services ToR:** No
- **Security compromised if server compromised:** Yes

9.4.2   DSN Adapter

Locating the DSN in domain-specific hardware inside the NIC is an optimal solution for high-performance servers that run VMs and containers, especially in a greenfield environment.

An example of this solution is the Annapurna Nitro card from AWS [10].

This solution does not require the presence of a hypervisor or a software virtual switch and, therefore, can be used for bare-metal servers, provided that NIC drivers are available for the particular OS installed on the bare-metal server.

Figure 9-3 shows a possible arrangement in which the NIC contains a fully self-sufficient DSN, including the switch, and uses SR-IOV toward the virtual machines.

This option can protect VMs and containers on the same server from each other and can also implement advanced features such as PCIe firewall. From a security perspective, if the server is compromised, the DSN maintains its integrity and continues to provide protection.

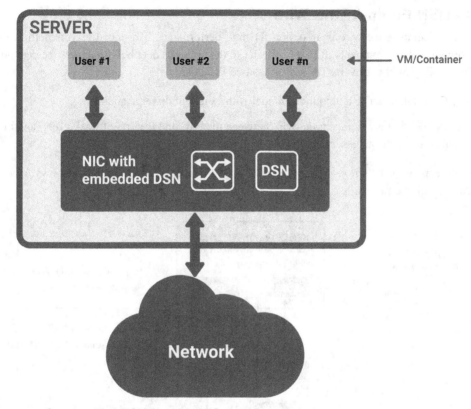

FIGURE 9-3 Server with a DSN-capable NIC

The following summarizes the characteristics of this solution for comparison with the other four proposed in this chapter:

- **Applicability:** Greenfield

- **Bare-metal:** Good support, if drivers are available

- **Performance:** Highest

- **Footprint on the server:** Minimal to nonexistent

- **Support for RDMA and storage:** Yes

- **Requires extra port on ToR:** No

- **Requires a distributed services ToR:** No

- **Security compromised if server compromised:** No

9.4.3   DSN Bump-in-the-Wire

The so-called bump-in-the-wire is an option for high-performance bare-metal servers both in green-field or brownfield environments. It is very similar to the previous one, but it removes the dependency on the availability of NIC drivers. The server has two PCIe cards:

- A NIC card that can be a ubiquitous model with excellent driver availability.
- A DSN card that is a bump-in-the-wire between the NIC and the Top of Rack (ToR) and implements all the distributed services.

DSN cards can be just "power-sucking aliens" on the server PCIe. Figure 9-4 shows a possible arrangement with the two cards.

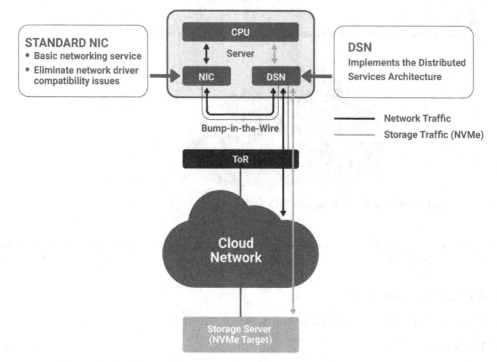

FIGURE 9-4   Bump-in-the-Wire

As in the previous case, if from a security perspective the server is compromised, the DSN maintains its integrity and continues to provide protection.

The following summarizes the characteristics of this solution for comparison with the other four proposed in this chapter:

- **Applicability:** Greenfield and possibly brownfield
- **Bare-metal:** Optimal support, independent of driver availability

- **Performance:** Highest

- **Footprint on the server:** Minimal to nonexistent

- **Support for RDMA and Storage:** Yes

- **Requires extra port on ToR:** No

- **Requires a distributed services ToR:** No

- **Security compromised if server compromised:** No

9.4.4 DSN in Switch

In the DSN in software and DS adapter solutions, the DSN was in the server; in the bump-in-the-wire solution, it was on the wire between the server and the ToR; in this solution, it is in the ToR. Conceptually, this solution is identical to bump-in-the-wire because the only difference is the place where the DSN is connected on the wire. There are two technical differences, however:

- The ToR provides the power and the cooling of the DSN instead of the server.

- The PCIe interface is not connected, and therefore, there is no support for RDMA and storage service.

This solution consolidates the DSN and the ToR switch (also known as a leaf switch) in a single box. Multiple DSN ASICs may be present in the DS switch and shared among the servers in the rack. This solution reduces the total cost of ownership, especially for enterprise applications, where it may be difficult to justify a dedicated DSN for each server because the volume of traffic is not as high as in the public cloud.

Figure 9-5 shows a possible arrangement with a DS switch built with a merchant switch silicon ASIC and four DSN ASICs.

Please note that from a management and telemetry perspective, nothing changes; there is still a policy manager that can work in any of these solutions and should support a mix of different implementations in the same network.

To implement security across VMs and containers in the same server, the server NIC should deploy SR-IOV and send all the traffic to the DS switch. Each VM or container can be tagged explicitly; for example, by adding a VLAN tag, or it can be tagged implicitly by its source MAC address.

Please note that this solution does not require using VXLAN encapsulation because the DSNs in the ToR are in the same layer 2 domain as the servers.

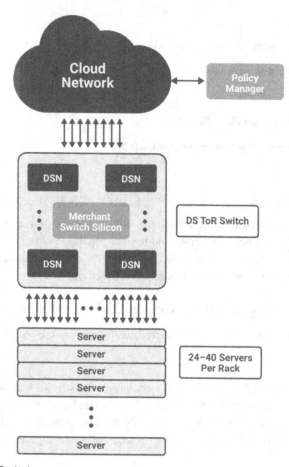

FIGURE 9-5   DSN in Switch

The following summarizes the characteristics of this solution for comparison with the other four proposed in this chapter:

- **Applicability:** Brownfield and greenfield

- **Bare-metal:** Optimal support, independent of driver availability

- **Performance:** High

- **Footprint on the server:** Minimal to nonexistent

- **Support for RDMA and storage:** No

- **Requires extra port on ToR:** No

- **Requires a distributed services ToR:** Yes

- **Security compromised if server compromised:** No

9.4.5   DSNs in an Appliance

An appliance connected through 100 Gbps Ethernet links to the ToR switch contains the DSNs. This solution is a variation of the previous one but targeted more toward the brownfield deployment where there is no desire to replace the ToR switch, and the ToR switch has extra Ethernet ports available. It is depicted in Figure 9-6.

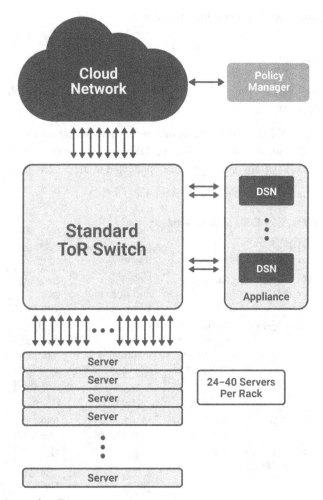

FIGURE 9-6   DSNs in an Appliance

Summarizing the characteristics of this solution and comparing it with the other four proposed in this chapter:

- **Applicability:** Brownfield and greenfield

- **Bare-metal:** Optimal support, independent of driver availability

- **Performance:** Intermediate

- **Footprint on the server:** Minimal to nonexistent
- **Support for RDMA and storage:** No
- **Requires extra port on ToR:** Yes
- **Requires a distributed services ToR:** No
- **Security compromised if server compromised:** No

9.5 Summary

In this chapter, we have analyzed the goals, constraints, target users, and possible implementation of a distributed services platform.

We have shown that the DSN may be implemented either in software on the main server CPU or in hardware. In the second case, we assumed that the DSN hardware could be hosted on a NIC, as a bump-in-the-wire, in a ToR switch, or an appliance connected to the ToR switch.

Table 9-1 summarizes the five possible ways to implement a DSN.

TABLE 9-1   Possible Ways for DSN Implementation

	DSN in Software	DSN Adapter	DSN Bump-in-the-Wire	DSN in Switch	DSN in an Appliance
Applicability	Greenfield and Brownfield	Greenfield	Greenfield and possibly Brownfield	Brownfield and Greenfield	Brownfield and Greenfield
Bare-metal	No support	Good support, if drivers are available	Optimal support, independent of driver availability	Optimal support, independent of driver availability	Optimal support, independent of driver availability
Performance	Low	Highest	Highest	High	Intermediate
Footprint on the server	Very high	Minimal to nonexistent	Minimal to nonexistent	Minimal to nonexistent	Minimal to nonexistent
Support for RDMA and storage	Dependent on the server NIC	Yes	Yes	No	No
Requires extra port on ToR	No	No	No	No	Yes
Requires a distributed services ToR	No	No	No	Yes	No
Security compromised if server compromised	Yes	No	No	No	No

In the next chapter, we will analyze possible hardware architectures for the DSN.

9.6 Bibliography

[1] IEEE 1588-2008, IEEE Standard for a Precision Clock Synchronization Protocol for Networked Measurement and Control Systems. https://standards.ieee.org/standard/1588-2008.html

[2] Yilong Geng, Shiyu Liu, Zi Yin, Ashish Naik, Balaji Prabhakar, Mendel Rosunblum, and Amin Vahdat, 2018. Exploiting a natural network effect for scalable, fine-grained clock synchronization. In Proceedings of the 15th USENIX Conference on Networked Systems Design and Implementation (NSDI '18). USENIX Association, Berkeley, CA, USA, 81–94.

[3] Bader, Andreas & Kopp, Oliver & Falkenthal, Michael. (2017). Survey and Comparison of Open Source Time Series Databases. https://www.researchgate.net/publication/315838456_Survey_and_Comparison_of_Open_Source_Time_Series_Databases

[4] Roy Thomas Fielding, "Chapter 5: Representational State Transfer (REST)." Architectural Styles and the Design of Network based Software Architectures (Ph.D.). University of California, Irvine, 2000.

[5] Swagger, https://swagger.io

[6] Open API, https://www.openapis.org

[7] M.Bjorklund, Ed., "YANG, A Data Modeling Language for the Network Configuration Protocol (NETCONF)," RFC 6020, DOI 10.17487/RFC6020, October 2010.

[8] gRPC, https://grpc.io

[9] Protocol Buffers, https://developers.google.com/protocolbuffers

[10] Simon Sharwood, "Amazon reveals 'Nitro'… Custom ASICs and boxes that do grunt work so EC2 hosts can just run instances," The Register, 29 Nov 2017, https://www.theregister.co.uk/2017/11/29/aws_reveals_nitro_architecture_bare_metal_ec2_guard_duty_security_tool

Chapter | 10

DSN Hardware Architectures

In this chapter, we analyze a few competing hardware structures that can be suitable for DSNs, according to the goals and constraints set in the previous chapter. We try to answer the question, "What is the best hardware architecture for a DSN?" reminding ourselves that the ideal DSN is a fully contained unit, with zero footprint on the servers, is programmable in three dimensions (data plane, control plane, and management plane), and performs at wire speed with low latency and low jitter.

The control and management planes' programmability don't really factor in, because they are not data intensive. All the DSNs include a few CPU cores, typically in the form of ARM cores, to execute control protocols and management interfaces.

Today, data plane programmability at speeds of 100 Gbps or more is still very rare, because it is difficult to implement in hardware. The P4 architecture, described in Chapter 11, "The P4 Domain-Specific Language," addresses this issue.

10.1   The Main Building Blocks of a DSN

Let's start with the description of some of the potential building blocks that might be needed to build a DSN, in no particular order:

- **2 x 100 growing to 2 x 200 and 2 x 400 Gbps Ethernet ports:** Two ports are the minimum to support the bump-in-the-wire configuration or to dual-attach a server to two ToR switches or two separate networks, and so on. It is desirable that they support the Pulse-Amplitude Modulation 4-Level (PAM-4) standard [1] to easily partition them in multiple 25 and 50 Gbps ports.

- **1 x 1 Gbps Ethernet management port:** We saw in the preceding chapter that the "network mode" is the preferred and most secure management mode, and some users want to run the management plane out-of-band as a separate network. A dedicated management port allows them to achieve this goal.

- **PCIe Gen 3 and Gen 4:** In section 8.1 we discussed how four Gen 3 lanes support a 25 Gb/s Ethernet connection, eight lanes support 50 Gb/s Ethernet, and sixteen support 100 Gb/s Ethernet. These bandwidth numbers double for Gen 4. If PCIe is limited to configuration and management, two lanes are enough; if it passes user data to and from the Ethernet ports, then an appropriate number of lanes is required, typically 16 or 32.

- **Internal switch:** An internal layer 2 switch capable of implementing SR-IOV is the minimum requirement. The internal switch is the central point of the DSN, and typically it is much more sophisticated, including layer 3, ACLs, firewall, NAT, load balancing, and so on. The final goal is to have a switch that is fully programmable in the data plane, allowing users to add proprietary functions or encapsulations.

- **SR-IOV logical ports (see section 8.4):** A sufficient number of physical functions (PFs) and virtual functions (VFs) need to be supported; a reasonable implementation may support, for example, 4 PFs and 256 VFs/PFs for a total of 1024 VFs. Each VF and PF is a separate logical port on the internal switch.

- **Memory:** A DSN requires memory to store state, data, and programs. For example, the state is stored in tables, the largest one being the flow table. A flow table entry contains multiple fields derived from the packet fields and various counters and timers associated with telemetry and other auxiliary functions. Assuming that one flow table entry is 128 bytes, 2 GB of memory is required to store 16 million flows. Considering all data and program storage requirements, a memory size between 4 GB and 16 GB looks reasonable.

- **Cache:** Some form of write-back cache is required to compensate between the high speed of the internal circuitry and the lower speed of the memory. Sizing a cache from a theoretical perspective is impossible; the larger the better, typically a few MB.

- **Network on chip (NOC):** All the components listed here need to communicate and share memories, and this is the primary purpose of the NOC that can optionally also guarantee cache coherency among the different memories on the chip.

- **Dedicated hardware for special functions:** Even with the best programmability in the data plane, some functions are best executed in specialized hardware structures, among them encryption and compression.

- **RDMA and storage support:** In Chapter 6, "Distributed Storage and RDMA Services," we discussed how RDMA and storage take advantage of particular hardware infrastructure to move data at very high speed without loading the main server CPU. If these services are required, a DSN needs to implement them in hardware.

- **Various auxiliary interfaces:** These are low-speed interfaces used for initialization and trouble-shooting, such as serial, USB, and I2C.

- **NVRAM interface:** This is needed to connect an NVRAM for storing DSN software images and other static data.

- **Embedded CPU cores:** These are required to run control and management planes.

10.2   Identifying the Silicon Sweet Spot

One of the challenges in designing a DSN is the identification of the "silicon sweet-spot": that is, of an area of silicon that has a reasonable cost, can provide exceptional services at high speed, and has a power dissipation that is compatible with the embodiments considered. How big this area is and how many logical functions can fit into it depends on the silicon process technology used in the fabrication.

Choosing the right technology is essential because it creates interdependencies among the silicon area, the number of gates, the clock frequency, the power consumption, and, ultimately, the cost. Figure 10-1 shows the significant interdependencies and also clarifies that the final performance of domain-specific hardware depends not only on the gate count but also on the chosen hardware architecture, which is the main topic of this chapter, starting from section 10.3.

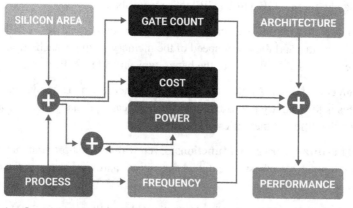

FIGURE 10-1   Major Considerations in Silicon Design

Usually, process technologies are classified according to the transistor channel length. Table 10-1 summarizes the integrated circuit (IC) manufacturing processes according to the year of introduction [2].

TABLE 10-1   Integrated Circuit Manufacturing Processes

2001	2004	2006	2007	2010	2012	2014[1]	2017	2018
130 nm	90 nm	65 nm	45 nm	32 nm	22 nm	16/14 nm	10 nm	7 nm

[1] The 14 nm and 16 nm are essentially the same process and are referred to as 16 nm in this chapter.

At the time of writing, the two technologies used to build most of the ASICs are 16 nm (nanometer) and 7 nm.

When you are evaluating a new process, several components must be considered carefully. Among them:

- **The Serializer/Deserializer (SerDes):** These are incredibly critical components used to input/output data from the chip at high speed. For example, they are the components at the base of the Ethernet MACs and PCIe lanes. In the case of Ethernet, two very desirable emerging standards are PAM-4 56G and PAM-4 112G [1]. PCIe Gen 3 and Gen 4 need to be supported, and, with respect to market trends, very soon Gen 5 will be required.

- **The memory interfaces:** These are also high-speed connections toward external memories. The desirable standards to be supported are DDR4, DDR5, and HBM.

- **CPUs:** All new ASICs include some form of general-purpose processors, and the ARM family of processors is often used for these applications. Frequency, architecture, cache size, and other parameters depend on the manufacturing processes.

- **Other logic infrastructures:** These include, for example, the availability of TCAMs, which are used for the longest prefix match or five-tuple ACL rules.

- **Availability of third-party intellectual property (IP):** These include, for example, libraries containing encryption and compression modules.

One significant consideration is always power dissipation. To keep the power budget around 25 Watts (which we have seen is a requirement for PCIe slots), the silicon area sweet spot is around 200 square millimeters, both at 16 nm and 7 nm.

How much logic and memory can be packed into that area depends first and foremost on the channel length, but also on which design path is chosen; a customer-owned tooling (COT), in general, produces smaller silicon areas, but not necessarily a lower power.

10.2.1   The 16 nm Process

The 16 nm process is the evolution of the 22 nm, and the first devices appeared in volume in products in 2015. For example, in 2015 the MacBook started to use the i7-5557U Intel processor, the Galaxy S6 began using a System on a Chip (SoC), and the iPhone 6S began using the A9 chips, all fabricated with this technology [2].

Ethernet interfaces up to 100 Gbps have been used in conjunction with PCI Gen 3 and Gen 4. Memory interfaces are typically DDR3, DDR4, and HBM. The availability of libraries with many modules is exceptionally mature, and ARM processors of the A72 architecture can be easily integrated with a clock frequency between 1.6 to 2.2 Ghz.

The 16 nm technology allows a transistor density of approximately 35 million transistors per square millimeter [3], a 2.5 times improvement compared to the previous 22 nm technology. When you consider that:

- At least four transistors are required to build a NAND gate

- Not all transistors can be used due to placement, routing, and other technological considerations

- Gates need to be accompanied by some amount of memory to produce a useful circuit

the net result is that—for example, with the 16 nm process—in one square millimeter it is possible to pack two to four million gates or 4 Mbit to 8 Mbit of RAM, or a combination of the two.

10.2.2   The 7 nm Process

The biggest challenges related to evolving the 16 nm process into the 7 nm process are in the area of lithography and, in particular, in the second part of the fabrication process called the back end of line (BEOL), where transistors get interconnected through the metallization layers.

The first devices in 7 nm were introduced in 2018 and are the Apple A12 Bionic [4] and the Huawei Kirin 980 [5]. They both have a transistor density of approximately 83 million transistors per square millimeter, and density up to 100 million transistors per square millimeter have been reported by Intel [3]. As a result, the 7 nm process can pack two to three times as many gates or memory bits as the 16 nm process.

Ethernet interfaces are typically 100/200/400 Gbps implemented using PAM-4 56G and PAM-4 112G. DDR5 and HBM2 memory interfaces are available in addition to the previous ones, and so is PCIe Gen 5. At the time of writing, the availability of libraries is maturing quickly and an ARM processor of the A72 architecture can be easily integrated with a clock frequency up to 3.0 GHz.

In a nutshell, at 7 nm it is possible to design devices that consume half the power with the same performance as 16 nm or with the same power and provide two to three times the performance.

10.3   Choosing an Architecture

Figure 10-1 showed how the final performance of domain-specific hardware is a combination of the gate count and of the architecture built using these gates. In the preceding sections, we explained the gate count and the availability of building blocks. In the following, we discuss which architecture is the best for distributed-service, domain-specific hardware.

Figure 10-2 illustrates the three major architecture possibilities: sea of CPU cores, field-programmable gate arrays (FPGAs), and ASICs. It also shows the presence of another interesting technology called P4 that adds data plane programmability to the ASIC architecture. Chapter 11, "The P4 Domain-Specific Language," presents the P4 architecture and the associated language.

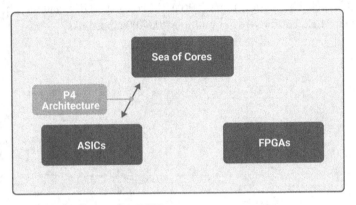

FIGURE 10-2 Possible Architectures for DSNs

10.4 Having a Sea of CPU Cores

The idea of having a limited number of CPU cores inside a DSN to implement control and management protocols and other auxiliary functions is widely accepted and deployed. This section does not discuss that; it analyzes the use of CPU cores in the data plane; that is, to parse, modify, drop, or forward every single packet that enters a DSN. The basic idea is to use all the silicon area for as many processors as possible combined with a hardwired, nonprogrammable NIC. Common processor choices are ARM [6] or MIPS [7] cores with associated caches.

The clear advantage of the sea of CPU cores architecture is easy programmability; for example, these processors can run a standard Linux distribution and can be programmed in any possible language. All the tools used to write and troubleshoot software on general-purpose CPUs are readily available and known to a large number of programmers. This option is very appealing for developers coming from the software world, but it has substantial performance drawbacks.

In this chapter, we base our discussion on the ARM A72 core [8], which is a widely used processor. The performance measurements refer to a complex of four ARM A72 cores and the associated cache memory. The size of this complex is approximately 17 million gates and 20 Mbits of RAM.

Using the sweet spot presented in the previous sections, it is probably possible to fit eight such complexes on a 16 nm, 200 square millimeters die, for a total of 32 processors at 2.2 GHz.

Figure 10-3 indicates that for a reasonable feature set with an average packet size of 256 bytes, an ARM A72 normalized at 1 GHz will process approximately a half Gbps of bandwidth [9]. Multiply that by 32 cores and 2.2 GHz, and the total bandwidth is 35 Gbps, clearly far from the processing capability required for a single 100 Gbps Ethernet link.

Moving to 7 nm it is probably possible to pack 96 ARM cores at 3 GHz, and this should be enough to process one 100 Gbps link, but for sure not multiple 200/400 Gbps links.

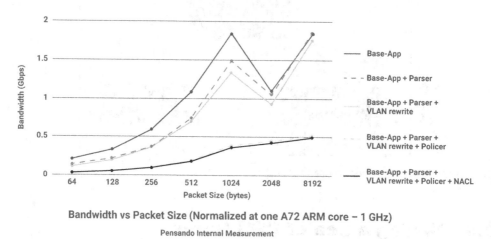

Bandwidth vs Packet Size (Normalized at one A72 ARM core – 1 GHz)

Pensando Internal Measurement

FIGURE 10-3   ARM Performance as a Packet Processor

Another way to think about these numbers is that one ARM core at 1 GHz is capable of executing one instruction every 1.5 clock cycles at best; that is, 666M instructions per second. With an average packet length of 256 bytes at 100 Gbps, it is possible to transmit 45 Mpps, equivalent to a budget of 14.8 instructions per packet per core. Assuming 32 cores at 3 GHz, the budget is 1420 instructions per packet, which is insufficient to program the data plane that parses, de-parses, forwards, and applies services. This analysis is optimistic because it completely ignores memory bandwidth and focuses just on the CPU.

Two other factors are even more critical: latency and jitter. We have previously discussed a goal of a few microseconds as the maximum latency introduced by a DSN with a jitter of less than a microsecond and as close as possible to zero.

General-purpose processors, when used as packet processors, are not good at minimizing latency and jitter. They run a standard OS, with a standard scheduler whose goal is to maximize throughput. They try to limit context swapping with techniques such as interrupt moderation that by definition increases jitter.

All the problems discussed in section 4.2.4 about using or bypassing the kernel are present, but now they are embedded inside a domain-specific hardware device, instead of being present on the main server CPU.

It is not uncommon to have jitter and latencies in milliseconds, three orders of magnitude worse than our goal. Just open a terminal window and type **ping google.com**. On my consumer home connection, I am getting an average latency of 15 ms, with a jitter of 2 ms; a DSN with latency and jitter of milliseconds is unusable.

To minimize jitter and latency, the OS can be removed from the processors and replaced by a technique familiarly called BLT (Big Loop Technology) in which a single code loop fetches the packets from the interfaces and process them. BLT reduces delay and jitter but negates some of the advantages of using general-purpose processors; the familiar toolchains, debugging, and troubleshooting tools don't work anymore. All the OS libraries are no longer available. What is still safe is the possibility of programming in high-level languages like C.

It should also be mentioned that ARM has cores that are more suitable for the BLT [10]. They don't support more advanced features such as virtualization (not required for BLT), but they have approximately the same packet processing power and are smaller, approximately half the size of an A72 core; therefore, it is possible to fit two of them in place of an A72, doubling the packet processing rate.

The sea of cores solution is not adequate for speeds of 100 Gbps or higher; It does not make the best use of the silicon area, and it provides inferior results in terms of throughput, latency, and jitter.

10.5 Understanding Field-Programmable Gate Arrays

Field-programmable gate arrays (FPGAs) [11] are integrated circuits that can be programmed to perform a particular function after they are manufactured. They have been around for many years and in their initial design were just an array of gates with a programmable interconnection. Using a CAD tool, system designers can develop a programming file that defines the interconnections between the gates, which can be downloaded into FPGA so it can perform the desired functions.

FPGAs carry the promise of perfect programmability because they can be entirely reprogrammed by downloading a new configuration file. Unfortunately, this programmability comes at a cost: FPGAs are less dense and more power hungry than ASICs. But more on this later.

Conventional FPGAs are not optimized for building a DSN; they have building blocks like digital signal processors that have no applicability in a DSN, and they lack standard blocks like Ethernet MAC and PCIe. This creates difficulties in obtaining a stable device at high speeds.

FPGAs have recently grown in size and complexity and are now available in a system on chip (SoC) version. These are combinations of hard and soft functions.

Examples of hard functions are an ARM core complex, PCIe interfaces, PAM-4 Ethernet interfaces, and DDR4 memory interfaces [12].

The soft part is the programmable one, which is generally expressed in terms of the number of logical elements (LEs) and adaptive logic modules (ALMs).

An LE, also known as a logical cell, is a four-input logical block that contains a programmable look up table (LUT), basically a four-input truth table, and a flip-flop (a memory bit).

An ALM is a more complex element that supports up to eight inputs, eight outputs, two combinational logic cells, two or four registers, two full adders, a carry chain, a register chain, and LUT mask. An ALM can implement substantially more complicated logical functions than an LE.

For example, the Intel Agilex AGF 008 [13] is an SoC that contains 764,640 LEs, 259,200 ALMs, DDR4 interfaces, 24x PAM-4, a quad-core 64-bit ARM Cortex-A53, and so on.

These features are desirable, but as we already mentioned, the most obvious drawbacks are high power consumption and high cost.

A dated study (2007) on the power consumption of FPGAs/ASICs [14] showed a ratio between 7.1 and 14; that is, approximately one order of magnitude. FPGAs have improved, but so have ASICs, and FPGA power consumption upto 100 Watts is typical, while some cards can use up to 215 Watts [15], very far from our target of 25 Watts for a DSN.

Cost is not relevant for small production, but it becomes crucial for high volumes. Here is where ASICs excel.

But there is another issue with FPGAs that is less understood and fundamental: programmability.

The term *programmability* is typically associated with processors that execute instructions sequentially. These instructions are the components of software programs that are written in a high-level programming language like C.

FPGAs are programmable, but not in the traditional way processors are. FPGAs are programmed using a hardware description language (HDL). The two most common HDLs are VHDL and Verilog. They describe hardware structures, not software programs. They may have a friendly C-like syntax that may induce you to think that you are writing C programs, but nothing can be farther from the truth. Software programs consist of a sequence of operations, whereas HDL code describes an interconnection of logic blocks and the functions performed by each block. HDL codes hardware structures, not software programs.

Suppose you write two software functions in C and want to use them in the main program; very easy: call them from the main. Now consider the case in which you have coded two hardware structures in Verilog, successfully tested them separately on an FPGA, and want to merge them in the same FPGA. It is not easy. You will need to redesign a manually combined structure. HDLs do not have a composable semantic!

Let's look at a more concrete example: two hardware structures to parse two network protocols. Each hardware structure has its packet parser, but in the merged structure, the FPGA needs to parse the frame only once, so you need to merge the two parsers manually.

FPGAs require a deep understanding of how hardware circuits and digital logic work. Merely asking a software engineer to write Verilog programs and hoping to get fantastic performance, high utilization, and low power consumption is unrealistic.

FPGAs are great devices for many applications, but in the author's opinion, they are not a suitable implementation for a DSN.

10.6   Using Application-Specific Integrated Circuits

An application-specific integrated circuit (ASIC) is an integrated circuit designed for a specific purpose and not intended to be a general-purpose device. Computer-aided design (CAD) tools are used to create and simulate the desired features and to produce a full set of photolithographic masks required to fabricate the IC. For DSN implementation, we only consider full-custom design ASICs, even if cheaper solutions exist for simpler applications [16]. The full-custom process requires a capable team of hardware and ASIC engineers and a non-recurring engineering (NRE) investment that for 16 nm and 7 nm technologies reaches several millions of dollars.

Additional advantages are the ability to integrate fully verified components from libraries; for example, analog components, microprocessor cores, encryption modules, and state-of-the-art SerDes.

Evidence that ASICs are the best solution for high-performance network, storage, and security devices is everywhere. All routers, switches, and NIC cards are built using ASICs; not a single successful network switch uses a sea of cores or an FPGA in the data plane.

ASICs have been criticized for being rigid and not as flexible as FPGAs. The introduction of a new feature requires a new generation of ASICs, and turnaround time may be an issue. The turnaround time is mostly dependent on the quality and determination of the ASIC team: I have seen ASIC solutions evolving faster than FPGA ones, but I have also seen designs stagnating forever.

In the specific case of ASICs used to implement a DSN, we have already seen that the ASIC is an SoC that includes processors. Therefore, it is the software that implements features in the management and control planes, providing all the desirable flexibility.

The data plane also requires flexibility to have an ASIC architecture that allows the addition of new features or the modification of existing ones without having to respin the ASIC. Here is where the P4 architecture, discussed in the next chapter, plays a vital role because P4 provides a programmable data plane.

ASICs are the best solution for proper silicon utilization; that is, to produce a DSN that has:

- Reduced area, with high transistor density, and high transistor utilization

- A lower cost per chip when mass-produced, and the NRE is amortized

- The best possible performance in terms of packets per seconds

- A packet latency that is known and limited to a low number

- The minimum packet jitter

- The minimum power consumption

10.7   Determining DSN Power Consumption

One criterion that has been proposed to compare all these approaches is to measure how much power is required by a DSN to process a packet in nanojoule.

The joule is a derived unit of energy in the International System of Units [19]. It is equal to the energy dissipated as heat when an electric current of 1 ampere passes through a resistance of 1 ohm for 1 second.

According to this definition, we can classify DSNs according to nanojoule per packet or nanowatt per packet per second. Because network device performance is expressed in pps (packets per second), this book uses nanowatt/pps, which is identical to nanojoule per packet.

In section 10.4 we saw that "an ARM A72 normalized at 1 GHz will process approximately a half Gbps of bandwidth." In 16 nm, a complex of four ARM cores at 2.2 GHz consume approximately 2.9 Watts and process 0.5 Gbps × 4 × 2.2 = 4.4 Gbps. With an average packet length of 256 bytes (plus 24 bytes of Ethernet interpacket gap, preamble, and CRC) or 2,240 bits, this is equal to 1.96 Mpps, thus resulting in average power consumption of 1,480 nanowatt/pps. At 7 nm, four quad-cores at 3 GHz consume approximately 12.4 Watts and process 0.5 Gbps × 16 × 3 = 24 Gbps, equal to 10.7 Mpps, equal to 1,159 nanowatt/pps.

In section 10.6 we didn't discuss the power consumption of DSN ASIC, but in Chapter 8, "NIC Evolution," we presented several modern NIC and SmartNIC cards that have a power consumption between 25 Watts and 35 Watts and implement some form of DSN in ASIC at 100 Gbps. It equates to 45 Mpps (100 Gbps / 2240 bit/packet) and power consumption of 560 to 780 nanowatt/pps. This also depends on the technology. In 16 nm, power consumption around 780 nanowatt/pps should be common; in 7 nm, the power consumption should be half of that, targeting 390 nanowatt/pps, but probably more realistically 500 nanowatt/pps.

In section 10.5 we discussed the fact that FPGAs consume on average four times the power of ASICs, placing them at approximately 2,000 nanowatt/pps. This seems to be confirmed by a 100 Gbps/ 45 Mpps implementation in FPGA that consumes 100 Watts; that is 2,222 nanowatt/pps. Table 10-2 tries to summarize the results, that are qualitative in nature and have significant variations among different implementations.

TABLE 10-2 DSN Power Consumptions

DSN at 100 Gbps Technology	Power Consumption nanowatt/pps or nanojoule per packet[2]
ARM A72 at 2.2 GHz — 16 nm	1,480
ARM A72 at 3.0 GHz — 7 nm	1,159
ASIC 16 nm	780
ASIC 7 nm	500
FPGA	2000

[2] 256 bytes per packet

10.8 Determining Memory Needs

Independently of the solution adopted, DSNs require large memories, including to buffer packets; to store flow tables used by firewalls, load balancers, NAT, and telemetry; and to store code for control and management planes. A DSN may need several gigabytes of memory, and these large amounts come only in the form of Dynamic RAM (DRAM).

DRAM speed is also critical, and it is typically expressed in Mega Transactions per second (MT/s) or GigaBytes per second (GB/s). For example, a DDR4-1600 does 1600 MT/s with a parallelism of 64 bits, equivalent to 12.8 GB/s. These numbers are the transfer rate, also known as the burst rate, but due to how the information is stored inside the DRAM, only a fraction of that bandwidth is usable in a sustainable way. According to applications and read versus write usage, utilization between 65 percent and 85 percent have been reported.

In critical cases, utilization can go down to 30 percent for random 64-byte reads and writes, which is a pattern observed behind an L3 cache running typical workloads on one CPU core.

DRAMs can have several form factors, as described in the next sections.

10.8.1 Host Memory

The host memory is an economical solution used by some NICs. The advantage is that host memory is abundant and relatively inexpensive; the main disadvantages are as follows:

- High access time and therefore low performance, because accessing host memory requires traversing the PCIe complex.

- The footprint on the host, because the memory used by the DSN is not available to the main server CPU, and it also requires a particular driver in the OS or hypervisor.

- Security, because the memory can be exposed to a compromised host. For this reason, in my opinion, this is not a viable solution for DSNs.

10.8.2 External DRAM

DSNs may integrate memory controllers to use external DRAMs in the form of DDR4, DDR5, and GDDR6 devices. This solution provides higher bandwidth than the host memory solution, and it is probably slightly more expensive, but it can host huge forwarding tables and RDMA context at very high performance.

Double Data Rate 4 Synchronous Dynamic Random-Access Memory (DDR4) is available with a parallelism of 64 bits from DDR-4-1600 (1600 MT/s, 12.8 GB/s burst rate) to DDR-4-3200 (3200 MT/s, 25.6 GB/s burst rate) [17].

Double Data Rate 5 Synchronous Dynamic Random-Access Memory (DDR5) has the same 64-bit parallelism, and it supports DDR-5-4400 (4400 MT/s, 35.2 GB/s burst rate). In November 2018, SK Hynix announced the completion of DDR5-5200 (5200 MT/s, 41.6 GB/s burst rate) [18]. DDR5 is still under development at the time of writing.

Graphics Double Data Rate type 6 synchronous dynamic random-access memory (GDDR6), initially designed for graphics cards, can be used by a DSN. It has a per-pin bandwidth of up to 16 Gbps and a parallelism of 2 x 16 bits, for a total bandwidth up to 64 GB/s. GDDR6 is still under development at the time of writing.

Of course, with external DRAM, it is possible to deploy two or more controllers, further increasing the bandwidth available.

10.8.3 On-chip DRAM

An ASIC cannot integrate all the DRAM required by a DSN. A solution used when an ASIC requires lots of DRAM with high bandwidth is to use a silicon interposer and insert into the same package a memory chip called high-bandwidth memory (HBM). Figure 10-4 shows this configuration [20].

Today, HBM exists in two versions: HBM-1 with a maximum bandwidth of 128 GB/s, and HBM-2 with a maximum bandwidth of 307 GB/s.

10.8.4 Memory Bandwidth Requirements

How much memory bandwidth is required is debatable.

All the previous solutions need to be complemented by on-chip caches to lower the average latency by exploiting temporal locality in packet flows.

For a cut-through solution that does not use the DRAM as a packet buffer, the memory bandwidth requirement is not huge. For example, 25 Mpps with ten table lookups per packet at 64 bytes equal 25 x 10 x 64 million = 16 GB/s, and all external DRAM solutions are adequate.

If packets need to be stored in DRAM for manipulation at 100 Gbps, this implies 100 Gbps of writing and 100 Gbps of reading, equivalent to 25 GB/s, plus the table lookup bandwidth, for a total of 40 GB/s–50 GB/s. Two channels of DDR5 or HBM-2 may be required for these solutions.

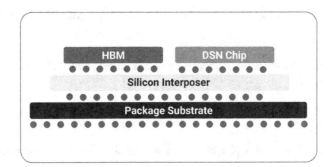

FIGURE 10-4   High-Bandwidth Memory (HBM)

10.9   Summary

In this chapter, we discussed that a DSN is an SoC that uses CPU cores (usually ARM cores) for implementing the control and management planes in software.

The data plane implementation differs. In the sea of CPU cores approach, more CPU cores are used to implement the data plane in software. In the ASIC approach, hardware structures implement the data plane for maximum efficiency and performance. In the FPGA approach, the same ASIC circuitry is implemented in a programmable structure that is inherently less efficient than the ASIC one.

For a DSN, the data plane is the most critical component, and the only acceptable implementation is an ASIC. The next chapter reviews the P4 architecture that adds runtime programmability to the ASIC data plane.

10.10   Bibliography

[1] Intel, "AN 835: PAM4 Signaling Fundamentals," 2019.03.12, https://www.intel.com/content/dam/www/programmable/us/en/pdfs/literature/an/an835.pdf

[2] Wikipedia, "14 nanometers," https://en.wikipedia.org/wiki/14_nanometer

[3] Rachel Courtland, "Intel Now Packs 100 Million Transistors in Each Square Millimeter," IEEE Spectrum, 30 Mar 2017. https://spectrum.ieee.org/nano-clast/semiconductors/processors/intel-now-packs-100-million-transistors-in-each-square-millimeter

[4] Apple A12 Bionic - HiSilicon, WikiChip.org, https://en.wikichip.org/wiki/apple/ax/a12

[5] Kirin 980 - HiSilicon, WikiChip.org, https://en.wikichip.org/wiki/hisilicon/kirin/980

[6] ARM Ltd., https://www.arm.com

[7] MIPS, https://www.mips.com

[8] Wikipedia, "ARM Cortex-A72," https://en.wikipedia.org/wiki/ARM_Cortex-A72

[9] Pensando, Private communication.

[10] ARM developers, "Arm Cortex-R Series Processors," https://developer.arm.com/ip-products/processors/cortex-r

[11] Wikipedia, "Field-programmable gate array," https://en.wikipedia.org/wiki/Field-programmable_gate

[12] Intel AGILEX FPGAs and SOCs, https://www.intel.com/content/www/us/en/products/programmable/fpga/agilex.html

[13] https://www.intel.com/content/dam/www/programmable/us/en/pdfs/literature/pt/intel-agilex-f-series-product-table.pdf

[14] I. Kuon and J. Rose, "Measuring the gap between FPGAs and ASICs," in IEEE Transactions on Computer-Aided Design of Integrated Circuits and Systems (TCAD), 2007.

[15] Intel FPGA Programmable Acceleration Card (PAC) D5005, Product Brief, https://www.intel.com/content/www/us/en/programmable/documentation/cvl1520030638800.html

[16] Wikipedia, "Application-specific integrated circuit," https://en.wikipedia.org/wiki/Application-specific_integrated_circuit

[17] Wikipedia, "DDR4 SDRAM," https://en.wikipedia.org/wiki/DDR4_SDRAM

[18] TechQuila, "SK Hynix Develops First 16 Gb DDR5-5200 Memory Chip," https://www.techquila.co.in/sk-hynix-develops-first-16-gb-ddr5-5200-memory-chip

[19] Wikipedia, "Joule," https://en.wikipedia.org/wiki/Joule

[20] Wikipedia, "High-Bandwidth Memory," https://en.wikipedia.org/wiki/High_Bandwidth_Memory

Chapter | 11

The P4 Domain-Specific Language

In the previous chapter, we explained that the application-specific integrated circuit (ASIC) architecture is best suited to implement a DSN, but we want to add data plane programmability, which is extremely data intensive and is still rare.

The P4 architecture will help us achieve this goal.

The Programming Protocol-independent Packet Processors (P4) architecture formally defines the data plane behavior of a network device, and it supports both programmable and fixed-function network devices. The idea derived from the SDN and OpenFlow movement (see section 4.2.1) and was first published in 2013 [1], [2].

In March 2015, the P4 language consortium was created [3], version 1.0.2 of "The P4 Language Specification" was posted, and in June 2015, Professor Nick McKeown hosted the first P4 workshop at Stanford University.

A lot has happened since then, and now the P4 project is hosted by the Open Networking Foundation [4], and the P4 specifications and any contributed code are primarily licensed under the Apache 2.0 License.

P4 adds to the ASIC architecture the missing data plane programmability aspect. Some of the benefits include the following:

- Adding support for new protocols is easy.
- It is possible to remove unused features and free up associated resources, thus reducing complexity and enabling the reallocation of resources for used features.
- It provides agility in rolling out updates on existing hardware.
- It offers greater visibility into the network.
- It allows the implementation of proprietary features, thus protecting intellectual property. This point is crucial for large users such as public cloud providers.

P4 programs can specify how the switch inside the DSN processes packets. It is possible to implement most of the services described in this book, except for those that require dedicated hardware structures; for example, encryption.

The first version of the P4 specification was called version 14 and had some significant limitations. It targeted a network device with an architecture like the one shown in Figure 11-1.

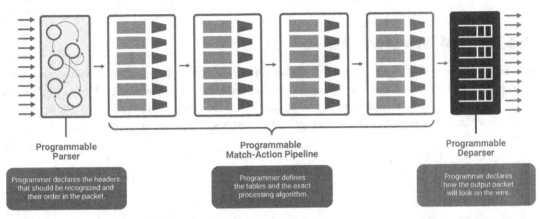

FIGURE 11-1 Example of P4 Version 14 Network Device

This device has three main components:

- **Programmable parser:** This is important because P4 does not have any predefined packet formats. It is composed of a state machine that specifies which packet format the switch recognizes and that generally has one state for each protocol. In each state, the parser extracts some protocol-specific information used in the rest of the pipeline. A classic example is the parsing of an Ethernet frame and then, as a function of the EtherType, parsing either an IPv4 header or an IPv6 header to extract the source and destination IP addresses. The programmable parser may extract and feed more than one header in the pipeline.

- **Programmable match-action pipeline:** The previously extracted headers are the inputs of a series of match-action tables that can modify them. While the headers go through the pipeline, they can carry with them metadata information generated in the previous pipeline stages. This match-action pipeline may also add new headers to the packet.

- **Programmable deparser:** It takes all the headers and constructs the output packet with the valid ones followed by the payload, and it serializes it to the destination port.

While the headers traverse the pipeline, metadata accompanies them. There are two kinds of metadata: standard and user defined. The standard metadata contains fields like input port, packet length, and time-stamp. The user-defined metadata can include, for example, the virtual routing and forwarding (VRF) value associated with the packets and derived from a table lookup in a previous stage of the pipeline.

The most common case is that a packet enters the P4 pipeline, goes through it, and a modified packet exits it. Of course, the packet can also be dropped; for example, due to an ACL. Other special operations are "cloning" a packet to send it to a switched port analyzer (SPAN) port, multicast replication, and "recirculating" a packet. This last operation is useful when, due to the complexity of the processing, the packet cannot be processed entirely in one pass, and consequently, it is reinjected at the input for further processing. Recirculation reduces performance.

11.1   P4 Version 16

In May 2017 P4 version 16 was posted, containing significant improvements to the previous version. P4 was extended to target multiple programmable devices with different architectures. Figure 11-2 shows that there are two groups of constructs: above the dashed line are general concepts that are common to all P4 implementations. Below the dashed line are architecture-specific definitions and components.

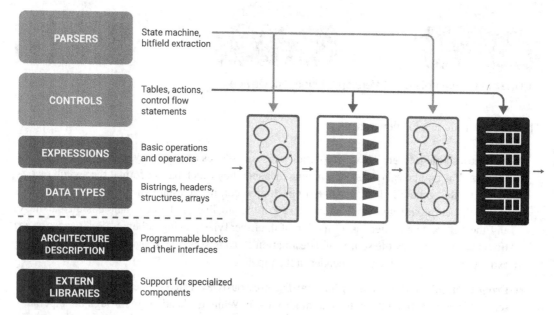

FIGURE 11-2   P4 Language Components

P4 version 16 introduces the following concepts[5]:

- **Architecture:** "A set of P4-programmable components and the data plane interfaces between them." The architecture is an abstraction of the underlying device, the way P4 programmers think about the device data plane.

- **Target:** "A packet-processing system capable of executing a P4 program." In general, it is a hardware device, but P4 16 also supports software switches such as OVS.

P4 16 main components are:

- **The P4 programming language:** P4 programs specify how the various programmable blocks of the data plane of a network device are programmed and connected. P4 does not have any preconceived packet format or protocol knowledge. A P4 program expresses how packets are processed by the data plane of a programmable network-forwarding element.

- **The Portable Switch Architecture (PSA):** A description of standard capabilities of network devices that process and forward packets across multiple interface ports.

- **The P4Runtime API:** A control plane specification for controlling the data plane elements of a device defined or described by a P4 program.

- **In-band Network Telemetry (INT):** A draft specification on how to collect telemetry data as a packet traverses the network.

11.2 Using the P4 Language

The P4 language [5] is a domain-specific language (DSL) targeted toward a high-performance hardware implementation. A modern network device processes billions of packets per second. This is achievable with a programmable infrastructure only if there is a functional coupling between the DSL and the domain-specific hardware. The P4 language has concepts like table lookups that match a hardware table lookup but, for example, even a table lookup cannot be invoked more than once to maintain the performance predictably. To improve hardware performance, P4 generally uses data structures of fixed size.

The core elements in the P4 language are shown in Figure 11-2 and are:

- **Parsers:** State machines to define the packet formats accepted by a P4 program. The parser is one place where the P4 language allows loops, because many headers may need to be extracted or reassembled.

- **Controls:** It defines a directed acyclic graph (DAG) of match-action tables. The term *DAG* indicates an if-then-else program structure that forbids loops.

- **Expression:** Parsers and controls are written using expressions. Expressions include standard expressions on boolean, bit-field operators; comparison, simple arithmetic on integer, conditional operators; operations on sets; operations on headers; and so on.

- **Data types:** P4 is a statically typed language. Supported data types are void, error, boolean, bit-strings of fixed width, signed integers, the match_ kind used for describing the implementation of table lookups, and so on. Constructors can be applied to these basic data types to derive more complex ones. Examples of constructors are header, struct, tuple, extern, and parser.

- **Architecture descriptions:** This is the description of the network device architecture. It identifies the P4-programmable blocks; for example, how many parsers, deparsers, match-action pipelines, and their relationship. It is used to accommodate differences; for instance, between a NIC and a data center switch. The P4 language is agnostic of the architecture; the hardware vendor defines the architecture.

- **Extern:** Objects and functions provided by the architecture. P4 programs can invoke services implemented by extern objects and functions. The extern construct describes the interfaces that an object exposes to the data plane. Examples of externs are CRC functions, random selector for ECMP, timestamp, and timers.

The hardware vendor provides the P4 compiler that produces configuration binaries for the P4 hardware. The binaries allocate and partition the resources of the P4 devices. These resources can be manipulated at runtime by the P4Runtime API. This API allows, for example, to add and remove table entries, read counters, program meters, inject and receive control packets, and so on.

11.3   Getting to Know the Portable Switch Architecture

Several P4 architectures have been developed and put in the public domain. The P4 Language consortium developed the Portable Switch Architecture (PSA) [6], a vendor-independent design that defines standard capabilities of network switches that process and forward packets across multiple interfaces. It establishes a library of types; externs for constructs such as counters, meters, and registers; and a set of "packet paths" that enable a P4 programmer to write P4 programs for network switches.

The PSA is composed of six programmable P4 blocks and two fixed-function blocks, as shown in Figure 11-3.

From left to right, the first three blocks are the "ingress pipeline," followed by a packet buffer and replication fixed-function box, followed by the egress pipeline, followed by the buffer-queueing engine fixed-function box.

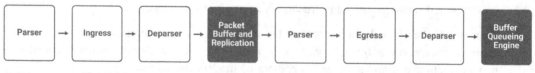

FIGURE 11-3   The PSA

The ingress and egress pipeline parse and validate the packet, pass it to a match action pipeline, and then pass it to the deparser.

After the ingress pipeline, the packet may optionally be replicated (for example, for multicast) and stored in the packet buffer.

After the egress pipeline, the packet is queued to leave the pipeline.

This architecture comes with APIs, templates, headers, metadata, and guidelines designed to maximize P4 code portability.

11.4   Looking at a P4 Example

The best way to learn P4 is to use the GitHub P4 Tutorial repository [7]. There you will find a set of exercises to help you get started with P4 programming, an emulation environment based on VirtualBox, and Vagrant where you will be able to run your code.

This section contains a brief description of the "Basic Forwarding" exercise, which uses a simple P4 architecture, known as the V1 model architecture, shown in Figure 11-4.

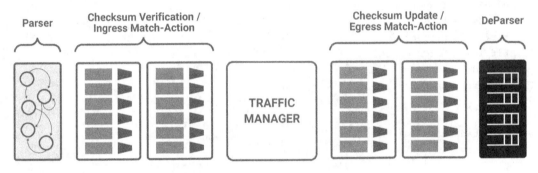

FIGURE 11-4   The V1 Model Architecture

Listing 11-1 spans a few pages and contains the necessary forwarding code of a switch based on the V1 model architecture. It starts by defining two headers: the Ethernet header and the IPv4 header. Then, following the V1 model architecture from left to right, it defines the parser that extracts the Ethernet (ethernet_t) and IPv4 (ipv4_t) headers.

LISTING 11-1   P4 Example

```
/* -*- P4_16 -*- */
#include <core.p4>
#include <v1model.p4>

const bit<16> TYPE_IPV4 = 0x800;
/***************** HEADERS ***********************/
typedef bit<9>  egressSpec_t;
typedef bit<48> macAddr_t;
typedef  bit<32> ip4Addr_t;
```

```
header ethernet_t {
    macAddr_t dstAddr;
    macAddr_t srcAddr;
    bit<16>
    etherType;
}

header ipv4_t {
    bit<4>     version;
    bit<4>     ihl;
    bit<8>     diffserv;
    bit<16>    totalLen;
    bit<16>    identification;
    bit<3>     flags;
    bit<13>    fragOffset;
    bit<8>     ttl;
    bit<8>     protocol;
    bit<16>    hdrChecksum;
    ip4Addr_t srcAddr;
    ip4Addr_t dstAddr;
}

struct metadata {
    /* empty */
}

struct headers {
    ethernet_t  ethernet;
    ipv4_t      ipv4;
}

/***************** PARSER ***********************/

parser MyParser(packet_in packet,
                out headers hdr,
                inout metadata meta,
                inout standard_metadata_t standard_metadata) {

    state start {
        transition parse_ethernet;
    }

    state parse_ethernet {
```

```
        packet.extract(hdr.ethernet);
        transition select(hdr.ethernet.etherType)
            { TYPE_IPV4: parse_ipv4;
            default: accept;
        }
    }

    state parse_ipv4 {
        packet.extract(hdr.ipv4);
        transition accept;
    }

}

/******** CHECKSUM VERIFICATION ********/

control MyVerifyChecksum(inout headers hdr, inout metadata meta) {
    apply { }
}

/*********** INGRESS PROCESSING **************/
control MyIngress(inout headers hdr,
                  inout metadata meta,
                  inout standard_metadata_t standard_metadata) {
    action drop() {
        mark_to_drop(standard_metadata);
    }

    action ipv4_forward(macAddr_t dstAddr, egressSpec_t port) {
        standard_metadata.egress_spec = port;
        hdr.ethernet.srcAddr = hdr.ethernet.dstAddr;
        hdr.ethernet.dstAddr = dstAddr;
        hdr.ipv4.ttl = hdr.ipv4.ttl - 1;
    }

    table ipv4_lpm {
    key = {
        hdr.ipv4.dstAddr: lpm;
    }
    actions = {
        ipv4_forward;
        drop;
        NoAction;
    }
```

```
        size = 1024;
        default_action = drop();
    }

    apply {
        if (hdr.ipv4.isValid()) {
            ipv4_lpm.apply();
        }
    }
}

/*********** EGRESS PROCESSING **************/

control MyEgress(inout headers hdr,
                 inout metadata meta,
                 inout standard_metadata_t standard_metadata) {
    apply { }
}

/********* CHECKSUM COMPUTATION **********/

control MyComputeChecksum(inout headers hdr, inout metadata meta) {
    apply {
    update_checksum(
        hdr.ipv4.isValid(),
          { hdr.ipv4.version,
          hdr.ipv4.ihl,
            hdr.ipv4.diffserv,
            hdr.ipv4.totalLen,
            hdr.ipv4.identification,
              hdr.ipv4.flags,
              hdr.ipv4.fragOffset,
              hdr.ipv4.ttl,
              hdr.ipv4.protocol,
              hdr.ipv4.srcAddr,
              hdr.ipv4.dstAddr },
            hdr.ipv4.hdrChecksum,
            HashAlgorithm.csum16);
    }
}

/***************** DEPARSER ********************/

control MyDeparser(packet_out packet, in headers hdr) {
```

```
    apply {
        packet.emit(hdr.ethernet);
        packet.emit(hdr.ipv4);
    }
}


/***************** SWITCH ************************/

V1Switch(
MyParser(),
MyVerifyChecksum(),
MyIngress(),
MyEgress(),
MyComputeChecksum(),
MyDeparser()
) main;
```

The next block is the checksum verifier followed by the ingress processing. This example does not specify a traffic manager. The following two blocks are egress processing and checksum computation. Finally, the deparser terminates the processing.

The definition of the V1 architecture is in the `v1model.p4` [8] included at the beginning of the example. The V1 architecture contains a construct package V1Switch<H, M> that lists the blocks of the V1 architecture. The `V1Switch()` at the end of the listing binds the P4 statements to the six blocks defined in the architecture.

From this example, it is evident that each P4 program must follow precisely the architecture for which it is written and that the compiler translates each section of the P4 program in code and configuration for the corresponding block on the architecture.

11.5 Implementing the P4Runtime API

The P4Runtime API [9] is "a control plane specification for controlling the data plane elements of a device defined or described by a P4 program." It is designed to be implemented in conjunction with the P4 16 language.

The significant P4Runtime features are:

- Runtime control of P4 objects (tables and value sets).

- Runtime control of PSA externs; for example, counters, meters, and action profiles.

- Runtime control of architecture-specific (non-PSA) externs, through an extension mechanism.

- I/O of control packets from the control plane.

The syntax follows the Protobuff format [10]. The client and the server communicate using gRPC [11], which is a perfect match for Protobuff (see section 3.4.2).

Figure 11-5 shows a complex solution in which three different servers manage the P4 pipeline: two remote and one embedded. For the target P4 pipeline, there is no difference between a P4Runtime client embedded or remote.

Both communications happen on gRPC and therefore on a TCP socket. Thus, there is no assumption that the control plane is collocated or separated from the data plane.

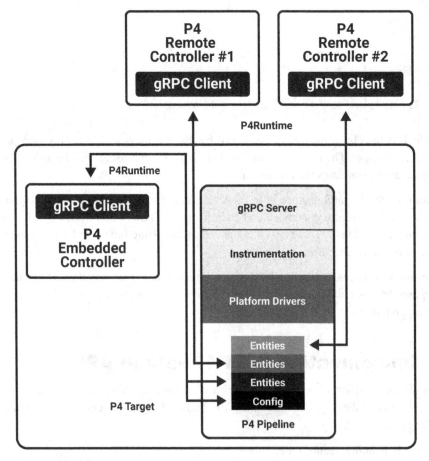

FIGURE 11-5   P4Runtime

11.6 Understanding the P4 INT

In P4 INT [12], a P4 device is instructed to add metadata information to each packet that it processes; for example, timestamp, device ID, and queue ID. The metadata is carried in the P4 INT header. This header can be hop-by-hop or end-to-end. P4 INT does not specify where to put the INT header in the packet.

The information inside the INT header helps answer questions such as:

- Which path did my packet take?

- How long was it queued on each device?

- Which other flows shared the queue with my packet?

There is no doubt that P4 INT allows an excellent understanding of packet propagation without requiring precise clock synchronization among network devices. The downside is the additional header that, depending on the placement on the packet, needs to be understood by different entities in the network and can potentially break implementations that are not P4 INT aware.

11.7 Extending P4

Although P4 is a good start, it could take advantage of some extensions to be better suited for implementing a DSN.

11.7.1 Portable NIC Architecture

Portable NIC Architecture (PNA) is the equivalent of a PSA for a NIC architecture. The P4 Architecture Working Group has discussed it, but at the time of writing there is not yet a final proposal.

To be able to model a NIC, one significant addition is a DMA engine capable of moving data to and from the host memory through the PCIe bus. The DMA engine should have the flexibility to assemble packets from data in memory through scatter and gather lists. A doorbell mechanism to interface the driver on the host should also exist.

A DMA engine is also crucial if a NIC needs to support RDMA and storage.

The availability of a PNA is essential to support a DSN implementation as a NIC.

11.7.2 Language Composability

Language composability is probably an overused term. In general, it refers to a design principle in which components can be easily selected and assembled in various combinations without any modifications to implement a specific set of features.

In this sense, P4 is not a composable language. It is similar to Verilog, strictly related to the hardware architecture; merging two P4 functions is a manual process that may involve a lot of rewriting.

Some preliminary attempts exist in this direction. For example, Mario Baldi's work at Cisco Systems [13] is a specific case of composability, as it allows a programmer to add features to an existing P4-coded data plane without having to have access to the existing source code, but the new feature must be written to fit the existing program.

In the most general case, composing functions that are written independently of each other would be desirable. A programmer should be able to add or remove features without having to rewrite the existing P4 code.

The P4 Language Design Working Group has discussed this issue in the past, but no solution has been adopted.

11.7.3   Better Programming and Development Tools

To make P4 successful, a large number of programmers need to have the means to design, write, compile, debug and profile P4 programs.

The P4 community provides an "alpha-quality reference compiler" that supports four standard backends. Each hardware vendor is in charge of adding its backend for its architecture. Unfortunately, we have already seen that the hardware architecture shapes how the P4 programs are written and limit their portability. If we want to address the aspect of "language composability," the backend needs to become much more sophisticated and be able to merge multiple programs and reallocate functions and resources in the pipeline.

These requirements seem to point in the direction of a P4 linker/loader that will also allow some programs not to be divulged in source form to protect intellectual property.

After a P4 program is compiled, understanding its behavior on real hardware may be tricky; for this reason, debugging and profiling tools are mandatory.

11.8   Summary

In this chapter, we reviewed the P4 architecture that brings runtime data plane programmability to ASIC. P4 is a domain-specific architecture targeted at network devices.

At the time of writing (2019), commercial P4 products are starting to be available; some of them are based on the Barefoot Networks Tofino switch [14] recently acquired by Intel [15].

The P4 language is a valuable way to specify the functionality of the data plane with a program for a manufacturer of network equipment or a large corporation, like a cloud provider. We have also discussed the fact that P4 is not a composable language, and unless this barrier is removed, it may be difficult for a small company or an individual programmer to add or remove features to a P4 network device.

11.9 Bibliography

[1] P. Bosshart, G. Gibb, H.-S. Kim, G. Varghese, N. McKeown, M. Izzard, F. Mujica, and M. Horowitz, "Forwarding metamorphosis: Fast programmable match-action processing in hardware for SDN," in ACM SIGCOMM, 2013.

[2] Pat Bosshart, Dan Daly, Glen Gibb, Martin Izzard, Nick McKeown, Jennifer Rexford, Cole Schlesinger, Dan Talayco, Amin Vahdat, George Varghese, and David Walker. 2014. P4: programming protocol-independent packet processors. SIGCOMM Comput. Commun. Rev. 44, 3 (July 2014), 87–95.

[3] P4 Language Consortium, https://p4.org

[4] The Open Networking Foundation (ONF), "P4," https://www.opennetworking.org/p4

[5] P4 16 Language Specification version 1.1.0, The P4 Language Consortium, 2018-11-30, https://p4.org/p4-spec/docs/P4-16-v1.1.0-spec.pdf

[6] P4 16 Portable Switch Architecture (PSA) Version 1.1, The P4.org Architecture Working Group, November 22, 2018, https://p4.org/p4-spec/docs/PSA-v1.1.0.pdf

[7] P4 Tutorial, https://github.com/p4lang/tutorials

[8] Barefoot Networks, Inc., "P4 v1.0 switch model," https://github.com/p4lang/p4c/blob/master/p4include/v1model.p4

[9] P4Runtime Specification, version 1.0.0, The P4.org API Working Group, 2019-01-29, https://s3-us-west-2.amazonaws.com/p4runtime/docs/v1.0.0/P4Runtime-Spec.pdf

[10] Protocol Buffers, https://developers.google.com/protocol-buffers

[11] gRPC, https://grpc.io

[12] Inband Network Telemetry (INT) Dataplane Specification, working draft, The P4.org Application Working Group, 2018-08-17, https://github.com/p4lang/p4-applications/blob/master/docs/INT.pdf

[13] Mario Baldi, "Demo at the P4 workshop 2019," May 2019, Stanford University.

[14] Barefoot Networks, "Tofino: World's fastest P4-programmable Ethernet switch ASICs," https://barefootnetworks.com/products/brief-tofino

[15] https://newsroom.intel.com/editorials/intel-acquire-barefoot-networks

Chapter 12

Management Architectures for DS Platforms

Distribution provides better resilience, scale benefits, and failure domain localization when compared to centralized systems. However, it poses a challenge of coherently managing a large number of DSNs. A well-architected management control plane not only provides management simplicity, but also offers a comprehensive view of the system and clusterwide insights. Simplification comes from providing intuitive abstractions of user concepts for configuring the system, showing relevant information for operationalizing the infrastructure, and extracting meaningful information from the vast amount of data collected over time. A comprehensive view of the system makes it easier to operate and aggregate information while hiding the unwanted details. A management control plane can provide insights from correlation and offer better visualization to operate infrastructure services efficiently.

Figure 12-1 describes the components of a distributed management control plane. To ensure resiliency and scale, DSN management system should be implemented as a distributed application running on multiple "control nodes."

As shown in Figure 12-1, DSNs are network managed, where each DSN communicates with the management plane over an IP network. Managing DSNs from the network is similar to how infrastructure is managed in a public cloud, separating consumers of infrastructure from the infrastructure itself.

This chapter describes the architectural elements of a distributed management services control plane and concludes with a proposed architecture, combining various concepts for a distributed management control plane.

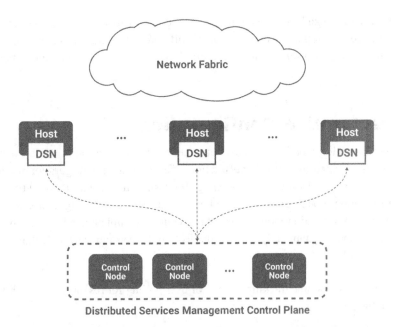

FIGURE 12-1 Distributed Services Management Control Plane

12.1 Architectural Traits of a Management Control Plane

If a management control plane were built like a modern multi-tier scale-out distributed application, then it would inherit all the benefits of such applications. Although the benefits, such as scale, composability, high availability, and so on are enticing, the challenges of debuggability, distribution, synchronization, and so on can be complex and time consuming. Simplification requires shielding the underlying complexity, especially for clusterwide services that require managing and coordinating multiple DSNs.

An architectural approach to address these challenges would offer a solution that can easily withstand the complexities that arise from scale, distribution, network partitioning, and operationalization. The elements of such a system would allow users to specify the intent declaratively and be built using a set of microservices. Consequently, they would provide a malleable cloud native application that could be deployed not only on-premise but also on any public cloud microservices platform. Microservices architecture can offer many benefits, such as decentralization, scale, upgradeability, resilience, and independence, assuming common pitfalls of application design are avoided. Generally speaking, if a microservice is built to serve a business function, it should offer a clean set of APIs that serves a user-visible feature and is likely to provide a simpler implementation. Therefore, a top-down approach, where business functions drive the APIs and functional abstraction, is preferred over a bottom-up approach of exposing engineering design to become a business function.

Although the term *service* can be confusing in the context of distributed services platform, this chapter uses the term *business function* to mean what really is offered as an infrastructure service by distributed services platform, and the term *service* may be referred to as a microservice that implements a business function.

12.2   Declarative Configuration

A declarative configuration model allows users to specify the desired intent while the system works toward achieving the desired intent. This abstraction offers a simpler configuration model to the user as the system constantly works toward reconciling the desired intent with the reality. In contrast, an imperative configuration model takes an immediate action before returning a success or a failure to the user. Imperative configuration models cannot be accurately implemented when a system grows to thousands of DSNs, some dynamically joining and leaving the system. The advantages of declarative configuration are as follows:

- System automates resource tracking instead of user polling for resource availability to instantiate the policy

- System can be optimized for policy distribution to the available DSNs

- Omission of tracking external dependencies; for example, workloads coming up and going away, integration with ecosystem partners, and so on

- Automation of failure handling, such as network disconnection, partitioning, reconciliation upon such events, and moving toward zero touch configuration management

- Scheduling future work; for example, upgrades and monitoring based on events

These advantages make it easier for the user to operationalize the system. In turn, the system offers full visibility about the status of the instantiated behavior for the specified intent. Figure 12-2 describes the mechanics of event watchers, a key concept in implementing a reconciliation loop.

The declarative configuration model is better suited for systems that offer generic resources at scale; for example, software-like scalable resources on DSNs. Not having rigid limits or specialized resources allows the control plane to accept the intent with a reasonable guarantee that the admitted policy will be instantiated, as long as there are no connectivity issues. Even upon disconnection and subsequent reconnection, the system could successfully reconcile the desired intent. The architecture to achieve declarative configuration requires upfront validation of any acceptable configuration, including syntax, semantics, authentication, authorization, and relational validations. The expectation from the system is that once the intent is admitted into the system, it can't be given back to the user for amendments. After this time, it becomes the system's responsibility to save and act upon the configuration. System services watch for user configuration changes and run reconciliation loops to instantiate the latest intent.

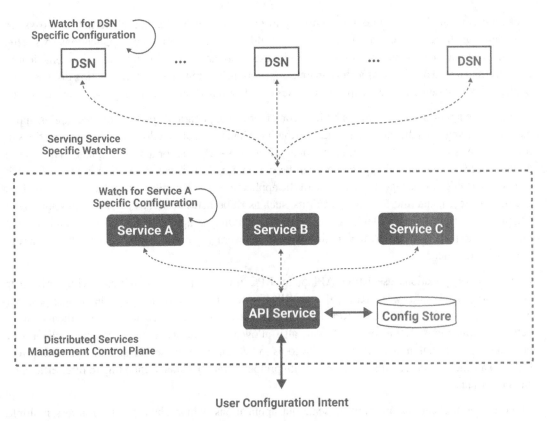

FIGURE 12-2 Implementation of Declarative Configuration

Declarative configuration is easy to back up and restore because the intent is inherently independent of the order in which the configuration was done. This presents a user with a simpler way to describe, copy, back up, and make changes to the configuration. Implementing transactional semantics in a declarative configuration also ensures that validation can be done across multiple objects together instead of having individual API objects configured into the system.

12.3 Building a Distributed Control Plane as a Cloud-Native Application

Cloud-native applications are portable, modular, exposed via APIs, scalable, and are policy driven. The most important aspect is their portability, making it easy to migrate between private and public clouds. The Cloud Native Computing Foundation (CNCF) [1] is a governing body under the Linux Foundation for many open source projects, which helps developers build cloud-native applications. Cloud-native applications are portable because they are implemented using normalized assumptions about the infrastructure resources they need to run on. They are built as stateless applications and, therefore, are easy to autoscale. They are built using functional component boundaries that interact with each other using backward compatible APIs, making them easy to grow independently. The cloud-native ecosystem provides a plethora of frameworks and tools to build, operate, and run such applications. Also, the vibrant open source community and the prevalent use in so many products makes it more practical to build the management system as a cloud-native application. The remainder of this section discusses the applicability of cloud-native concepts as it relates to a distributed services management control plane.

Cloud-native applications are always built as containerized applications to allow for decoupling application packaging from the underlying OS distribution. Containerization allows building applications in the developer's language of choice, be it Golang, Rust, C++, Python, or a new language that is yet to be developed. Containerized applications can be run on a microservices orchestration platform, such as Kubernetes [2], to manage the life cycle of the application. The benefits of containerization, such as use of Docker [3], and microservice platforms, such as Kubernetes or Mesos [4], are well known (see Chapter 3, "Virtualization"). One obvious benefit for building an application as a set of containerized microservices is to speed up the feature delivery, while leveraging mature open source software to run, upgrade, and scale.

Cloud-native applications use REST API or an RPC framework to communicate with each other (see sections 3.4.1 and 3.4.2). gRPC [5] is an RPC framework, often built alongside Google protocol buffers (protobuf) [6], to define the RPC messages and marshalling and demarshalling of the messages between applications. Using protobufs can also allow using various tools to generate client API bindings, documentation, and other code for tools to help manage the services. Although JSON over REST is a generic user-friendly API, gRPC with protobuf employs binary encoding to offer efficiency and performance.

Cloud-native applications are built as scale-out applications, which share the load across multiple instances. To share the load of incoming API requests, microservices are often accessed via a network or an application load balancer. A load balancer function can be implemented as a proxy software, such as Envoy [7] or Nginx [8], intercepting the messages between two applications using service discovery mechanisms. Alternatively, a load balancer can also be a logical function that is packaged as a library within the application itself, often referred to as client-side load balancing. Client-side load balancing is implemented as part of the RPC layer; for example using Finagle [9] or gRPC. Client-side load balancing offers lower latency and efficiency than an external Network Load Balancer (NLB) because it avoids one extra hop, but it requires application architecture to use the prescribed RPC mechanism. In contrast, independently running load balancers can be inserted in an application topology without the need to change the applications.

Cloud-native applications need sophisticated troubleshooting tooling because of their distributed nature. To trace the path traversed by messages between microservices, the tooling must carry the message context across the RPC messages. Then it can correlate message context information with observed failures and help the developer diagnose problems. Tools such as OpenZipkin [10] utilize the OpenTracing [11] protocol and methods to offer integration with gRPC and/or HTTP layers to allow message tracing across services and improved troubleshooting capabilities.

To summarize, building a management control plane as a cloud-native application is not only beneficial for the features it offers, but also speeds development given the mature, open source tooling available.

12.4 Monitoring and Troubleshooting

Observability and troubleshooting capabilities are essential in the management control plane as well as the architectural aspects required to build these capabilities natively in the control plane.

DSNs can be expected to provide highly scalable data paths; for example, hundreds of thousands of network sessions, a large number of RDMA sessions, and storage service functions. The amount of data gathered on just one DSN can be inundating. Therefore, the amount of data collected within the entire cluster, consisting of thousands of DSNs, would need sophisticated data collection, query, and presentation techniques. Use of a distributed database as a part of a management control plane helps with increased scale and redundancy. In addition, using multiple kinds of databases may be needed, such as a:

- **Time series database:** To help observe usage and trends over time

- **Search database:** To help with arbitrary text search of events, logs, and configuration

- **SQL database:** To help manage system inventory

- **Graph database:** To help track data relationships

Most of these databases offer a query language and mathematical functions to help perform aggregate functions to get meaningful insights.

The mechanisms discussed here can be useful for both monitoring applications on the system and for troubleshooting the system itself. For example, trends on resource usage or failures can proactively provide hints about the potential problems. The data collected about applications can provide insights such as top users of the resources, workloads with highest security violations, and network or storage latency between applications. Given that the management control plane has full view of all workloads and their locality, it can offer automation tools to troubleshoot the network-wide issues by examining the collected data or sending stimulus data and measuring the behavior within the network. This can help troubleshoot network issues, storage performance measurements, or provide data that can lead to identifying and addressing anomalies.

Architecturally, the system should be designed to proactively notify the user when the first signs of the problem are detected. Traditional "reactive troubleshooting" takes place only after a problem (soft failure or a hard failure) has surfaced and requires domain expertise to properly diagnose. The availability of historical data can play a significant role here in helping determine anomalies, thus leading to a proactive nature of system diagnostics and troubleshooting application connectivity, performance, or latency. The notion of normalcy and definition of exception path is very relative to deployment and user. Therefore, providing a way for the user to define or help learn the anomaly could train the system, possibly by leveraging self-learning mechanisms to take out any false positives.

To promote easy consumption of data, the metrics should be associated with a configured object. This makes metrics a first-class concept available for every configured object, even though metrics can be internally managed differently from the status of an object.

12.5   Securing the Management Control Plane

The management control plane communicates highly sensitive information to the DSNs over an IP network. If this information is tampered with, blocked by, or even read by unauthorized actor, it can lead to a severe security lapse and implications that can have long-lasting consequences. Although the typical recommendation is to keep the management network isolated from the rest of the infrastructure, it breaks the security model if the management network is compromised. Instead, a security framework for the management control plane should be responsible for ensuring the identity management, authentication, authorization, and encryption of the traffic independent of the underlying network connectivity and assumptions.

Identity establishment and identity verification is the most important first step in ensuring the security posture of the system. Distributed entities like DSNs and control plane software components would need to be given cryptographic identities. Then, a mechanism should be in place to have these entities prove their identity to each other before they start to exchange information. First, DSNs should be able to prove their cryptographic identity, using an X.509 certificate, for example, that the management control plane can trust. DSNs can use hardware security modules such as the Trusted Platform Module (TPM) [12] or latch on to the trust chain of underlying booted root of trust to assert their identity. Second, microservice applications running within the control plane across a set of compute nodes need to provide their identity to each other to establish trust. Secure Production Identity Framework for Everyone (SPIFFE) [13] is an open effort that attempts to standardize the application identity and mechanisms to perform mutual authentication among those entities using a common root of trust before they communicate over an untrusted network.

Using mutual Transport Layer Security (TLS) for all communication between control plane services and DSNs should be an integral component of the security architecture. RPC frameworks, such as gRPC, support TLS natively, paving a way to secure the communication. The management control plane must become the certificate authority (CA) for all the components and is also responsible for providing mechanisms to sign the certificates; the system should ensure that this can be done without ever having to share the private keys. TLS is proven to provide security across the Internet; it ensures all user data is encrypted and can never be eavesdropped on by a middle man. It also provides non-repudiation for auditing and traceability. Figure 12-3 shows the key management and TLS between various entities within the cluster.

In addition to authentication, an authorization layer is needed to help ensure proper permissions for communication; for example, a list of permissible connections and API operations. Typically, one doesn't need a very elaborate authorization policy between the components of a microservices platform, but a basic authorization would define which communication is permitted, respecting the application layering of the infrastructure.

The Role-Based Access Control (RBAC) layer defines what an external user of the management control plane can or cannot do. An external user can be a human making modifications to the control plane via GUI or CLI, or it can be an automation script or software component interacting with the system using a REST or gRPC API. The control plane must define the notion of users, roles, permissions and allow assigning permissions to the roles and eventually users having access to those roles. The users may need to be obtained from the organization's database, using integration with Lightweight Directory

Access Protocol (LDAP) servers. Furthermore, the granularity of these roles needs to be sufficient to permit a variety of operations on individual objects or object categories. Naturally, keeping an audit log of all API calls into the system also becomes an important aspect of authorization.

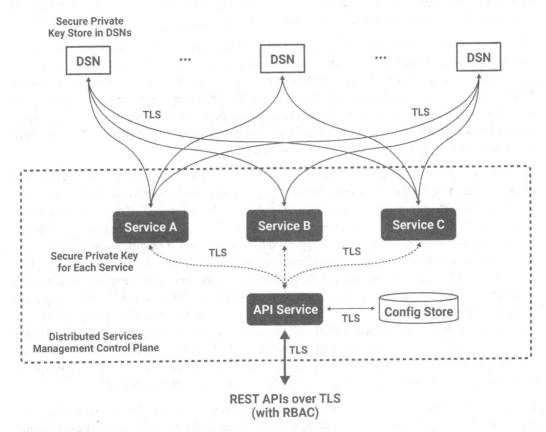

FIGURE 12-3   Security Model of Management Control Plane

12.6   Ease of Deployment

A management control plane has multiple independent services, making it complex to deploy and operate. However, a well-designed system will be easy to install, configure, and operationalize, while hiding the underlying complexity. Unwanted details are often forced upon users, possibly exposing them to architectural deficiencies. Designing for simplicity does not necessarily require trade-offs around security, functionality, scalability, and performance. This section discusses the architectural elements of the management control plane that can make it simple to use, yet not compromise on other attributes such as security, scale, and so on.

To make it easy to deploy the control plane software, the packaging should include all components with minimal configuration to bootstrap the control plane. This can be done if the software is bundled to bootstrap easily on a physical or virtual machine. After the control plane is started, it then can kick-start all the required services and provide a startup wizard to perform day-0 setup. In situations when a user has brought up a microservices deployment platform such as Kubernetes, the management control plane can be deployed using tools like Helm [14]. Deploying on Kubernetes can be easier in a public cloud as most of the public clouds provide a managed Kubernetes service.

DSNs are expected to be added or removed dynamically from the cluster, presenting another day-0 operation requiring simplification to accommodate detection, discovery, and admission of DSNs into the management control plane. When a DSN is brought up, it must discover the management control domain-name address to be able to communicate with it. This discovery can be automated by having a network service that is expected to be always up, either in a public cloud or on-premise responding to the beacons sent by DSNs. Other network-based discovery mechanisms, such as DHCP service, may also be employed for DSN to discover the control plane.

Simplification of day-1 and day-2 operations, such as configuring, troubleshooting, upgrading, and so on, require many architectural considerations. Specifically, the system must provide an object model that accurately captures business functions, offers visibility into the system, and allows ease of migrating to new features in a backward-compatible way. The system should also build ample API integration points and client libraries ensuring smoother integration into existing software tools. Most of the software and systems, both commercial and open source software used in deployment and operations, provide APIs and infrastructure to add plugins; for example, pre-baked recipes to be used with configuration management tools such as Ansible, Chef, or Puppet. Integration with syslog importers can help users unify their logging analysis tools. Creating recipes for application deployment and for upgrade operations, using tools such as Helm or charts for Kubernetes, can help users to use validated packaging. Many users bring their own metrics analysis tools. Therefore, design goals should focus on easy integration of metrics and schema with visualization tools such as Grafana, or Kibana. Providing plugins for integrated stacks, such as ELK [15] or TICK [16], could help, if applicable.

To simplify operations, troubleshooting and diagnosis tools offered by the management control plane must provide an end-to-end perspective and stay operational even in the case of partial failures within the system itself. To achieve the highest resilience, the diagnostic software and tools require operating within a context of "reserved" resource allocation and isolation, so that diagnostic tools can operate even when the system is under unusual stress, failure, or resource exhaustion. Ensuring stability and reliability of diagnostic tools is paramount for troubleshooting the broader infrastructure via the management control plane. Conversely, the diagnostic tools should not cause any instability. Section 12.4 discusses some of the tools that can be used to troubleshoot infrastructure problems.

12.7 Performance and Scale

Scaling a distributed system is a topic of heavy research and exploration [17] with a focus on achieving consensus, replication, high availability, transactions, concurrency, performance, and scalability. The techniques include distributed consensus building, lock-free synchronization, workload distribution sharding, caching and cache invalidation, division of a work with parallelism, data replication consistency, and so on. A discussion on these techniques is outside the scope of this book; readers are encouraged to look at the references. These techniques have been successfully used in consistent key-value store implementations such as Zookeeper [18] or Etcd [19], distributed time series databases such as Prometheus [20] or InfluxDB [21], distributed NoSQL databases such as Cassandra [22], MongoDB [23] or Redis [24], distributed SQL databases such as CockroachDB [25], distributed object stores such as Minio [26], distributed search DBs such as ElasticDB [27], and distributed message buses, such as Kafka [28] or NATS [29]. The plethora of the tooling is somewhat inundating, but as we get deeper into the use cases and their architectures, one thing becomes clear: Different solutions exist to solve different business problems. Therefore, choosing the right database, key-value store, or message bus should be based on the nature of data produced by the DSNs and within the management control plane. In fact, microservices architecture calls for using these elements for individual business functions instead of combining all the requirements into a single back-end database. Splitting these functional aspects not only allows the independent scaling of each business function, but also facilitates horizontal scaling of each entity, improving control plane performance. Furthermore, architecturally it allows the control plane to solve scalability by merely adding more general-purpose compute resources, without creating a single point of failure or performance bottleneck.

The scale of a distributed platform is defined by the following factors:

- **Number of DSNs:** This measures the control plane's ability to serve a large set of DSNs. Each DSN is a managed entity in itself and, therefore, requires additional work to manage their life cycle, such as discovery, monitoring, upgrading, and so on. Every DSN within the cluster increases the management plane's burden to handle more events, generate more metrics, and distribute policies to a larger set of entities. On the other hand, this scale parameter should be as high as possible to avoid splitting the cluster, which is a burden for the operator. However, note that multiple management domains or clusters may be applicable where there are limits based on connectivity regions or the maximum size of the failure domain.

- **Number of objects:** Configuration is typically managed using Create, Read, Update, and Delete (CRUD) operations on published REST APIs. Each configured object represents a conceptual instance of the desired function. Therefore, increases in cluster size or workload density result in more objects being instantiated within the system. More objects result in more data to be saved, increased number of metrics, and, most importantly, an increase in the quantity of objects to be distributed to the applicable recipients.

- **API performance:** This is the control plane's ability to serve a large number of user requests per second. More is always better; however, care should be taken to determine the nature of requests on various objects. To serve an API request successfully, the management plane would need to authenticate, authorize, and perform validation checks on the API call. Thus, scaling the rate of APIs may require running multiple entry points into the cluster, and/or improving the caching to serve the read operations much faster.

- **Metrics scale:** This is the control plane's ability to ingest the millions of metrics produced every second by the system either on DSNs or within the control plane and requires selecting an appropriate metrics database with enough redundancy and horizontal scale built with sharding methodologies. Time series databases (TSDBs) are a good choice to manage metrics and perform queries on the data, perform aggregation functions, and so on.

- **Events scale:** This is the control plane's ability to handle the vast number of events generated by various distributed entities in the cluster. The aspects of handling the scale of events in a distributed system include dealing with the sheer volume of the events generated by various entities in the system, and the control plane's ability to find user-actionable tasks from those events. In addition, all events and logs may need to be exported to an external collector. When events are produced at very large scale, the greatest challenge becomes finding ways to take meaningful action and ways to create correlation between certain events, system state, metrics, and user actions. This correlation and analysis is best done using sophisticated tooling, described earlier in this section.

- **Data plane scale:** This is the management control plane's ability to handle the data generated by the data path; for example, metrics, logs, searchable records of data path activity, and so on. Ultimately, the purpose of the distributed services platform is to provide services in the data path for the workloads; therefore, the ability to deal with a scalable data path is critical.

Later in the chapter, we discuss how to test the scale of such a system.

12.8   Failure Handling

A system is incomplete without its ability to handle various internal or external failures. Therefore, architecting a system with the assumption that failures will occur is the most natural way of dealing with the problem. Although failure handling complicates the system architecture, it is required to ensure reliable operation.

The mechanisms to handle failures vary depending on the problem, but the balance between providing redundancy, efficiency, and performance is important. These mechanisms include:

- **Data replication:** Data replication can avoid loss of data due to a single failure. Of course, n-way replication may result in better resiliency, but at the cost of reduced performance. Most of the distributed databases that we discuss in this chapter are capable of replicating the data and continue to be fully operational in case of failure(s).

- **Network redundancy:** Redundant network connectivity can easily handle link failure, network element failure, or a DSN failure and will ensure the infrastructure can converge using alternative connectivity with minimal disruption.

- **Resource acquisition on demand:** Providing the system with extra processing capacity ensures that system can overflow into spare available resources that can be acquired on demand.

Implementing the control plane as a cloud-native application, such as via Kubernetes, helps with resource acquisition and scheduling on demand by the infrastructure software.

- **Reconciliation:** Network failures can result in distributed entities going out of sync. After the network connectivity is restored, distributed entities must reconcile with the latest user intent. As discussed earlier, a declarative model helps distributed entities reconcile the system to the latest intent.

- **In-service upgrade:** Rollout of newer versions of the management control plane can be done leveraging the underlying features of the cloud-native infrastructure capabilities, such as via Kubernetes, to upgrade the microservices components one at a time to allow for the older version to be phased out without requiring any disruption to the applications. Doing this upgrade requires building backward-compatible APIs so that applications don't need to be upgraded together. We discuss more about API architecture in the subsequent section.

The minimum expectation from a management system is to handle any single point of failure without disruption and be able to recover the system from multiple simultaneous failures with minimal or no impact to the users. There are nonrecoverable failures and recoverable failures. Recoverable failures generally happen due to software malfunction such as a process crash; a correctable human error such as a configuration error; or connectivity issues such as network miscabling. Nonrecoverable failures happen due to hardware failures, such as memory errors, disk failures, transmission device failures, or power supply failures. Nonrecoverable failures can be hard failures or soft failures. A hard failure is abrupt and typically unpredictable; for example, system halt. Therefore, failure handling must take into consideration that it may never get a chance to predict the failure. Failures that start slow and grow over time are referred to as soft failures (not to be confused with soft*ware* failures). Examples include deterioration in a disk's life, bit errors increasing in the I/O hardware, or a software memory leak slowly degrading the usability of the system. Ideally, soft failures can be detected based on trends of relevant metrics going in a specific direction (either non-increasing or non-decreasing, depending on the metric).

Placing all control nodes behind a load balancer with a discoverable IP address ensures the best possible serviceability of the management control plane. Doing so allows the serving of the external users without any disruption and can also improve the overall performance by sharing the incoming API requests among multiple instances of the service.

12.9 API Architecture

APIs are the user-facing programmable interface into the management control plane. Graphical user interface (GUI) and command line interface (CLI) use the APIs to provide other mechanisms to manage the system. APIs ought to be simple to use, intuitive to understand, be highly performant, and ensure security with authenticated and authorized access into the system. The APIs must also be backward compatible, self-documenting, and scalable. Figure 12-4 describes a sample set of components comprising the API layer of the management control plane.

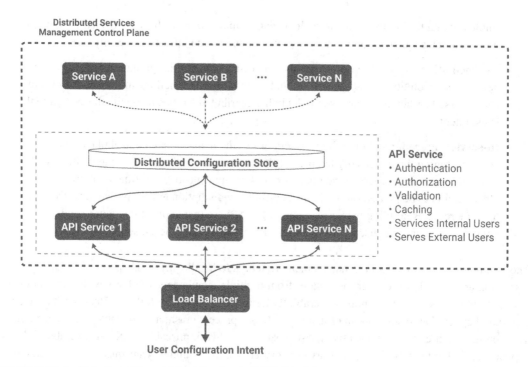

FIGURE 12-4   Functionality and Architecture of API Service

Now, we discuss the design choices to achieve these desired attributes:

- **Simple to use:** System APIs should be easy to learn; for example, REST/JSON APIs may be a familiar interface to many users. Another important aspect of making the APIs simpler is if the documentation itself is available as part of the API, which describes the objects and their fields. Although not always possible, if the structure of the API objects uses a familiar semantic structure, it could simplify understanding the APIs. Providing client bindings in popular languages to access the APIs can ease the integration challenges. The importance of APIs returning meaningful error messages can be very helpful in improving the API usability. Using automation tools to generate the client bindings or documentation can also avoid the human errors in translating the repeatable part of things. A simplified URL path for various objects in the REST APIs can provide an easy way for the user to interact with the system using commonly available tools to manage REST APIs.

- **API security:** The API being the entry point into the system exposes an attack surface. It is important to tie every single object/API access to the users and their roles. Further, the granularity of various actions, including create, update, get, delete, and so on, should also be tied to the RBAC model. The API should only be accessible over an encrypted transport such as HTTPS/TLS. The mechanism must employ short-lived certificates or time-limited JSON Web Tokens (JWT) [30] given to specific users for a configurable time period. This ensures that even when credentials are compromised, the impact of the compromise is limited. Only very specific user roles must be able to alter the credentials of the user; that is, modify the RBAC objects. And in case of a compromise, users should be able to revoke the credentials right away. The control plane can also be subjected to DoS attack, where a huge number of API requests can prevent authorized users from accessing the system; therefore, it can help to employ rate limiting to restrict the number of API calls per object(s) per user. Finally, simple proven measures like accepting all incoming requests on one TCP port can help reduce the attach surface, and, of course, not leaving any backdoors open to unauthorized access. Note, however, that RBAC not only controls the rights to perform CRUD operations, but also what data is returned based on the user role.

- **API auditing:** It is an important security aspect of the system to be able to audit all API calls into the system; therefore, preserving the audit logs for the longest possible period with all required details can offer the user a glimpse of answers to who accessed the API, when it was accessed, why it was permitted, what operation was performed, and from where it was done. A searchable audit log goes a long way in improving the security posture of the management control plane.

- **Performance and scale:** API performance comes from a reduction in the amount of back-end processing to perform the functions such as authentication, authorization, object syntax validation, semantic validation, auditing, and so on. Therefore, employing caching can improve the performance. Doing multiple validations and other error checks in parallel threads can result in quicker response. In addition to improving the overall API processing times, serving the APIs in all scale-out instances in the control plane nodes can also allow for horizontal scale.

- **Backward compatibility:** API compatibility becomes relevant as the adoption and ecosystem around the APIs start to build. As a general rule, the API should have a very good reason to break the compatibility, and when this is needed it should be versioned; that is, a new version should support the new API while the control plane continues to support the older version of the API to ensure older users can use the system without any impact, yet providing them a chance to move to the newer version if they want to move to newer functionality. Using the REST/JSON structure can allow adding incremental fields to existing objects easily without breaking backward compatibility. However, a semantic change in the object relationship or a change in the meaning of the field would need a version update.

- **Debuggability:** Dry-runs on API calls without impacting the system behavior gives users a way to play with the APIs and ensures that the understanding of various fields and parameters is correct. Furthermore, precise error codes and crisp error messages can improve API debuggability significantly.

- **Transactional semantics:** Often, the user may want to commit creation or modification of multiple objects atomically. The API backend would need to support transactional semantics to allow the user to create these objects together, validate them as a single unit, and then commit them all at once.

12.10   Federation

This section explains the concept of federation of multiple software defined services platforms (SDSPs). We cover some common reasons for adopting a federated policy-driven management architecture.

Before talking about federation of management, it's worth reviewing common nonfederated service management. Perhaps the most common architecture is "centralized management," because it works well in small to midsize environments in a single location. In a centralized management system architecture there is typically one SDSP (which itself could consist of multiple distributed control nodes) located in a single location or data center.

One of the core responsibilities of the SDSP is to perform full life-cycle management of DSNs, which includes the following:

- Admission, or allow a DSN to join the SDSP management domain
- Inventory
- Monitoring
- Upgrades and downgrades
- Policy distribution; services, rules and behaviors, and so on
- Decommission, or remove a DSN from the SDSP

The SDSP typically also provides other crucial functions such as:

- RBAC
- Multi-tenancy
- Systemwide monitoring and alerting
- Systemwide telemetry correlation and reporting
- Auditing
- Log collection of distributed services (such as firewall, workloads and load-balancers, and so on)
- Tools for diagnostics and troubleshooting
- Systemwide software and image management

In this architecture, the SDSP is considered to be the "single source of truth" for all the policies and configurations in the domain. That said, it is common that the actual source of truth for rules and desired behaviors and so on comes from an external system, such as a custom configuration management database (CMDB). Rules and configurations are often pushed to the SDSP via a REST-based API or gRPC from an orchestration engine or similar.

12.10.1 Scaling a Single SDSP

A SDSP can become resource constrained in aspects such as capacity (space for logs, events, audits, policies, stats, and so on) or performance (processing of policies, events, telemetry, and other system services) due to factors such as an increased number of managed DSNs in the domain and/or an increased number of workloads or services enabled such as firewalls, load balancers, and so on. Typically, a SDSP can be scaled in a scale-out or scale-up fashion. But in practice, single SDSP scales only to a certain point, for reasons we will discuss later.

Scale-up is often the simplest solution, where each distributed node gets upgraded (or moved to a different compute system) with more resources such as CPU cores, memory, and storage. However, this often becomes an expensive solution compared to scale-out, and it is typically neither practical nor possible to scale up nodes indefinitely.

Scale-out is often a better solution, where additional controller nodes are added to the SDSP, allowing for redistribution of microservices as well as increasing the number of microservices, therefore reducing the average load on each controller node. However, adding too many nodes to a SDSP may cause challenges, as well, especially when data needs to be persistent and consistent across all the nodes. Such systems are built to scale linearly, but at some point, adding too many nodes can result in increased latency or reduced performance benefit for each added node (that is, non-linear scaling), often caused by system updates such as events, statistics, states, and config changes, as more nodes participate in the update. Building a large scale-out distributed system that maintains low latency as it scales is a lot more challenging than building one targeted for delivering high throughput; see Figure 12-5.

There are other reasons why having a single SDSP may not be practical. A single SDSP domain does provide resiliency against failures (for individual or multinode failures), but a single SDSP can be considered a failure domain in itself. Even the most sophisticated and stable systems are not guaranteed to be protected against bugs and infrastructure failures. For many customers, the SDSP size is limited by an acceptable security zone size to reduce the attack surface. Also, in consideration of managing DSNs across multiple data centers with disaster recovery (DR) in mind, a single SDSP may not be practical.

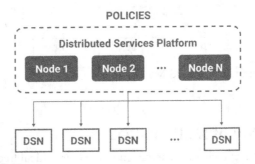

FIGURE 12-5 A Single DS Manager

To address these challenges, we propose using multiple SDSPs as the preferred approach. A multiple SDSP approach can be architected by using a distributed SDSP architecture or by a federated SDSP architecture. Both options are discussed in the following sections.

12.10.2   Distributed Multiple SDSPs

One approach to reduce a domain size is to create multiple distributed SDSPs. Such an approach can be done within a single data center or across data centers. In this architecture, each SDSP acts as an independent system, and the SDSPs coexist as peers. In this approach, global policies are distributed and applied across these independent systems. This is a common architectural approach for such systems, because there are typically few modifications needed with respect to the centralized single domain model. However, this approach does introduce certain complexity: As the architecture scales out to larger numbers, it increases the risks for consequential configuration drifts and potential policy consistency issues across the SDSPs due to synchronizations or human configuration drifts. Visibility and troubleshooting can be challenging, because each SDSP has its own view of the world and works independently of others. Troubleshooting and correlation of events between these systems can sometimes be challenging; see Figure 12-6.

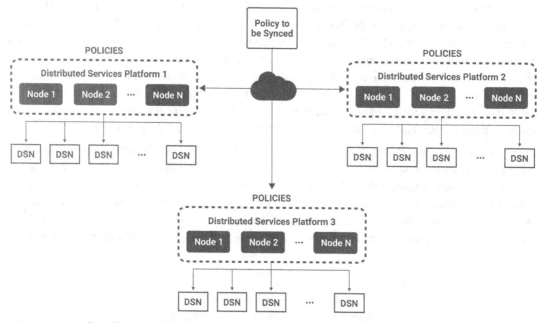

FIGURE 12-6   Distribution of Multiple DS Managers

12.10.3   Federation of Multiple SDSPs

Federation is a different concept where the architecture is a hierarchical treelike structure rather than a peer architecture, operating more as a single system across multiple domains; see Figure 12-7.

The Federated Service Manager (FSM) would typically provide centralized systemwide services and manage high-level policy definitions, rather than individual domain-specific data such as local IP addresses, networks, and so on. These polices use high-level descriptors like names or labels to describe the intent. A high-level policy terminates on a named reference, rather than an actual attribute value. These names or labels are later resolved into something meaningful and specific with respect to the SDSP domain itself (domain-specific data). Examples of high-level policies can be:

- Authorization policies (for example, no local user authentication allowed, only external authentication via RADIUS or LDAP)

- Network services, such as security policies

- Backup schedule definitions

- Optional versus mandatory network services (for example, load balancer is optional; firewall is mandatory)

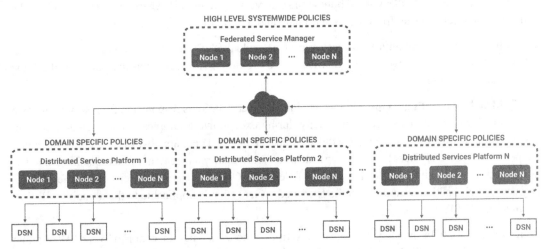

FIGURE 12-7 Federation of Multiple DS Managers

Each SDSP contains domain-specific policies and configurations relevant to its own management domain and resources. Individual SDSPs also have their own understanding of how to resolve a named reference in a high-level policy definition (the attribute value or data). In this way, the system can work in harmony and reduce the risk of drifts and policy inconsistency.

For example, if each SDSP has two networks labeled Database and AppX, and each SDSP domain uses different subnets and VLAN IDs for these networks. And let's say there is a high-level FSM policy describing firewall rules for the two networks, Database and AppX. Each SDSP receives the high-level FSM policy and will then individually resolve these labels based on its own definition of subnet and VLAN IDs; the SDSP then applies the rules based on its knowledge of the definition. From an FSM level the rules are the same, but on the SDSP level the definitions are different.

This architecture brings systemwide benefits, including:

- Global policy definition and enforcement
- Visibility
- Event correlations
- Troubleshooting
- Reporting
- A centralized software and image repository

The architecture enforces system policies top down and policies are inherited if they could not be provided locally within SDSP. Global policies also serve as "guidelines" where the system resolves the policy in a hierarchical way from the local domain and up into the scope of the parent.

The policy would first attempt to be resolved at individual SDSP level (in a hierarchical way) if it exists. If it cannot be resolved at the SDSP level, it would be resolved from the policy in the FSM instead (also hierarchical).

The FSM and the SDSPs are typically loosely coupled. Each SDSP is responsible for resolving its own policies and each domain can act individually during exceptions. Examples would include a disconnection from the federated system (scheduled or unscheduled). There are always exceptions that could happen, where a SDSP must be able to operate as an individual management system outside the federation for a period of time and later rejoin the federation. Once the SDSP has rejoined the federation, any new policies added or updated in the federated system (that is applicable to the domain) will flow down to the SDSP.

Policy relevance can be managed through a subscription model and pull mechanism by the SDSP, rather than by push from the Federated Service Manager. Each SDSP would be responsible for requesting policies from the federated system. However, if the SDSP has made local changes to any existing policy (during a disconnected state) that conflicts with the high-level policy in the Federation Service Manager, the system needs to detect and identify any conflicts that require a resolution. The action to resolve the conflict is typically taken from the SDSP rather than the FSM. The system should provide insight into what the conflict looks like, provide impact analysis, and propose various resolutions.

One caveat or anti-pattern is to refrain from having domain policy definitions synced up to the federation level, because this could conflict with other SDSPs in the same federation. Similar challenges would also exist for the distributed SDSP model, discussed previously.

Explicitly overriding inherited policies may not be recommended either, but may be necessary in certain circumstances, such as if a change was made that violates some fundamental security setting; for example, a local authentication exception.

There are numerous ways to resolve global versus local policy conflicts. In some instances, conflicts can be automatically resolved. But there are no single "silver bullets" or axioms to apply automatically for resolving policy conflicts. In general, resolution will come down to human intervention and common sense from the administrators involved. Time is also an important factor in policy conflict resolution. Sometimes resolution can be delayed; sometimes resolution needs to be immediate, depending on the conflict.

A federated system monitors the health of the individual SDSPs and related components in the system. The FSM can also often provide centralized services such as a repository of secure and verified software images for the SDSP to consume. The FSM typically has some kind of dashboard, which provides a single systemwide, correlated view of all the individual domains as well as troubleshooting tools. The common pillar is seamless management of individual domains, tenants, and users.

Please note: *A Federation Service Manager typically does not bring up all the data such as logs, telemetry, events, and statistics from all the individual SDSPs. Doing so would not be efficient because the amount of data could be very large depending on number of domains, number of DSNs, network services, and so on. Instead, the FSM would contain a subset of the data and query individual SDSPs for specific data in real time, processing the received data before presentation to provide the impression that the data is stored centrally.*

In summary, federation is a way to span multiple SDSP systems across multiple data centers or to reduce the failure domain/security zone within a single data center. Federation provides high-level policies (non-SDSP specific attributes) and systemwide services. An FSM provides global services (for example, a software image repository) across all SDSPs participating in the federation. The federation provides cross-SDSP management and is able to correlate information such as events, alerts, and logs.

In addition to federation, other distributed system architectures are common and provide similar capabilities but can sometimes be challenging to manage as their distribution scale increases.

12.11 **Scale and Performance Testing**

A SDSP system should be designed to handle a large number of endpoints or DSNs. Therefore, all of the functions and components of a SDSP system need to be thoroughly tested for realistic scale, performance, and resiliency during its development cycle.

The testing should confirm that the architecture is valid and that it can provide the scale, performance, and robustness as expected. The testing should aim to find weaknesses and critical bottlenecks. Studies show that failures in these systems tend to be caused by their inability to scale to meet user demand, as opposed to feature bugs. Therefore, load testing at scale is required in addition to conventional functional testing.

Scale and performance testing are critical aspects during the development of a SDSP. This is an ongoing process, starting as early as possible in the development phase. Simulating individual components is needed for development and integration testing. Simulation also helps with testing scale and architectural validation.

Scale testing can be thought of in three phases:

1. Scale test design (defines what a realistic load looks like)
2. Scale test execution (defines how the tests will be run)
3. Analysis of the test results

All the components in an SDSP are expected to work in harmony, especially at full scale. Buffers, caches, processes and services, and so on should be balanced relative to each other, so the system behaves accurately under heavy load. With proper design, systems can handle burstiness and provide predictability. Realistic full-scale testing is a common way to make sure the system operates in an optimal way at full scale.

A SDSP system should be easy to scale for performance and/or capacity, easy to troubleshoot, and easy to manage at scale. An effective design hides the internal complexity and makes the management of one SDSP almost as easy as multiple thousands of SDSPs. The end user should not experience increases in complexity and slower performance as the scale of the system increases. Intent-based, policy-driven management has proven itself to be an excellent choice. A good example is Cisco UCS Manager for solving management at scale.

A SDSP architecture consists of many different "moving parts," and there are many aspects to consider during the design of the architecture, such as how the different components interact with each other, how they scale internally, and how to make them efficient and resource effective. For example, here are some components that should be considered:

- Control plane
- Data plane
- Management plane
- Security (interaction between the various components)
- Microservices with their different functions
- Intercommunication and synchronization between services and between nodes
- Load distribution of service requests, both internally and externally
- Transactional data (user intents, policy mutations, and other state changes)
- Non-transactional data that needs to be processed or analyzed (logs, events, and so on)
- User interfaces such as API, GUI, and CLI with respect to usability, scale, and responsiveness

- Failure detection and handling

- Number and size of internal objects

- Size of logs and other forms of internal data

All system aspects and components need to be tested at full scale. However, most test environments do not have the luxury of full-scale test beds with real physical compute nodes or DSNs. Performing realistic testing of SDSP systems at scale requires other means to be used, like simulators utilizing various virtualization techniques, such as VMs or Containers.

When architecting a full-scale test bed, it is important to understand what a full-scale customer implementation would look like in terms of the capability and functionality of the SDSP, supported network services, and so on.

There are many different data points in a SDSP system. All data points should be considered both from MAX/Burst and Average values. Table 12-1 describes a few common data points. At a very high level it can be divided into three simple areas: scale, workload, and management/monitoring characteristics.

TABLE 12-1 Scaling

Area	Description
Scale: Number of DSNs per SDSP	This helps determine the scale of the test bed needed, number of simulators, and so on
Workload Characteristics: Number of connections per second Number of active flows Number of endpoints	This is defined per DSN, and it indicates the amount of data that will be generated by telemetry and stats collections per second. This data is typically rolled up into a systemwide workload map.
Management/Monitoring: Number, types, and sizes of policies Number of updates per second Number of calls per second	This helps to estimate the size and the required number of updates for the policy database, as well as the policy distribution and enforcement for the different DSNs. It will also indicate the number of expected API calls per second expected to be handled by the API gateways.

To give headroom for future feature enhancements of the system, it is important that the architecture is designed for scalability well beyond what the initial requirements are.

Based on the data points described previously, certain test data parameters can be sized for aspects such as events, amount of telemetry data to process, state changes, flows, log entries and sizes, user requests, and so on. This sizing provides useful information on what the target test topology should look like and how the tests should be run.

A test topology consisting of real and simulated components provides many benefits. Simulators are economical, easy to scale, and easy to control. Another important aspect is the ability to perform various forms of fault injection. Simulators can report simulated hardware failures, states, temperatures, misbehaviors, and so on, which are often hard to accomplish with physical hardware.

During testing, both physical and simulated DSNs pass real traffic and test the actual required network, storage, and RDMA traffic per DSN. Containers and other virtualization technologies are excellent for running simulators. The number of simulators that can run on a single physical host varies depending on the physical host resources as well as the simulator's resource consumption profile. Typically, multiple hundreds of simulators can be run per physical server.

To generate an effective simulation test topology at scale, configuration generation and traffic generation for a given configuration is essential. This can be thought of as a description of an "infrastructure and traffic pattern map" with the validation capability for verifying expected behaviors. This enables creating realistic test scenarios at scale, testing individual or aggregated workloads, and testing for specific use cases.

The testing infrastructure itself should be dynamic and be designed to easily scale for larger testing purpose, to easily inject new tests, and to be fully automated. The following are some common guidelines that can be used in large-scale test design:

- Run multiple scenarios; for example, starting with a small-scale test and increasing the scale and/or load test up toward the full-scale testing. Upon completion, the results should be compared to obtain better insight into the system behavior, as scale and load increases.

- Run tests for extended periods of time to ensure the target system will not degrade in performance and functionality over time with massive load at scale.

- Use multiple parallel test beds for parallel testing of different scenarios.

- Take advantage of AI/ML and other forms of analytics to help produce test result reports and to analyze both individual DSN's behaviors as well as clusterwide behavior (SDSP).

- Run tests at larger scale than are required to find limitations, including larger log data than expected. During the tests run user-realistic operations of the data, such as various reporting, trending analysis, and various searches to verify an acceptable responsiveness.

The tests are often broken into three different categories: performance testing, stress testing, and load testing. Tests should be run individually as well as in combination of these types of tests:

- Load testing aims to verify the functional correctness of the system under load.

- Performance testing aims to verify the performance of the architecture—services, algorithms, and so on—during normal conditions.

- Stress testing aims to test abnormal conditions such as higher latency and lower bandwidth than expected.

All components of the system need to be considered, and the test results should be analyzed for individual components (DSNs, algorithms, services, and so on) as well as systemwide behavior.

12.12   Summary

In this chapter, we presented a management control plane architecture, built using containerized microservices, that is secure, scalable, high performance, debuggable, resilient, and extensible. It is a system built to run on a container orchestration system such as Kubernetes, running microservices that interact with each other using backward-compatible APIs presenting a scalable, resilient, and upgradable deployment model. We presented the design choices for an implementation that can allow business functions to be created and evolved independently. We presented how using mutual TLS between all the components of the system present a highly secure architecture. We also presented mechanisms to federate the policies consistently and allow debugging in a multisite deployment. Finally, we discussed the challenges of building the management system as a cloud-native application and discussed techniques to mitigate those challenges.

12.13   Bibliography

[1] Cloud Native Computing Foundation, "Sustaining and Integrating Open Source Technologies," https://www.cncf.io

[2] Kubernetes.io, "Production-Grade Container Orchestration," https://kubernetes.io

[3] Docker, "Docker: The Modern Platform for High-Velocity Innovation," https://www.docker.com/why-docker

[4] Apache Software Foundation, "Program against your datacenter like it's a single pool of resources," http://mesos.apache.org

[5] Cloud Native Computing Foundation, "A high performance, open-source universal RPC framework," https://grpc.io

[6] GitHub, "Protocol Buffers," https://developers.google.com/protocol-buffers

[7] Cloud Native Computing Foundation, "Envoy Proxy Architecture Overview" https://www.envoyproxy.io/docs/envoy/latest/intro/arch_overview/arch_overview

[8] Nginx, "nginx documentation," https://nginx.org/en/docs

[9] GitHub, "finagle: A fault tolerant, protocol-agnostic RPC system," https://github.com/twitter/finagle

[10] OpenZipkin, "Architecture Overview," https://zipkin.io/pages/architecture.html

[11] Cloud Native Computing Foundation, "Vendor-neutral APIs and instrumentation for distributed tracing," https://opentracing.io

[12] Wikipedia, "Trusted Platform Module," https://en.wikipedia.org/wiki/Trusted_Platform_Module

[13] Cloud Native Computing Foundation, "Secure Production Identity Framework for Everyone," https://spiffe.io

[14] Helm, "The Packet manager for Kubernetes," https://helm.sh

[15] Elastic, "What is the ELK Stack? Why, it's the Elastic Stack," https://www.elastic.co/elk-stack

[16] InfluxData, "Introduction to InfluxData's InfluxDB and TICK Stack," https://www.influxdata.com/blog/introduction-to-influxdatas-influxdb-and-tick-stack

[17] Distributed Systems Reading Group, "Papers on Consensus," http://dsrg.pdos.csail.mit.edu/papers

[18] Apache Software Foundation, "Zookeeper," https://zookeeper.apache.org

[19] Cloud Native Computing Foundation, "etcd: A distributed, reliable key-value store for the most critical data of a distributed system," https://coreos.com/etcd

[20] Prometheus, "From metrics to insight," https://prometheus.io

[21] Universite libre de Bruxelles, "Time Series Databases and InfluxDB," https://cs.ulb.ac.be/public/_media/teaching/influxdb_2017.pdf

[22] Apache Software Foundation, "Cassandra," http://cassandra.apache.org

[23] MongoDB, "What is MongoDB," https://www.mongodb.com/what-is-mongodb

[24] Wikipedia, "Redis," https://en.wikipedia.org/wiki/Redis

[25] GitHub, "CockroachDB - the open source, cloud-native SQL database," https://github.com/cockroachdb/cockroach

[26] GitHub, "MinIO is a high performance object storage server compatible with Amazon S3 APIs," https://github.com/minio/minio

[27] Wikipedia, ElasticSearch, https://en.wikipedia.org/wiki/Elasticsearch

[28] Apache Software Foundation, "Kafka: A distributed streaming platform," https://kafka.apache.org

[29] Github, "NATS," https://nats-io.github.io/docs

[30] JSON Web Tokens, "JWT," https://jwt.io/introduction

Index

Numbers

3D Xpoint, 120
7 nm circuit-manufacturing process, 178
16 nm circuit-manufacturing process, 177–178
802.1Q tag, 12

A

Access-Aggregation-Core model, 10
ACLs (access control lists), 28, 157
active-active mode, 39
active-standby mode, 39
adapters, DSN, 164–166
adaptive logic modules (ALMs), 182
ADD API (CNI), 50
AES (Advanced Encryption Standard), 89, 125
AI (artificial intelligence), 4–5
ALGs (application layer gateways), 79
Alibaba Cloud, 36, 46
ALMs (adaptive logic modules), 182
alpha-quality reference compiler (P4), 202
Amazon Web Services (AWS), 36, 46
AMD
    Epyc processor, 137
    xenproject.org, 46
Amdahl, Gene, 135
Amdahl's Law, 135–136
Ansible, 57, 212
APIs (application programming interfaces), 215–217
Apple A12 Bionic, 178

speed, distributed services platforms, 158

SPF (shortest path first), 64

SPIFFE (Secure Production Identity Framework for Everyone), 210

SQ (Send Queue), 106–107

SR (segment routing), 23–24

SR-IOV (Single Root Input/Output Virtualization), 45–46, 149–153, 175

SRP (SCSI RDMA Protocol), 121

SSDs (solid state drives), 119–120

SSL (Secure Sockets Layer), 88, 93

Starovoitov, Alexei, 76

stateful NAT (network address translation), 79

stateless offloads, 150

static bonding, 40

storage
  data plane model of storage protocols, 120–122
  efficiency of, 125–126
  NVMe-oF (NVME over Fabrics), 120
  offloading and distributing, 126–127
  persistent memory as, 127
  reliability of, 126
  SCSI (Small Computer System Interface), 119
  security, 125
  SSDs (solid state drives), 119–120
  storage services by type, 124
  virtualization and, 122–124

Storage Networking Industry Association (SNIA), 127

Sun, 103

Swagger, 54, 160

Swift module (OpenStack), 56

switched port analyzer (SPAN) ports, 192

switches. See also bridging and routing
  distributed services platforms in, 169–170
  ToR (top of rack), 168
  vSwitches
    BPF (Berkeley Packet Filter), 76
    classification of, 69
    DPDK Generic Flow API, 74
    eBPF (extended Berkeley Packet Filter), 76
    overview of, 39–40
    OVS (Open vSwitch), 70–73

  summary of, 78–79
  tc-flower, 73–74
  VPP (Vector Packet Processing), 75
  XDP (eXpress Data Path), 76–77

symmetric encryption, 89

synchronization, time, 152

System on a Chip (SoC), 177

T

Tandem Computers, 103

target users, determining, 163–164

TCAM (ternary content-addressable memory), 13, 139

tc-flower, 73–74

TCP (Transmission Control Protocol), 19, 91

TCP segmentation offload (TSO), 150

telecommunications, 57

telemetry, 8, 80–81

ternary content-addressable memory (TCAM), 13, 139

ternary matches, 13–14

TICK, 212

time series databases (TSDBs), 214

Time Server, 29

time synchronization, 152

time to live (TTL), 12

TLS (Transport Layer Security), 87–89, 91, 93–94, 210

top of rack (ToR) switches, 14, 168

topologies, Clos, 14–15

ToR (top of rack) switches, 14, 168

Torvolds, Linus, 96

TPM (Trusted Platform Module), 210

traffic shaping, 150

transactional semantics, 217

transistor count
  Amdahl's Law, 4
  Dennard scaling, 4, 134–135
  historical perspective of, 130–131
  historical trend data, 131–132
  Moore's law, 4, 103, 132–134, 138
  single-thread performance, 137–138
  technical factors limiting, 136–137